D1327569

London in the
Age of Reform

London in the
Age of Reform

Edited by John Stevenson

BASIL BLACKWELL · OXFORD

© Basil Blackwell, 1977

The City of London and the Opposition to Government, 1768–74
© Lucy S. Sutherland 1959

All Rights Reserved. No part of this publication
may be reproduced, stored in a retrieval system
or transmitted, in any form or by any means,
electronic, mechanical, photocopying, recording
or otherwise, without the prior permission of
Basil Blackwell & Mott Limited.

British Library Cataloguing in Publication Data

London in the Age of Reform.
　1. London – History – 1800–1950
　2. London – Politics and government
　I. Stevenson, John
　942.1′07　　　DA682
　ISBN 0–631–17820–1

78-16334 01

Printed in Great Britain by
Richard Clay (The Chaucer Press) Ltd
Bungay, Suffolk.

Contents

Acknowledgements

This book owes a considerable debt to a variety of persons. The idea for the volume arose out of attending the eighteenth-century history seminar in Oxford and I would like to thank Peter Dickson, Paul Langford, and John Roberts for the stimulus which this provided. A number of people gave generously of their advice and encouragement, including Dame Lucy Sutherland, Ian Christie, John Dinwiddy, Marianne Elliott, and William Thomas. I am especially grateful to Betty Kemp for her unfailing encouragement of my work on London. In a difficult publishing climate, Jim Feather has been the model of a patient and helpful publisher.

We are grateful to the Athlone Press for permission to reprint Dame Lucy Sutherland's Creighton Lecture in History, 1958.

Notes on Contributors

J. Ann Hone is a graduate of Melbourne, Monash and Oxford Universities. She is the author of numerous entries in the *Australian Dictionary of Biography* and an article on William Hone, the early nineteenth century bookseller and publisher, in *Historical Studies* (1974). She is a Lecturer at the Canberra College of Advanced Education.

Paul Langford was educated at Monmouth School and Hertford College, Oxford. He is the author of books on The First Rockingham Ministry, 1765–66, the Excise Crisis of 1733 and British Foreign Policy in the Eighteenth Century, as well as articles on the Elder Pitt and the American Revolution. He is currently editing the *Writings and Speeches of Edmund Burke*. He is Fellow and Tutor at Lincoln College, Oxford.

David Large was educated at Caterham School and Worcester College, Oxford. He is the author of several articles in the *English Historical Review*, *Irish Historical Studies* and other periodicals. A contributor to P. Hollis (ed.), *Pressure from Without*, he is currently working on a study of 1848 in the United Kingdom. He is Senior Lecturer in History at the University of Bristol.

Alice Prochaska is a graduate of Somerville College, Oxford and completed her doctorate on Westminster Radicalism in 1975. Her publications include *London in the Thirties* and reviews in *Victorian Studies* and the *London Journal*. She is working on a commissioned history of the General Federation of Trade Unions from 1899 to the present and is an Assistant Keeper at the Public Record Office.

Nicholas Rogers read history at St. Edmund's Hall, Oxford and took his doctorate at the University of Toronto with a social study of London politics in the mid-eighteenth century. He has contributed articles on London politics to *Past and Present* and *The London Journal*. He is an Assistant Professor in the Department of History, York University, Toronto.

D. J. Rowe is a Lecturer in Economics at the University of Newcastle upon Tyne. His research interests are on Chartism and on the economic development of the north-east. He has published several essays on radicalism in the 1830s and 1840s and edited *London Radicalism, 1830–43* (1970).

John Stevenson was educated at the Boteler Grammar School, Warrington, and Worcester and Nuffield Colleges, Oxford. His publications include *Popular Protest and Public Order* (edited with Dr. R. Quinault 1975); *Social Conditions in Britain between the Wars* (edited, 1977); and contributions to a number of collections of essays. He is preparing for publication a study of popular disturbances and public order in London during the late eighteenth and early nineteenth centuries. After teaching for five years at Oriel College, Oxford, he is now Lecturer in History at the University of Sheffield.

Dame Lucy Sutherland D.B.E., D.Litt., has contributed many studies to the eighteenth century field, including the *East India Company in the Eighteenth Century* (1952), the *Correspondence of Edmund Burke* volume II (edited, 1960), and *The University of Oxford in the Eighteenth Century* (1973), as well as a number of articles in the *English Historical Review*, the *Economic History Review*, and the *Transactions of the Royal Historical Society*. She is an Honorary Fellow of Lady Margaret Hall.

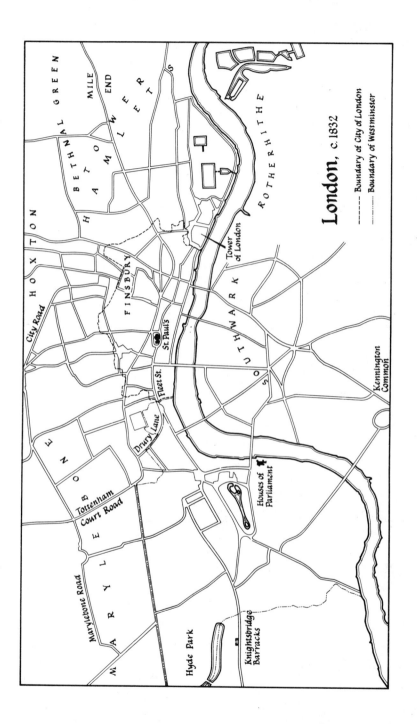

London, c. 1832

------- Boundary of City of London
———— Boundary of Westminster

MILE END

BETHNAL GREEN

HAMLETS

HOXTON

City Road

FINSBURY

ROTHERHITHE

Tower of London

St. Paul's

Fleet St.

SOUTHWARK

Drury Lane

Kennington Common

MARYLEBONE

Tottenham Court Road

Marylebone Road

Houses of Parliament

Hyde Park

Knightsbridge Barracks

JOHN STEVENSON

Introduction

This volume aims to bring together some of the work which has been
completed on the political history of London in the period from the
ascendency of Walpole to the Chartist agitation. For the country at
large, this was an era of great social and economic change. Politically
too, it witnessed the rise of the reform movement, the impact of the
French Revolution, the passing of the First Reform Act, and the
agitations of the 1840s. The role that London played in the political
developments of this period and their manifestations in the political
history of the capital are the main themes of this group of essays.

By 1750 London had emerged as the largest city in Europe, if not in
the world. Its population then was estimated at 575,000 people and
almost one Englishman in ten lived in the capital. By 1801 its
population had passed the million mark and was more than twice that
of Paris and more than ten times as great as the population of
Liverpool, the second largest city in the country. By the middle of the
nineteenth century a combination of natural increase and large-scale
migration had increased its population to over two and a half million
people. As the centre of government, the largest port, a major manufacturing centre, and the greatest concentration of population in
the British Isles it had achieved a unique position in the life of the
nation.

The sheer size and diversity of London present many challenges to
the historian and its continued growth in the eighteenth and nineteenth centuries make it difficult to discern the complex dynamics of
its political structure. London was not one political centre, but several.
At its heart lay the City of London, for so long the traditional
expression of the capital's prestige and influence. London was the
centre of the 'monied interest', the financial and commercial hub of the

nation, and also a proud civic entity with jealously guarded privileges and 'rights'.[1] *

The City's position as the financial centre of the country and the major source of credit remained a crucial aspect of its importance. The nineteenth century saw the rise of the Bank of England to become the hub of the national monetary system, confirmed in the Bank Charter Act of 1844. In addition, the City housed an increasingly sophisticated money market in which credit was raised through the great mercantile companies and from a small number of individual contractors, operating through the Stock Exchange, men such as the Baring brothers and the Rothschilds. Even in the eighteenth century, however, the 'monied interest' had become firmly wedded to the administration of the day, the prosperity of many of its members being dependent upon the favour of the Government. This accounted for the alliance of the richer citizens, those represented in the City's Court of Aldermen, with the ruling Ministry. The City of London acted in the seventeenth and early eighteenth centuries as the focus for metropolitan opinion as a whole, using the machinery of its constitution to voice the interests of a much wider section of opinion than was represented by the City itself.

The City elected four members of Parliament, on a franchise which included the 8,000 liverymen of the City companies. But its Parliamentary representatives were only one part of a complex constitution which gave scope for the expression of a wide range of political, social, and economic interests. The City was governed by its three Courts, the Court of Aldermen, Court of Common Council, and Court of Common Hall. Aldermen were elected by wards, and it has been estimated that a fortune of at least £30,000 was a necessary qualification for election.[2] Though there were always some radical aldermen, the great majority were effectively representatives of the 'monied interest', who tended to side with the administration and provided oligarchic leadership of the City. The Court of Common Council was made up of twenty-five aldermen and 210 Common Councillors elected by the freemen ratepayers of each ward. Common Council was more representative of the 'middling men', the class of small merchants tradesmen and artisans, than the Court of Aldermen. An inquiry in 1739 revealed that 152 were tradesmen and 'artificers' and only thirty of higher status. In addition, the Common Councillors had to be freeman householders of their wards, leading many of them in the early and mid-eighteenth century to play a prominent part in City politics

* Notes are to be found at the end of the relevant chapter.

at both ward and parish level. During the course of the eighteenth century, Common Council assumed a greatly enlarged legislative and administrative role with salaried staff, regular committees, and considerable responsibility for the day-to-day running of the capital. Sidney and Beatrice Webb described how in the course of the period 1746 to 1832, Common Council's position grew 'from a sort of consultative legislature, dependent for its Executive upon the Lord Mayor and the Aldermen, into a supreme organ of administration, itself wielding the whole power of government, and reducing the Lord Mayor and Aldermen to a mere magistracy'. This marked a considerable shift in power within the City: the starting date for which was the repeal of the London Election Act of 1725 which had imposed the 'Aldermanic Veto' upon decisions of Common Council. At the base of the City's constitution lay the Court of Common Hall. Common Hall was open to all freeman members of the livery companies, approximately two-thirds of the 12,000–15,000 freemen of the City. It has been described as 'the backbone of City democracy', with the right to elect the Lord Mayor, the two Sheriffs of London and Middlesex, and the City's four members of Parliament. Although Common Hall did not assume the same degree of municipal responsibility as Common Council, it provided an important focus for meetings, debates, and resolutions.[3]

Two other organs of City influence require mention. In the past the local Courts of Wardmote had provided a focus for opinion within each ward of the City. They were presided over by the aldermen and open to all ward ratepayers, their functions being to elect ward officers, to nominate the ward's Common Councilmen, and fill any aldermanic vacancies. During the course of the eighteenth century, the wardmotes lost most of the administrative duties, such as direction of the nightly watch, to Common Council. Moreover, where once the wardmotes had been an important element in the mobilization of grassroots opinion within the City, by the end of the century the great majority of wardmote meetings were routine and poorly attended. The last instance upon which they made a concerted political effort was in opposition to the Property Tax. Thereafter only one or two wardmotes had an effective political role, usually under the aegis of a particularly active alderman. Another traditional source of organized opinion within the City had been the City companies. Like the wardmotes, however, they were decaying as political organizations in the course of the eighteenth century, becoming increasingly dominated by prosperous master craftsmen whose principal interests were closely associated with the wealthier citizens. Their records for the nineteenth century breathe a spirit of oligarchic control, consisting mainly of reports of banquets, donations to charity, and occasional disputes with journeymen.

Below the administrations of the counties and the twin cities of Westminster lay the parochial organization common to the whole capital. In the seventeenth century, many parishes in the capital had played an active part in politics. In the following century, their importance as centres of political expression tended to decline some-what, but was never completely eclipsed. In the City of London, most civic duties had been taken over by the Court of Common Council. In other areas, such as Westminster, the county administration had taken over the most important functions of the parishes, whereas the 'five villages' of metropolitan Surrey and many of the out-parishes of Middlesex were still effectively run by their parish vestries. The involve-ment of the inhabitants of a parish depended upon whether it was open or closed. By the end of the eighteenth century over half of the parishes in the metropolitan area were closed or select vestries in which the bulk of the parishioners had little or no say. The prosperous parish of St. George, Hanover Square had a vestry composed primarily of resident gentlemen and nobility, including seven dukes, fourteen earls, two viscounts, seven barons, and twenty-six other titled persons. Yet other parishes remained open to all ratepayers occupying premises of a value of £15 per year. On the other hand, Bethnal Green was administered by a group of about 2,000 householders. So that in some areas at least, the parish could still act as an important vehicle of grassroots opinion.

In the seventeenth and eighteenth centuries the City of London developed a powerful tradition of political involvement. It had played a prominent part in the opposition to Charles I, when its train-bands, puritan sympathies, and financial wealth had been put into the service of the parliamentary cause. During the Exclusion Crisis, City politi-cians and the London mob were recruited to the aid of Shaftesbury's 'country party'. Moreover, the City's influence was frequently thrown against the administration of the day; between the 1720s and the 1780s the City was almost continuously in opposition. The spirit of opposition can partly be explained in terms of divisions within the City itself, the 'middling sort' opposing administrations with which the richer citizens were allied. The smaller merchants and tradesmen were also more vulnerable to the consequences of an unsuccessful war or foreign policy which seemed antithetical to their commercial interests. Even more important in explaining the persistence of opposition from the City in the eighteenth century, however, was the use to which opposi-tions within parliament could put the organized expression of opinion from the City. The City was frequently called upon to provide the 'support without doors' which Burke considered essential to successful opposition in parliament. With its long experience of corporate action, the City of London could be a useful means of orchestrating extra-parliamentary pressure. As Dame Lucy Sutherland has written:

> City leaders were expert, from long experience of organizing commercial agitation affecting both London and the 'outports', in the art of bringing pressure to bear on authority from without. Petitions, instructions, from the Common Council to the City representatives, pamphlets and press campaigns were rapidly planned there, while whenever political excitement ran high the London crowd could be relied on to emerge and give the added support of their clamour to the Opposition cause.[4]

The highpoint of the City's involvement in extra-parliamentary agitation came with the Wilkite agitation of the 1760s and 1770s when political organization and propaganda reached new levels of sophistication. In this agitation and in opposition to the American War, the City of London reached what has been called 'the climax of the influence of London on the political life of the country during the century'. Rudé has suggested that the politics of the City developed in three significant directions in the latter part of the eighteenth century. Firstly, it developed a more independent line of its own, often at variance with traditional parliamentary groups, be they either Ministry or opposition. Secondly, the City radicals, in conjunction with the Associations of the counties, also began to articulate a programme of parliamentary reform, including shorter parliaments, reform of the 'Rotten' boroughs, and a widening of the franchise. Thirdly, they extended their appeal to those parts of the nation who did not possess the vote. Although the crowds who rioted during the Wilkite agitations may have had economic grievances, Wilkes had nonetheless harnessed these grievances to a programme of constitutional change.[5] But the City's radicalism petered out with the events of 1779–82. Wilkes dropped out of radical politics after he acquired a sinecure as City Chamberlain in 1779. By 1784 he had declared for Pitt, as had other radical leaders, such as Brass Crosby. The Gordon Riots of 1780 also acted as a brake upon the use of the London mob in extra-parliamentary agitation. The loss of lives and property occasioned by the riots led to a marked reluctance on the part of city politicians to take up the role played by Wilkes. Its effect was to lead some of them to 'shut their ears against the voices of popular clamour'. In addition, the passing of 'economical' reform removed much of the whiggish support that had existed in the capital and in the country. When Pitt was called into office in 1784 the City entered a period of more amicable relations with the Government which lasted until the last years of the Napoleonic Wars.

With the outbreak of war against revolutionary France, the City pledged its support to King and constitution, offering bounties to seamen and funds for the sea and land campaigns. However, with the failures of the campaigns in the low countries, the corn scarcity of 1795–6, and increasing commercial dislocation, sections of Common Hall began to show signs of opposition. In January 1795, Common Hall demanded peace with France and this was echoed in a milder address from Common Council. The failure to obtain peace in 1796 led to some stormy resolutions in Common Hall, calling for the dismissal of Ministers and reminding the King that it was for the 'peace and felicity of the Kingdom that your family were placed upon the throne'.[6] The City's opposition to the war was temporarily cut short by the panic created by the naval mutinies. Nonetheless, Common Council opposed the Income Tax Bill of 1798 and the Livery petitioned for an acceptance of Napoleon's terms in January 1800. When peace was finally signed in March 1802 there was general rejoicing in the capital.

During the second phase of the Napoleonic Wars, the City remained suspicious of the conduct of the administration, but the complexion of its parliamentary representation and Lord Mayors remained predominantly Tory. Nonetheless, the City remained antagonistic towards the war and Common Council refused to attend Pitt's funeral. City opposition was stirred into life by the Convention of Cintra and the Walcheren campaign leading to a number of bitter addresses to the throne, demanding inquiries into the conduct of the war. All the old ingredients of war-time mismanagement, evil advisers, and wastage of 'blood and treasure' were invoked. In February 1810 Common Council was refused an audience with the King and claimed that a barrier was being placed between 'the King and the People'. In 1812 Common Council was demanding 'radical reforms' and the removal of ministers. Yet with the cessation of the war, the City lapsed into a quieter phase. Opposition to the administration of Lord Liverpool was left to a small group led by Matthew Wood and Robert Waithman. They provided a nucleus of radical support which was used to oppose the Income Tax, the suspension of Habeas Corpus in 1817, and the Six Acts.[7] The last great agitation in which the City gave a lead was the Queen Caroline affair, but at least since the end of the Napoleonic Wars, the City was being challenged by the rise of other bodies acting within the metropolis.

Unlike the City of London, Westminster had never become a municipality with a Lord Mayor and Court of Aldermen. It was effectively governed by the vestries of the nine parishes and the Middlesex justices who sat for Westminster. But although the inhabitants of Westminster had little part in the conduct of municipal affairs – in contrast to the inhabitants of the City of London, they enjoyed a very wide parliamentary franchise, open to all resident householders or 'pot-wallopers'. It was this which underlay the rise of 'radical Westminster'. Thomas Oldfield dated the rise of an 'independent' Westminster from the 1780s, but the renewed radical stirrings became apparent in 1790 when Horne Tooke obtained 1,779 votes as an 'independent Reformer'. The election of Sir Francis Burdett in 1807, aided by the electoral organization of Francis Place, marked a new departure for metropolitan politics. Westminster, rather than the City, became the dominant partner in 'radical politics'. Other Westminster MPs such as Lord Cochrane and John Cam Hobhouse carried on a radical tradition which was to last until the Reform Act of 1832 when the 'pot-walloper' franchise was ended. Even before then, however, divisions between the socially superior MPs, especially Burdett and Hobhouse, and their lower class supporters had diffused the impact of Westminster radicalism. Place regarded Burdett as an 'amateur . . . too rich, too high, and too lazy' and came himself increasingly under the influence of the utilitarians, including Jeremy Bentham and James Hill. Burdett became increasingly conservative in his sympathies, eventually becoming Tory MP for Wiltshire.[8]

Other strands of political influence were also emerging towards the end of the eighteenth century. London's workmen and artisans had a long tradition of collective action in defence of wage rates and in pursuit of their established patterns of work. Groups such as the Spitalfields silk-weavers, the framework knitters, coal-heavers, tailors, and printers were frequently involved in industrial disputes during the course of the eighteenth century. Wilkes was the first person to harness the socioeconomic demands of the 'inferior set' to the cause of parliamentary reform, but by 1792 the first lower-class political organization was formed when the London Corresponding Society was set up at the Bell Tavern in the Strand. With a weekly subscription of 1d., modelled upon that of the trade organizations of the capital, it was open to 'members unlimited'. Most of its members were composed of 'tradesmen, mechanics and shopkeepers', reflecting the range of craft trades to be found in the capital. The great majority of its members, at least in the early years, were artisans, skilled workers of a higher status and income than the common labourers. At its peak, the LCS had ninety 'divisions' in the capital, providing a forum for debates and 'correspondence' with societies in the provinces. By the mid-1790s it was calling for annual parliaments and universal suffrage and held a number of successful, mass meetings in the capital. Although the society was 'utterly suppressed and prohibited' in 1799 by an Act against Unlawful Combinations and Confederacies, its activities were taken up in the formation of the London Hampden Club in 1812 and the survival of a group of early members, such as Francis Place and John Thelwall, who continued to play a part in London politics.

In spite of the Combination Laws many trade organizations continued to flourish during the Napoleonic Wars and the post-war period. Strikes and combinations were conducted openly, though always at the risk of prosecution. Such activity was mainly confined, however, to the skilled artisans, particularly groups such as the shipwrights, printers, coopers, and cabinet-makers. The Webbs concluded that the skilled trades had 'never been more completely organized in London than between 1810 and 1820'. The unskilled groups were largely unorganized, although there were occasional stirrings among the London dock-workers and other groups of labourers. Under the leadership of men such as John Gast and Francis Place, the London artisans began to involve themselves in political affairs. During the post-war period Cobbett's *Political Register* and *Twopenny Trash* and the publications of the radical printers, such as Hone and Wooler, provided the politically conscious artisans with a steady stream of radical literature. *The Gorgon* acted as sounding-board for the trade groups, while *The Black Dwarf* and *The Yellow Dwarf* had an important impact in disseminating radical ideas and freeing the Press from government restriction. By the 1820s the trade groups were becoming better organized and more articulate. The repeal of the Combination Laws in 1824 led to a rash of strikes and the participation of London artisans in many of the Utopian and Co-operative schemes of Owen and Lovett.

The growth of political organizations among the London trades marked one of the major developments in the political life of the capital during the first half of the nineteenth century. In addition, London was also one of the major areas of influence for men such as Henry Hunt and Major Cartwright, both of whom were heavily involved in metropolitan politics. Many different strands went to make up the complex fabric of London radicalism. In the post-war period there was also a small revolutionary group based on the Spenceans. Its leaders were Dr. James Watson and Arthur Thistlewood. They followed the insurrectionary tradition of Colonel Despard, aiming to precipitate a nation-wide revolution by an insurrection in the capital. Although acquitted from a charge of High Treason for their involvement in the Spa Fields Riots of 1816, Thistlewood ended his days on the scaffold for his part in the Cato Street conspiracy of 1820, when the assassination of the Cabinet while they were at dinner was to signal the introduction of a revolutionary regime.[9]

But one of the most striking features of the first half of the nineteenth century was the way in which the focus of attention shifted away from London and to the provinces. As one historian has commented, 'London became a centre of journalistic propaganda rather than of effective action'.[10] Several historians have noticed the way in which the provincial cities began to play a far more effective role in political agitation in the years after 1815. E. P. Thompson, for example, has written of the demonstrations in London in 1831 that 'while the numbers called out were impressive, they compare poorly with the even greater demonstrations at Birmingham, drawn from a smaller population'.[11] F. Sheppard has also argued that the impact of London on the course of the reform struggle was 'relatively small'.[12] Similarly in the Chartist agitation, although the capital provided the scene for the climaxes of the movement, London's involvement has commonly been regarded as disappointing in relation to its size and importance. Place himself expressed this view when he reported to Cobden in 1840 that:

> London in my time, and that is half a century, has never moved. A few people in different parts have moved, and these, whenever they come together, make a considerable number – still a very small number indeed when compared with the whole number . . .[13]

Why was London to play a less significant role after the 1820s in the political life of the nation? Two arguments have often been used. One suggests that the issues of the mid-century, especially Reform, had less appeal in London than elsewhere. Others have argued that London was not a 'manufacturing' centre in the same sense as those of the midlands and north. Yet neither point can be fully sustained. Almost every political grouping in the metropolis was involved in the demand for parliamentary reform at some time or another in the period from 1760 to 1832. Even the City of London, far and away the most conservative body from the 1780s until the 1800s, was eventually won over again to a pro-reform stand. In addition to the City, Westminster and the trade groups of the working districts provided strong support for reform in the years up to 1832. Although London had political representation already, it was, as Thomas Oldfield had pointed out in 1792, grossly under-represented in terms of seats in relation to its population. Even after the 1832 Reform Act increased the capital's representation from ten to twenty-two, London remained under-represented. Nor did London lack leaders. It was, as we have seen, the focus for the activities not only of indigenous reformers, but also of prominent national figures such as Cobbett and Hunt. In addition, reformers in the capital had the backing of the capital's print shops and publishing houses, one of the most potent forces in the radical movement.

Moreover, it has been convincingly argued that London remained an important manufacturing centre during this period. F. Sheppard has described the capital as 'the greatest manufacturing centre in the country' until the middle of the nineteenth century.[14] London remained the centre of a large number of traditional craft industries, such as printing, coachbuilding, furniture-making, tailoring, silk-weaving, and skilled metal-working. But the capital was not confined to the craft trades which could be found in any centre of consumption. The docks upon which London's prosperity was based were estimated to have employed 20,000 men by the early nineteenth century. Hardly a surprising figure when the total number of ships using the port had risen to 23,618 by 1824. Many of the early docks had a permanent workforce of several hundred men as well as large numbers of casual workers. London's trade brought in a host of products for refining and process-ing, such as sugar, tobacco, and coffee. It had large scale factories for brewing, tin-plating, dying, and food-processing. Clothing trades employed 197,000 people in 1861 and London remained the pre-eminent shipbuilding centre in the country until the middle of the nineteenth century. London's growth had created a vast construction industry which supported a large pool of skilled and unskilled labour. By 1861 the capital contained almost half a million workers engaged in manufacturing, 14·9 per cent of the total for the country as a whole.[15] Nor was lower class organization lacking, for the London trades were by the 1820s among the best organized in the country, forming an artisan élite unrivalled for its experience and range of contacts with radical politicians. London was a city with a large manufacturing population, well-organized, politically active, and seemingly capable of playing a decisive role in the political struggles of the first half of the nineteenth century.

There were, in fact, other reasons why London failed to realize its political promise of the eighteenth century. Its sheer size and diversity was one feature which Place saw as critical, writing in 1840, 'isolated as men are here, living as they do at considerable distances, many seven miles apart, and but seldom meeting together, except in small groups . . .' He went on:

> London differs very widely from Manchester, and, indeed, from every other place on the face of the earth. It has no local or particular interest as a town, not even as to politics. Its several boroughs in this respect are like so many very populous places at a distance from one another, and the inhabitants of any one of them know nothing, or next to nothing, of the proceedings in any other, and not much indeed of those of their own.[16]

This process of stratification and localization had been reflected in the politics of London over the past hundred years. The City of London, which had once acted as the focus of political action in the capital, was an increasingly specialized part of the whole. The capital's fragmentation into a number of distinct political groupings was one of the most important developments during the course of the nineteenth century. Studies of population change in London during the first half of the nineteenth century have shown that there was a continuous movement of population from the central areas to the outer parishes. An important influence here was the pressure of increasing ground rents which drove the poorer sections of the population to the out-parishes. On the eastern side of the capital the most important growth was to be found in the districts of Mile End, Spitalfields, Bethnal Green, and Whitechapel. In the north, Clerkenwell, St. Pancras, and Hoxton showed large increases in population, while along the river, Blackwall, Poplar, Wapping, and Rotherhithe were also growing rapidly. In the central districts of the capital, there was a trend towards the segregation of occupations and classes, so that the City of London was increasingly given over to offices, warehouses, and shops. Although many of its wealthy citizens retained houses in the 'square mile', others moved to the fashionable parishes of Kensington, Chelsea, and Hammersmith and to the squares and town houses of the West End. Thus while the population of the capital as a whole increased, that of the City actually declined in both absolute numbers and in as a proportion of the total population. In 1750 it had approximately 150,000 inhabitants, but by 1821 this had fallen to about 120,000 and continued to fall throughout the remainder of the nineteenth century. As well as the movement 'upwards and outwards', to use Professor Dyos's phrase, there was also a concentration of the poorest sections of the population in the notorious 'rookeries' of east Smithfield, Moorfields, and St. Giles.[17]

Thus London was becoming an increasingly complex community

and there were many difficulties in the way of mobilizing its full weight on a particular political issue. The creation of new parliamentary constituencies in 1832 in Finsbury, Lambeth, Greenwich, Marylebone, and Tower Hamlets further emphasized the scale of metropolitan politics. The capital, however, remained an important 'stage' for political activity. The events of the Reform crisis and the Chartist agitation showed that London could still be the focus of attention, even if it was not the main source of the political movements to which it was host. Fears that London might be the scene of revolution were expressed pithily by Lord Liverpool when he remarked to Chateaubriand that 'One insurrection in London and all is lost'. In fact, London never developed the scale of revolutionary activity associated with some continental cities, most notably Paris. In part, at least, this was the result of important differences in the traditions and context of London politics and the nature of London as a political centre. Inevitably, the political history of the capital has an important bearing upon the development of the country at large in the era of reform.

Each of the essays which follow must speak for itself, but they all approach important problems and themes in the political history of the capital during this period. Nicholas Rogers examines the forces which underlay the City's opposition to Walpole and his successors. He shows the part played by the Tory-radicalism of the 'Patriots' and assesses reactions to the Jacobite Rising of 1745. Rogers illustrates the role of the City in Walpole's fall and the legacy of political organization left by the 'Patriots'. Dame Lucy Sutherland takes up the development of London radicalism at the time of Wilkes. Her contention is that London was at the forefront of eighteenth-century radicalism because it alone possessed the traditions, organization, and leaders which were essential to its emergence. In exploring this theme, Dame Lucy examines the development of radicalism in London and the role of John Wilkes and William Beckford. The relationship between the City of London and the reform movements in the counties is considered, as is the nature of the link between the popular leaders of the City and the parliamentary 'Opposition'.

Paul Langford deals with the impact of the American crisis upon London. He shows that as well as genuine sympathy and support in the capital, there was also a considerable degree of calculation in the responses of some sections of opinion. Langford suggests that there was a discrepancy between the support which the colonists believed existed in London for their cause and the actual manifestations of discontent in the capital as war approached. He concludes that the American issue was largely incidental to the course of political development in the capital, but that the expressions of support by London politicians provided important encouragement to the American colonists in the years leading up to the War of Independence.

The years of the French Revolution and the Napoleonic Wars provide the background for Dr. J. Ann Hone's essay. Hone re-examines the evidence for the survival of radicalism in period after 1796. She suggests that there has been an over-emphasis upon the retreat of popular radicalism in the years between the passing of the Two Acts in 1795 and the Middlesex Election of 1802. She points to the continuation of radical activity, seen in the formation of new associations and the continuity of radical personnel, culminating in the Middlesex Election campaign and the emergence of Sir Francis Burdett as a popular figure. Alice Prochaska looks at one of the practical manifestations of London radicalism in the early years of the nineteenth century. She analyses the educational schemes of the Westminster radicals and their relationship to their political programme. She sees their approach to the task of educating the poor as symptomatic of a wider vision of politics and society, illustrating many of their political methods and ideals.

My own essay considers the place of the Queen Caroline affair in the development of London radicalism. The last of the traditional agitations based upon a popular figure-head, it also marked one of the last occasions upon which London was the main source of an agitation which affected the country at large. My examination of the agitation argues that Caroline bound together various strands of reformist and radical opinion within the capital, but that it also displayed many of the features which were to limit London's role in future movements.

D. J. Rowe's essay is concerned with the nature of the popular reform movement in London at the time of the Great Reform Bill. He examines the activities of the political unions and the background of public meetings which took place in the capital. Rowe shows that there were important divisions between different groups in the capital and that a basic problem for reformers was to achieve an effective compromise which would provide a united, powerful movement for reform. Finally, he examines the possibility that the reform agitation might have extended into violence or even revolution. He suggests that this was unlikely. David Large takes as his theme the place of London in the Chartist agitation of 1848. He considers the confrontations between the authorities and the Chartists in London during that year. He traces the fear of Chartist violence in public opinion and examines its role in depriving the Chartists of support in the capital. He concludes by contrasting the experience of Paris and of London in the 'year of revolutions'.

Notes

1. See L. S. Sutherland 'The City of London in Eighteenth-Century Politics', in *Essays presented to Sir Lewis Namier* (ed. R. Pares and A. J. P. Taylor, London, 1956); G. Rudé, *Hanoverian London, 1714–1808* (London, 1971), especially chapter 8.
2. L. S. Sutherland, *op. cit.*, p. 55, n. 3.
3. See G. Rudé, *op. cit.*, chapter 7.
4. L. S. Sutherland, *op. cit.*, p. 59.
5. G. Rudé, *op. cit.*, pp. 162–74; see also G. Rudé, *Wilkes and Liberty* (Oxford, 1962).
6. See R. R. Sharpe, *London and the Kingdom* (London, 1895), vol. iii, pp. 209–33.
7. For the revival of City radicalism and Waithman's career see J. R. Dinwiddy, 'The Patriotic Linen-Draper: Robert Waithman and the Revival of Radicalism in the City of London, 1795–1818', *Bulletin of the Institute of Historical Research*, vol. xlvi (1973).
8. See F. Sheppard, *London, 1808–1870: The Infernal Wen* (London, 1971), pp. 298–300. For the persons mentioned see G. Wallas, *The Life of Francis Place, 1771–1854* (5th imp., London, 1951); M. W. Patterson, *Sir Francis Burdett and his times* (London, 1931); R. E. Zegger, *John Cam Hobhouse: A Political Life, 1819–1852* (Columbia, 1973).
9. See T. M. Parsinnen, 'The Revolutionary Party in London', *Bulletin of the Institute of Historical Research*, xlv (1972).
10. F. Sheppard, *op. cit.*, chapter 8.
11. E. P. Thompson, *The Making of the English Working Class* (2nd edn., London, 1968), p. 894.
12. F. Sheppard, *op. cit.*, p. 319.
13. G. Wallas, *op. cit.*, p. 393.
14. See F. Sheppard, *op. cit.*, pp. 158–9.
15. *Ibid.*, chapter 5.
16. G. Wallas, *op. cit.*
17. See F. Sheppard, *op. cit.*, chapter 1 and K. Grytzell, *Population Changes in London* (Lund, Sweden, 1969).

NICHOLAS ROGERS

Resistance to Oligarchy:
The City Opposition to Walpole and his Successors, 1725–47

During the last decade or so historians of the eighteenth century have paid increasing attention to the political public beyond parliament. The revival of interest in political ideology, in the modes of political communication, and in the structure and behaviour of the electorate itself, has inaugurated a welcome departure from the almost obsessive preoccupation with high politics which characterized the historiography of the Namier school. Within this context London looms large. By virtue of its capital status, its commercial supremacy, its size, heterogeneity, and unceasing magnetism, London dominated the popular political arena for much if not all of the eighteenth century. Of its variegated constituencies the City was, until the eighties at least, the most important. By reputation and history, it was the embodiment of the independent political community, testily suspicious of any infringement of its liberties. Comparatively democratic by contemporary standards, armed with special privileges of petition and address,[1] the City of London was a natural rallying-point for broader appeals to the electorate. Responsible for law and order within its own confines, it could also influence, through encouragement, connivance, or suppression, the dimensions of political protest.

The City of London's unique position in English society enabled it to play a singularly influential role in metropolitan and national politics. And it is hardly surprising that it should feature so strongly in the history of early extra-parliamentary radicalism. Its conduct and significance in mid-century politics, however, are less well known. There has admittedly been one monograph on Walpole's relations with the City, a useful though somewhat superficial work based largely on newspaper sources, while Dame Lucy Sutherland has mapped out the various phases of City politics.[2] But there has been no detailed examination of the social context of City politics during the first half of the century. And certainly nothing that incorporates recent research on the development of Whig oligarchy after a period of striking political vitality. In this essay I propose to re-examine the background to the formation of the anti-Walpolean coalition in City politics, its subsequent successes, and final fragmentation during the political crisis of 1745. At the same time I will endeavour to note certain precedents in political organization upon which Wilkite radicals built, and also highlight the relations between City politics and commercial capital.

Historians are right to see 1725 as marking a new point of departure in London politics. That year witnessed the beginnings of a broadly based opposition to Walpole's Election Act which sought to remodel the constitution of the City and circumscribe its democratic tendencies. The new opposition to the Court was not, however, strictly Tory, if we adopt a narrow political definition. Although broad party configurations remained a characteristic feature of London politics, there was nevertheless a growing relaxation of party ties. During the first thirty years of the century, the strictly non-partisan vote more than doubled, from around 10 per cent in the years 1710–13 to 24 per cent in 1727.[3] Among the floaters, in particular, split voting increased. The careers of Sir John Barnard and several well known Tories illustrate the general trend. For the first time in many years a politician emerged who was able to straddle traditional party differences. In 1722 Barnard ran as a 'Whig' and picked up 47 per cent of the stray votes. In the following general election he stood as an opposition candidate and attracted substantial support from the ministerial fold. By contrast, confirmed Tory candidates fared indifferently at the polls. In 1727 for example, Humphrey Parsons, a local brewer and farmer of the City markets, scrambled home by less than thirty votes, although in the subsequent election his avid attack on the Excise bill greatly enhanced his electoral popularity. In 1734, the intransigent Tory John Barber, whose defiant support of anti-Excise demonstrations while Lord Mayor won him ministerial opprobrium and popular acclaim, failed to win a seat. According to my calculations, derived from newspaper reports, for no polling lists have survived, the die-hard Tory vote, those that supported Parsons and Barber alone, numbered less than 1,000, about 15 per cent of the electorate.[4] City politics in the late twenties and thirties were therefore conspicuously different to those of Queen Anne's reign. One notes an attenuation of old party distinctions, and a substantial sector of moderate voters uncommitted to either of the old parties. If we examine the composition of the Livery we should not find this surprising, for the turnover at Common Hall ran at about 20-25 per cent every five years. By 1734, 65 per cent of the voters had joined the Livery since the Hanoverian succession.[5] If we assume that liverymen received their political education in the decade prior to membership, admittedly a questionable assumption, then we can say that by 1734, 37 per cent of the Common Hall electorate had no direct experience of the great Whig–Tory battles of bygone days.

Statements about the fluidity of party configurations in the twenties and thirties, however, cannot explain the realignments and issues which surrounded the City Elections Act. They can only outline the background. The controversy itself demands further exploration. The Whig objective in 1725 was to arrest the advance of popular Toryism. This resurgence in grass roots Toryism dated from the late seventeenth century, when the Whigs shed their radical coat for a more establishment cut. Several factors contributed to it. There was, firstly, the widespread feeling that William III and his ministers had been too indulgent towards the Protestant Dissenters and that a tougher policy was required to protect the realm from the threat of rabid sectarianism. Allied to this theme were a series of economic issues which were of great importance to London citizenry. The great expansion of the suburbs, which grew apace after the Fire, was not wholeheartedly welcomed by many of the domestic trading companies, for it ultimately jeopardized their ability to control their clientele and maintain their privileged position in the metropolitan market.[6] Indeed it was precisely in those areas where craft and retailing privileges were persistently undermined, in the wards beyond the walls, that popular Toryism was most pronounced. This grievance was compounded by the financial strain of continental war, and by the growing unpopularity of the new financial aristocracy, whose fortunes, notwithstanding the odd Tory tycoon, had been intertwined with the Whigs since the 1690s. The monied interest, in particular, became a Tory bugbear; not only on grounds of political parasitism, but because their interests appeared antipathetic to domestic trade and also to the City proper, since they had superseded the Corporation and the livery companies as the major government creditors and at the same time showed a marked reluctance to contribute substantially to the municipality's welfare.[7] Together these factors fostered a Tory populism, which, notwithstanding the volatility of party life during Queen Anne's reign, made a permanent imprint on City politics.

By the 1720s, Whig dignitaries, who had been well entrenched within the City hierarchy since the Revolution, saw themselves threatened on all flanks. The Whig landslide of 1715 proved temporary, notwithstanding persistent efforts to flaunt the Jacobite bogey before the Livery. In an expanded electorate, which had more than doubled during the second half of the seventeenth century, reaching a highpoint of 8,500 in 1722, Tory candidates proved singularly successful in capturing the votes of the newer and lesser companies.[8] Two seats fell to the Tories in 1722 and in the next two years, Common Hall politics appeared so finely balanced that even shrieval elections, which determined the next returning officers, assumed new dimensions.

It was in the wards, however, that Whig hegemony was most threatened. Notwithstanding the ability of a Whig-dominated bench to materially influence freeman politics, ward after ward fell to the Tories. In 1710 they held six out of a total of twenty-five; by 1722 twelve. Successive Tory Common Councils helped matters considerably, for under two by-laws they introduced stricter electoral procedures and transformed the mode of electing aldermen, replacing the elaborate system of nomination and co-option by direct elections. Sometimes their efforts produced litigation not results. In the years 1711-19 Londoners witnessed a protracted legal feud between a Tory Council and a Whig Court of Aldermen, the one financing suits at King's Bench, the other replying with writs of prohibition. There is no doubt that Whig· obstruction and legal stalemate prevented the Tories from capturing the marginal wards.[9]

In the City Elections Act the Whigs hoped to find a solution to their predicament. The freeman franchise was defined as narrowly as was practicable, overriding custom and disqualifying perhaps 3,000 voters. Proposals were also formulated for the restriction of the livery electorate, but the government backed down in the face of unanimous protests from the City companies.[10] Ultimately the Common Hall franchise was merely clarified by the introduction of a twelve month qualification and due payment of livery fines. Most controversial of all was clause fifteen of the Act. This imposed an aldermanic veto on all legislative acts and resolutions of the Common Council, a power which had been rescinded during the Civil War, and while tacitly binding after 1683, had never hitherto been reasserted. In practical terms, the negative prohibited the Common Council from adopting an independent role as government critic and potentially at least, reaffirmed aldermanic control over ward politics.

The 1725 Act was a flagrantly partisan measure designed to cut City Toryism from its popular roots and immobilize the principal bastion of support, the Common Council. It revealed, in its transparency, the reciprocity of interests between the Court and the plutocracy, for Walpole's ability to guarantee a majority on the City bench greatly depended upon his deft manipulation of financial patronage. To the City radicals, the 1725 measure represented yet another statutory control which facilitated the path to Oligarchy. It also, however, evoked moderate opposition, for it raised the vexed question of the City's political autonomy. During the first decade of Hanoverian rule there had been clear signs of a general disposition to clarify the freeman franchise and to introduce a semblance of order in City elections. In 1723, for example, a Common Council committee had been established to resolve the ambiguities of the ward franchise, particularly the contentious issue of what constituted paying Scot and bearing Lot.[11] The Whigs forestalled these efforts, and used their majority in parliament to do so. Walpole's Act could thus be interpreted as an affront to independency, a denial of the City's right to put its own house in order without outside interference. One opponent described it as 'the highest attempt of its nature that was ever made, and much beyond the taking away of charters in King Charles and King James days'.[12] This was a flamboyant statement indeed, but one which showed some grasp of the Act's wider implications.

The remodelling of the City's constitutional structure by parliamentary authority for indisputably partisan purposes thus engendered a realignment in City politics. After 1725, several well known independent Whigs gravitated to opposition ranks. In the next general election a conscious effort was made by anti-Walpolean forces to eschew traditional party affiliations to attract a wider base of support. The Opposition quite deliberately set up a 'Country' list, and through the *Craftsman*, Bolingbroke's new journalistic venture, directed their attention to the need for representatives who would uphold the general trading interests of the City rather than those of high finance. In a special pre-election edition, the weekly urged the Livery to discriminate between 'fair Merchants and notorious Stock-jobbers, between the true promoters of our Manufacturers and most beneficial Commerce, and overgrown Monopolies which are the destruction of both'.[13] Indeed it was the Court Whigs rather than their opponents who deliberately emphasized traditional divisions and fears, delaying the election until the coronation of George II and disseminating the report that Sir John Barnard, a former Quaker, was wholly unsympathetic to the post-Revolution religious settlement which gave Dissenters a qualified toleration. One Dissenter, Andrew Pitt, in an attempt to revive old religious and dynastic animosities, even circulated the rumour that Barnard had been an enthusiastic supporter of Sacheverell.[14] This strategy combined with deft electoral organization, appears to have been successful. For a time the Court Whigs arrested their decline in popularity, and by posing as the party of order and dynastic loyalty, made considerable headway among the older voters.[15]

Within six years, however, Court fortunes once again slipped. In February 1733, Lord Mayor Barber surprised the ministerial party by promoting a Common Council resolution instructing the City MPs to vote against Walpole's Excise proposals, and in collusion with a number of well-known parliamentarians, mounted a huge campaign against the ministry. Tobacco and wine importers, linen drapers and brewers, Dutch and Hamburg merchants, mobilized against the Monster Excise. So too did the populace at large, who paraded wooden shoes through the streets, jostled Walpole at the door of the Commons, and burnt him in effigy. According to Charles Howard, the crowd 'broke all the windows at the Post Office, rung their bells in all the churches, made bonfires, stopt every coach that came by, and made them cry "No Excise"'.[16] The electoral consequences of this successful agitation, which rippled through the provinces, became apparent a year later. In March 1734, the Opposition candidate and tobacco merchant John Bosworth unexpectedly defeated the ministerialist and former Tory William Selwin in the contest for City Chamberlain. As a result of this decisive setback, which so embittered Walpole, no ministerial supporter ventured to stand in the City general election two months later.

Judging from the March poll, whose turnout astounded contemporaries, the Court continued to win the allegiance of the directors of the major monied companies, who, in conjunction with the government departments in the City were able to amass a substantial retainer vote. The ministerial Whigs could also count upon the support of influential sectors of mercantile opinion, part of the wider superstructure of the money market: Lombard and Fenchurch Street bankers; textile manufacturers and middlemen; merchants in the more traditional spheres of overseas enterprise – the Levant trade, for example – who tended to diversify their activities and had developed close connections with the cosmopolitan plutocracy of London. In fact one notes a clear congruence between Whiggery and the financial establishment. Nevertheless, their opponents were not bereft of merchant-financier affiliations and were able to marshal an impressive galaxy of business interests. Goldsmith-bankers displaced by Revolution finance, wine importers, independent insurers and industrialists, Atlantic merchants outside the matrix of the greater business syndicates, all gave their votes to Bosworth in 1734. Together with the petty bourgeoisie and a substantial section of the middling liverymen engaged in either the professions or domestic trade, they constituted a powerful phalanx in City politics, an anti-establishment with a genuinely popular base, which gradually assumed command of the corporations's elective institutions.

The decade following the City Elections Act thus saw the emergence of a broadly-based anti-ministerial coalition, a 'Patriot' party as it was called, united in opposition to the political and economic policies of Walpole and his financial allies. This predominantly populist front appealed to those who wished to broaden the base of anticipatory finance and free private credit from the control of the plutocratic élite. It attracted the allegiance of merchants in the more dynamic sectors of overseas enterprise who considered Walpole's continentalist foreign policy inhibited commercial expansion in the trans-Atlantic trades and who distrusted trading monopolies. And it embraced those sections of domestic trade, the food retailers in particular, who campaigned for a more determined defence of traditional economic controls in the metropolitan market. To some extent it preyed upon sectarian animosities; indeed the ethnic orientation of conspicuous sectors of high finance and textile manufacture rekindled old religious antagonisms. From a more general perspective, however, City Patriotism represented a protest against political and economic centralization, a vindication of the wider interests of trade and manufacture and a defence of the City's independence and democratic traditions.

During the years 1738–42 the anti-Court coalition consolidated its position in the City. The background to this significant development is well known.[18] It concerned the popular campaign for a war with Spain to bolster British commercial enterprise in Spanish–American waters, a campaign which irrevocably undermined all confidence in Walpole's ministry and finally forced him from power. The struggle for commercial privileges in Spain's old American empire was a long-standing issue. Since the second half of the seventeenth century English merchants had continually baulked the restrictive regulations which governed their trade in the area. Spanish efforts to contain the lucrative contraband trade between her territories and British dominions, and her unwillingness after 1713 to redefine the terms on which legitimate commerce could be conducted, became a smouldering grievance within the trans-Atlantic mercantile community. The employment of *guarda-costas* to police Spanish waters and search British vessels on the open seas brought the situation to crisis point. Redress for the British merchant, even where legitimate, proved virtually impossible. Litigation was endless. And negotiations through diplomatic channels appeared ineffectual. The commissaries established by the Treaty of Seville in 1729 to arbitrate on the question of unlawful seizures had by 1737 produced no significant result.

Indeed traders in American and Caribbean waters grew alarmed at the increasing scale of confiscations, and in October 1737, 153 merchants signed a petition drawn up by the colonial agent of Jamaica complaining of Spanish privateering. Early the following year, merchant lobbies were organized at the Ship tavern behind the Royal Exchange to press the government to take firmer action.[19] And on 3 March, Micajah Perry, a London alderman and tobacco merchant who had played a leading part in the anti-Excise agitation of 1733, presented a petition to the Commons from the London American and West India merchants condemning the continued disruption of British commerce and demanding a tougher response from the administration. He was seconded by Sir John Barnard, who advocated war rather than 'a dishonourable peace'.[20] Within weeks the London petition was joined by others from the outports, from Liverpool, Glasgow, and Bristol, confronting the ministry with the formidable array of mercantile opinion.

Although Walpole successfully fought off the demands of Atlantic merchants, Tories, and opposition Whigs for a parliamentary review of government and an unambiguous affirmation of British rights to freedom of navigation during the spring of 1738, the campaign for tougher measures gathered momentum. The dispute between the merchants and the Spanish authorities was quickly caricatured as a struggle between English liberty and foreign absolutism. Comparisons were made between the operations of *guardacostas* abroad and excise officers at home. 'No Search', the popular abridgement of freedom and navigation, became a new libertarian slogan.[21] And the hardships inflicted upon British sailors, idealized in Richard Glover's poem 'London' as the 'chosen train of Liberty and Commerce', were well orchestrated in the anti-ministerial press. The *London Evening Post*, for example, run by a Tory Common Councilman named Richard Nutt, declared there were 'no less than 71 in Irons in one Prison a-starving and God knows how many more in the same misery in other gaols both in Spain and America' and a subscription for their dependants was quickly opened at Lloyd's Coffee House.[22]

It was the Spanish Convention, however, which gave the campaign its real fillip. The agreement merely confirmed the opposition's worst fears concerning Walpole's accommodating policy. Mercantile reparations were substantially reduced; rights guaranteed by earlier treaties remained ill-defined; and the principle of freedom of navigation was still not recognized. Brushing aside the argument that the Convention was but a prelude to a more comprehensive settlement which would settle mercantile grievances without the burden of war or the disruption of trade, Opposition spokesmen believed it would 'dwindle away in a few months to peaceable Pen and Paper again'.[23] Without doubt, the Convention inaugurated a new wave of protest. A masquerade at the Haymarket satirized the Court's servility to Spain. Ballads portrayed Walpole bribing the Don for hollow concessions. And a ministerial sympathizer who cried out 'No Merchants, but Conventions and Treaties for ever' was attacked outside the Commons.[24] In the paper war which followed the publication of the agreement, ministerial writers found themselves very much on the defensive. 'The clamours raised against this Convention,' declared Bishop Hare in March, 'have been carried to the greatest height both within doors and without.'[25]

Although Walpole's success in the Commons disheartened the parliamentary Opposition and led to their secession, London opinion remained as resolute as ever. The Common Council had already petitioned against the Convention, and had been lampooned as a trifling band of shopkeepers for their pains.[26] Once the measure became law, it campaigned at the grass roots to oppose the mayoral ambitions of Sir George Champion, one of the two aldermen in parliament who had voted for the Convention. Since Champion was next in line for mayoral office, this move implied a radical departure from the usual custom of nominating the two most senior aldermen below the chair as prospective candidates. Sir George countered these initiatives by sending a letter to the *Daily Advertiser* in which he argued that he was not accountable as a member of the corporation for his actions as MP for Aylesbury.[27] But his opponents in the City were not impressed by his reasoning, and were determined to make a political example of him. In this they succeeded. Notwithstanding the extensive campaign mounted in his favour – the Court Whigs were said to have rallied the Customs, Excise, and Post Office and distributed 4,000 circulars on his behalf – he was decisively defeated at Common Hall.[28] Ministerial reaction was one of consternation. Bishop Hare was shocked by the Livery's defiant denunciation of the Spanish compact which, he emphasized, had received parliamentary assent. And Newcastle feared the Convention would continue to dominate City elections. 'If we go on despising what people think and say,' he confided to Harwicke, 'We shall not have it long in our power to direct what measures shall be taken.'[29]

The Livery's clear repudiation of the Convention in September 1739 set the scene for an electoral landslide. To the accompaniment of a well organized campaign against Walpole and his allies in which every tactical retreat by the administration was readily exploited, the Patriots gradually penetrated the Court strongholds within the Corporation. In 1739, the Court party could muster seventy-one supporters on the Common Council to the Patriot's 110, a slight advance on their position both immediately before and after the City Elections Act. Determined efforts were made to improve this situation. In December 1739, for example, Sir John Eyles, the Postmaster General and former South Sea director, launched a new Court offensive in several wards where big business retained considerable electoral influence, denigrating the anti-ministerialists as a narrow party caucus which arrogated to itself all lucrative City contracts and offices. This counter-offensive failed. In Bishopsgate, where the contest resembled an open parliamentary election replete with broadsides and ballads, the voters proved insensitive to the protestations of 'placemen, pensioners and conventioners', and rejected all Court candidates at both the precinct meetings and the wardmote.[30] Indeed, within two years, the Patriot bloc had made major inroads into the predominantly financial wards surrounding the Exchange, where for twenty years Whig supremacy had been unquestioned. Cornhill, the home of Jonathan's and Garraway's, social centres of high finance and marine insurance, fell to the opposition. So too did Broad Street after the litigious aldermanic contest of 1741. Even Langbourn, the bankers' ward, witnessed the election of four Patriots; so that by 1742, the Whig bloc on Common Council was smaller than at any time since the Hanoverian accession.[31]

The chronicle of Patriot victories was not, however, of unwavering success. Following the Livery's rejection of Sir George Champion, the ministerialists on the bench flouted opposition opinion by deliberately rejecting the nomination of Sir Robert Godschall, a wine merchant and brother-in-law to Sir John Barnard. On these successive occasions between September 1740 and March 1741, the Court of Aldermen refused Godschall mayoral office. Nevertheless, this reversal of Patriot fortunes proved counter-productive, for Godschall's ostracism by the Court of Aldermen only highlighted the isolation of the Court party from the mainstream of City politics. This became clear in the general election of 1741. Notwithstanding Court efforts to rally the support of moderate as well as solidly ministerial opinion and to divide their opponents by promoting the candidature of the popular Admiral Vernon, the Opposition swept the polls. Even Godschall, who came bottom of the poll in 1734, received over 3,000 votes, approximately 1,100 more than the combined vote of the two principal Court candidates.[32] It was brought home, too, four months after the election, when the ministerial patriciate capitulated to popular pressures and allowed Sir Robert to assume mayoral office. And it was emphatically reaffirmed the following year when Edward Gibbons' election as

Alderman of Vintry ward gave the Opposition a clear majority on the bench. The Court party had reached the nadir of its fortunes. For the first time since the Revolution, Court hegemony on the aldermanic bench, the linchpin of Walpole's policy of containment, was decisively broken.[33]

Two central features emerge then, in a study of London politics during the years 1738–42. Firstly, one notes a convergence of forces in opposition to Walpole embracing American and West Indian merchants, the City élite, particularly the Common Council, and the unenfranchised. Secondly, one sees a dramatic disintegration of ministerial influence in the City, even within the Court of Aldermen. Two further themes deserve comment, not only because they have been largely overlooked in the conventional historiography of the period, but because they denote a subtle change in London's stature as an extra-parliamentary force: the emergence of a more coherent anti-Walpolean platform radiating from the capital to the provinces, and the promotion of novel forms of political association to achieve this aim.

One of the most significant aspects of City politics during this period was its role within the wider political arena. From the spring of 1738 until the general election of 1741, the parliamentary Opposition was deeply divided over its strategy towards the administration, and it befell the constituencies to sustain the momentum of the campaign against Walpole. In this respect the City of London made an invaluable contribution. By rejecting Champion, defending Godschall and rallying to Admiral Vernon, whose early victories underlined the merits of retaliatory action against Spain, the City Patriots animated the opposition to Walpole.[34] Through the medium of the Press, their activities penetrated the provinces. The *Norwich Gazette* kept its readers in touch with London developments.[35] And the London newspapers themselves, whose circulation was by no means confined to the metropolitan area, continually expatiated upon the national significance of City politics. Such a claim was hardly new. The idea that London was a barometer of national opinion had been a commonplace during the reign of Queen Anne. But in the oligarchic climate of the Hanoverian era, The more vibrant and mettlesome character of City politics assumed a new significance. London became the champion of independent opinion, the vindicator of a more open conception of politics. In the City, one pamphleteer argued, it was possible 'to distinguish betwixt a popular Cry carr'd on and encouraged by a Faction, and the just complaints of a People'. A judicious observer would discover 'that the Sense of the Whole Nation breath'd thro' all her Remonstrances, and animated all her Resolutions'.[36]

One important tactic adopted by the City opposition was the formulation of instructions to its parliamentary representatives. First utilized at the turn of the century, instructions became a fairly regular feature of City politics. Normally they were promoted at Common Hall, after a parliamentary election. During the years 1739–42, however, they were used more extensively as an alternative political medium to the City petition or address, which could be frustrated by an aldermanic veto. On no less than five occasions instructions were passed by Common Hall or Common Council.[37] Organized from the Half Moon tavern on Cheapside, the centre of opposition activity, they broadened the attack upon Walpole to embrace the political system he had helped to inaugurate, outlining a series of political reforms designed to recapture the vitality of the early Augustan era and offset the power of the executive. Instructions not intended as mere expressions of local sentiment. Furthermore, there was no consensus about their constitutional implications, certainly no move, at Common Hall, to pledge candidates to specific issues before their election.[38] They were principally propagandist devices, designed to rally support, through the agency of the Press, within the metropolis and beyond. In this respect they were quite successful, setting precedents which local factions could exploit and sometimes emulate. The Livery's instructions of October 1739 calling for a place bill were re-echoed by twelve boroughs and five counties. The Common Council resolutions of June 1740 became a rallying point at the summer assizes, particularly in those counties where grass-roots Toryism was strong. And the City instructions at the culmination of the campaign against Walpole provided a context for similar resolutions from at least thirty-six constituencies, including many of the larger freeman boroughs and the Welsh, Scottish, and south-western counties.[39] Although it is impossible to gauge the precise extent of London's influence on these occasions, there is little doubt that it was impressive, evoking strong opposition from the ministerial press and bitter comments from Court grandees.

The City of London thus played a valuable role at the vanguard of the 'unofficial opposition' to Walpole's administration. In helping to co-ordinate the extra-parliamentary agitation against the first minister and extending its social base, it proved of invaluable service to Walpole's opponents in high politics. The City Patriot coalition did not, however, act as simple latimer to its parliamentary allies. It was not bedevilled by the divisions which beset the anti-ministerial group in parliament. There is no evidence that the dispute over Sandys motion for the dismissal of Walpole in February 1741, for example, weakened the resolve of the City Opposition, even though two leading aldermen followed the Shippen coterie in repudiating the measure.[40] Indeed it seems that the City patriots pursued an increasingly independent course. Under the leadership of the Half Moon club, the City adopted a more strident radical posture.[41] While continuing to rally support for a more adventurous foreign policy attuned to Britain's expanding commercial interests in the New World, the City Opposition campaigned for a Country programme of constitutional reform, the repeal of the aldermanic veto, the repudiation of standing armies in peace time and the relaxation of excise controls. Such a programme appealed to a wide range of economic interests within the City, retailers as well as merchants. It was singularly relevant to a community which prided itself upon its independence of Court and government, had a keen sense of its historic role as a watchdog of the constitution, and fully appreciated its importance within the mercantilist system.

By 1742, the City of London was firmly committed to a campaign of political reform as well as the dismissal of Walpole. In conjunction with the newly formed political association in Westminster, the City Patriots demanded a vigorous inquiry into Walpole's mismanagement of public affairs and the implementation of measures designed to eliminate the stultifying aspects of the political system he had helped to fashion. Neither wish was fulfilled. The Commons committee of inquiry died a natural death in the summer of 1742. The modest place bill proved a token gesture. And the realignments and accommodations which accompanied Walpole's displacement from power frustrated further reform. The City's reaction was one of bitter indignation. Pulteney in particular was sharply denounced. A deluge of ballads lambasted his desertion of the Patriot camp for a peerage, lacing their criticisms with ironic quips about the political game. And the Common Council, in a more solemn manner, condemned Pulteney and his fellow-travellers for their unrepentant apostacy.[42]

Walpole's fall thus saw little abatement of the tide of anti-ministerialism. If anything London opinion hardened. City discontent quickly found a new focus in the administration's continentalist foreign policy, which raised traditional fears about the subordination of British to Hanoverian interests. In October 1742 the Common Council condemned 'the parade of Land Armies and the Hire of Foreign Forces' and contrasted the lavish commitment to Europe with the poor protection of British overseas dominions. And in the final month of the year, five of the six City aldermen in parliament joined forces with the Tories and the rump of Patriot Whigs in opposing the hire of 16,000 Hanoverian troops.[43] The inactivity of the Pragmatic army the following winter and the battle of Dettingen brought a fresh upsurge of anti-Hanoverianism. Prints and ballads exposed the neglect of British troops. One cheap pamphlet, bitterly critical of the king's partiality towards his Electoral troops at Dettingen, was distributed from Pater Noster Row by the thousand.[44] In March, two leading anti-ministerial aldermen, George Heathcote and William Calvert, attended a Tory rally at the Fountain Tavern on the Strand where toasts were drunk to the 'promotion of true interest in HM's BRITISH DOMINIONS'; and the Common Council deliberately snubbed George II by ignoring his victory at Dettingen in their summer address.[45] Jacobite observers were elated by these events. Thomas Carte was so overwhelmed by the ferment against the Court that he believed 'the only distinction left' was 'that of Englishmen or Britons, and Hanoverians'. 'Were you in London to hear what is said there openly every day and in the most public places,' he reported in July, 'you would not think there was a man for the present Government.'[46]

Even allowing for Jacobite optimism, there is little doubt that the conduct of the war on the continent had alienated a wide section of metropolitan opinion. Henry Fox told Ilchester in October 1743 that the ferment against Hanover had grown so serious as 'to disturb as sanguine a Politician as I am'.[47] The threat of a French–Jacobite invasion in 1744, however, inevitably silenced anti-Hanoverian protest. The suspension of Habeas Corpus and the arrest of Lord Barrymore curbed the inflammatory diatribes of the following year. The City aldermen in parliament still continued to oppose the British financing of Hanoverian troops, although three of them, Sir John Barnard, William Calvert, and Daniel Lambert, were not prepared to embarrass the ministry on other issues. They opposed, for example, Dodington's motion for a naval inquiry in February 1744.[48] Nevertheless, relations between the government and the City of London remained strained, and Pelham's willingness to modify Carteret's pro-Hanoverian foreign policy did not inaugurate a new climate of reconciliation. Indeed, Court opposition to the repeal of the aldermanic veto, an issue which the City had raised with increasing urgency since 1740, thwarted even the possibility of a *rapprochement* with moderate elements within the corporation.[49] At the outbreak of the 1745 rebellion therefore, the Court found itself well isolated from the mainstream of London opinion. The Courts of Common Hall and Common Council were firmly in Opposition hands. And of the twenty-five aldermen, only eight were ministerial stalwarts. At a time when the government was fully aware that the Jacobites entertained high hopes of a metropolitan insurrection, this was a disturbing situation.

Government supporters did all they could to bolster loyalism in the metropolis during the autumn of 1745. The Press and the pulpit inundated the public with the stock in trade images of anti-Catholicism, and reasserted the traditional arguments of Whig orthodoxy, the threat of a Stuart Restoration to commerce, credit, and liberty.[50] Pope-burning ceremonies were revived. The War Office staged a regular sequence of military parades as the troops came home from the continent, and the local militia regiments were quickly if ineffectually mobilized. Within the City's own Lieutenancy Commission, the only body appointed by the crown, ministerialists numbered in force. The committee set up to reorganize the trained bands was packed with courtiers.[51] It included four directors of the East India and South Sea Companies; William Selwin, the Receiver-General of the Land Tax and the unsuccessful candidate in the Chamberlain's election of 1734; and Edward Ratcliffe, a Turkey merchant and London Assurance director, who had stood on the ministerial slate in the Bishopsgate Common Council election of 1739. Ministerial supervision of the City militia, moreover, was accompanied by the zealous activities of the cosmopolitan plutocracy. Over seven hundred merchants and financiers, including representatives of the Dutch, Huguenot, and Jewish communities as well as directors of the major monied companies, signed a loyalist address to the Hanoverian crown and resolved to uphold the public credit at a time when there was an alarming run on the Bank.[52] In addition, many of them supported the loyalist associations and subscription funds for government troops in the north. Although several aldermen played a leading role in these transactions – Sir William Baker, for example, acted as an intermediary between Newcastle and the Spitalfields volunteer regiments, while Sir Joseph Hankey helped sponsor the first subscription scheme – it was the financial élite rather than the City's political community who formed the backbone of loyalist support.[53]

What then was the response of the City of London? How did the opposition in particular react to loyalist initiatives? All the evidence suggests that the City was divided over political strategy. Whereas the moderates within the Opposition camp showed a willingness to shelve their political grievances during the rebellion and collaborate with the government, the radicals made co-operation conditional upon political concessions. National harmony they argued, could best be fostered by some gesture towards the political demands set out in 1742, by popular remedies designed to break the sinews of Court influence and to arrest the anti-libertarian tendencies of thirty years' Whig domination. Such aims, embracing the repeal of the Riot Act, the elimination of standing armies and the National Debt, and the full implementation of the Act of

Settlement as well as the better known panaceas of the Patriot programme – Place and Pension bills and the restoration of Triennial Parliaments – had been regularly voiced during the aftermath of Walpole's fall. They were set out in the rejoinders to the Earl of Egmont's *Faction Detected*, a tract which not only defended the political *volte-face* of the Pulteney faction, but condemned the activities of London and Westminster radicals and warned that further constitutional reform would undermine the equilibrium of powers in the state and open the door to popular anarchy and Jacobitism.[54] And they were restated at the outbreak of the Forty-Five both in the City and in Parliament, where Sir Francis Dashwood pressed for 'anti-corruption' bills to bolster popular loyalism.[55]

The first signs of a schism within the City Opposition came in early September when news of the rebellion reached London. Even before the City had received official confirmation of the insurrection, the Lord Mayor Sir Henry Marshal and Sir John Barnard prepared the ground for a loyalist address from the Court of Aldermen, assuring the King of their 'Zeal and Readiness to Oppose his Enemies and every attempt against the Rights of his Crown and our present happy Constitution.'[56] Three days later, as Marshal and Barnard rallied support for a similar address from the Common Council, the radicals were better prepared, George Heathcote refusing to support any motion 'unattended with a representation of our grievances, or the least hint to the crown of its obligations to the people'.[57] His objections, however, were overruled, and another controversial and conciliatory resolution was passed. How genuine a reflection of City opinion this gesture was is difficult to assess. Heathcote claimed the meeting was poorly attended, many members being out of town, and accused his colleagues of bamboozling the Council. Nevertheless, his testimony is suspect. Although Barnard helped to draw up the address, the eight commoners on the committee included three who had been responsible for the City instructions of 1742 and two others who had been regular members of the two committees on the repeal of the aldermanic veto.[58] Clearly certain influential Opposition spokesmen were prepared to postpone their long term political objectives and rally unconditionally to the crown.

A similar polarization of opinion occurred over the question of loyalist associations and subscription funds to aid the government's military effort against the Jacobites. First launched in Ireland, these schemes were ostensibly designed for local defence or for the promotion of volunteer regiments supplementary to the government's regular forces. The associations, for example, were intended as alternatives to the militia, which proved difficult to raise owing to certain legal and

financial impediments.[59] In practice, however, their military importance was slight. In reality they were intended as loyalist and inevitably
pro-ministerial rallies. Archbishop Herring, for instance, alarmed by
public diffidence in Yorkshire, quite consciously set up an association
'to animate the King's Friends'.[60] The Earl of Hardwicke, too, placed
'more weight upon the Evidence & Eclat that will arise from such
Meetings & associations of ye Zeal & Spirit & good assertions of His
Majesty's Subjects in support of the Governmt & agst the Pretender
than upon the military utility of their Troops'.[61] Although the loyal
associations could and sometimes did play a modest military role during
the   rebellion – quite   apart   from   the   question   of   internal
vigilance – there is little doubt that they were of greater political
significance. Their avid promotion during the early months of the
insurrection – no less than twenty-five counties and twelve provincial
towns set up loyalist organizations – undoubtedly put many opponents
of the ministry on the defensive. To refuse to join an association was a
courageous act. Political neutrality in such a crisis, claimed Theophilus
Cibber in his poem *The Association: or, Liberty and Loyalty*, was 'a
Crime'.[62]

Notwithstanding the obvious dangers of dissent, quite a few Tories
and indeed several independents objected to these activities. The
prospect of swearing unconditional allegiance to the crown even
disturbed the libertarian consciences of gentlemen whose loyalism was
unswerving and hitherto unquestioned. Sir George Seville for instance,
described by Herring as 'perfectly in the King's Interest', confessed to
the Earl of Malton that he was 'really diffident' about joining the
Yorkshire Association. 'I fear the very strong terms the Association is
couch'd in,' he confided, 'may frighten many, who wou'd otherwise,
while the danger lasted, cheerfully and heartily stand by their Leader to
the last.'[63] In addition, many militia enthusiasts believed the associations denied them the opportunity of reorganizing the local levies into
a truly constitutional force, a counterpoise to both standing armies and
mercenaries; a grievance that was aggravated by the government's
sponsorship of thirteen regiments of foot under aristocratic command,
described by Sir John Phillips in the Commons as a 'pretty play thing'
which would only feather noble nests and further the ambition of
ministerial sycophants.[64] Earl Poulett, writing from Tory country,
reported that the Somerset gentry believed the associations, set up by
royal warrant, 'were contrary to the nature of Parliament, unparliamentary and unconstitutional'. 'There was a bull baiting, wch
made a good deal of noise at the time of our meeting,' he added, 'and
was supposed by some to have been contrived on purpose.'[65] Similar

objections were raised about subscriptions. Tory-radicals denounced them as an illegal tax, controverting the Commons' right to scrutinize supply, and denying them the opportunity of examining the government's overall defence policy in detail. In parliament Thomas Carew and George Heathcote compared the subscriptions to the benevolences of Charles I's reign, and declared 'they opened the door to the infringement of the most sacred privilege of parliament, the power of granting money'. The Welsh Tory, Sir Watkin Williams Wynne, also concurred with this view. According to William Ellis, he 'did not speak but on the Topick of subscriptions cried Hear & gave the hint to some of his people to do the like'.[66]

Opposition to the associations and subscription plans was deep rooted in the City of London notwithstanding the strength of popular loyalism and the unanimous enthusiasm of the mercantile community.[67] The corporation appears to have been singularly lethargic in setting up its own subscription fund, even though it was under considerable pressure to do so, and it was not until late November that it agreed to establish one in conjunction with earlier projects at Jonathan's and Garraway's. Similarly the City's loyalist association took some time to germinate, in spite of an early declaration of intent and pointed exhortations from leading London preachers.[68] Nevertheless, a substantial section of the City Opposition did support the various loyalist associations which blossomed in the final months of 1745. Nineteen aldermen, including eleven members of the former anti-Walpolean coalition, signed the declaration of 4 October pledging their support for 'our Present Happy Constitution'. Twelve contributed to the Guildhall fund to aid government troops in the north, among them three City MPs, Sir John Barnard, Sir Daniel Lambert, and Sir William Calvert, all of whom had played influential roles at the vanguard of the Patriot faction.[69] Of the Common Councilmen, ninety-two out of a total of 236 supported the loyalist declaration. Approximately half were members of the Patriot bloc, including several important committee men: James Hodges, a bookseller on London bridge, later to become Town Clerk; James Heywood, a linen draper from the same ward, an aldermanic candidate in 1746 and Master of the Drapers' Company in 1747-8; and Richard Sclater, a druggist of Newgate Street, Master of the Grocers' Company 1743-4, deputy of Farringdon Within and its alderman in 1745. Fewer commoners tended individual contributions to the Guildhall Fund (the Council itself donated £1,000), but of those that did, Opposition sympathizers outnumbered ministerialists by a ratio of two to one. Significant contributions also came from the two leading Opposition livery companies, the Goldsmiths' and the Vintners'; from Cordwainer, a ward which had swung over to the Patriots in the years 1739-41; and from St. Bride's, Fleet Street, a parish in the traditionally Tory ward of Farringdon Without. The Guildhall subscription fund, like the loyalist declaration, was never monopolized by the ministerial Whigs. Although the financial and mercantile bourgeoisie outside the City political élite provided the impetus for the project, it was organized with the help of moderate Patriots such as Sir Richard Hoare, the Lord Mayor and a banker of Tory lineage, who was later thanked for his efforts.[70]

The political crisis of 1745 thus divided the City Opposition. While a conspicuous minority of Patriots joined forces with the administration in buttressing loyalism in the metropolis, the radicals eschewed all co-operation with a ministry insensitive to their political demands. Such a tactic inevitably opened them to the charge of crypto-Jacobitism. Was it in any way justified? Recent commentaries on mid-century Toryism have taken Whig and indeed Jacobite propaganda at their face value, and the City in particular has been portrayed as a hot-bed of disaffection. The evidence for such a view, however, is extremely ambiguous. It is clear that the Pretender's minions hoped for a fifth column uprising in London; in fact the Jacobites had to make a case for metropolitan disaffection in order to win French support.[71] But it is by no means certain that the Stuarts had a strong following in the City, notwithstanding Murray's subsequent testimony and Sempil's enthusiastic reports to Rome while the rebellion was in progress.[72] Although Jacobite agents had re-established contact with City politicians in the summer of 1743, their reports, often sensational and politically naïve, leave us with a dubious record of their reception. Even Balhady's detailed list of Common Council affiliations, drawn up in May or June 1743, is peppered with minor flaws, overlooks the complexity of political configurations within the City and evades the central issue of dynastic commitment.[73] Certainly his optimistic forecast that 70 per cent of the Council were potential converts to the Pretender's party does not easily square with the known *behaviour* of City patriots. Admittedly there is marginal evidence that George Heathcote flirted with Jacobitism during the insurrection.[74] But once again the evidence is inconclusive. Even if one accepted his complicity, the spectacle of a disaffected capital would remain unsubstantiated. Indeed, unless one is prepared to adopt a wholly conspiratorial view of opposition politics and reduce anti-ministerial arguments to the specious rationalization of troublemakers and fifth columnists, the Jacobite thesis cannot be sustained.

Rumours of disaffection were nevertheless rife during the rebellion and its aftermath. It was widely feared that substantial sums had been raised for the Young Pretender in London and the City élite was strongly suspected of harbouring crypto-Jacobite sympathies. The radicals, in particular, came under attack. Several broadsides accused the Westminster Independents of conspiracy and condemned the refractory and by implication treasonable behaviour of some of their allies in the City, notably aldermen William Benn and George Heathcote.[75] Even their former conduct was censured. 'Did not the Common Language and Behaviour of too many of our Countrymen,' asked one pamphleteer, encourage the Stuart exiles and the French, 'to hope for that success from a murmuring, discontented, and divided nation.'[76] Such invective fulfilled its purposes. It created a climate of fear, questioned the legitimacy of criticism, and sapped the will to oppose.

In this manner the Whigs prepared the way for the impending general election. Public interest in the rebellion was maintained at fever pitch by a series of well-executed scenarios. At the impeachment of the Jacobite Lord Lovat but a few months before the election, John Murray, the former secretary of the Pretender, disclosed that a number of prominent Tories well entrenched in Westminster radical circles had collaborated with Lord Traquair, a Jacobite agent. The Tories shrugged off the charge; the government never pursued it; but it had the desired effect. 'You may easily imagine that Murray's evidence makes a great noise,' wrote Elizabeth Yorke to her brother, 'and it is not unlikely but it may have further consequences.'[77]

Two further incidents helped to maintain public interest in the trial and emblazon the standard of patriotic Whiggery. On 24 March 1747, the Commons ordered an investigation into the conduct of the Westminster Independents at their annual dinner at Vintners' Hall, where the landlord of the White Horn, Piccadilly, had apparently been assaulted for harbouring one of the principal prosecuting witnesses in the Lovat trial.[78] Nothing came of the incident, but in a climate fraught with the Jacobite menace, only the Whigs could turn it to good account. The final attempt to exploit the trial for political ends came in early April when Newcastle directed the London sheriffs to hold up the head of the traitor Lord Lovat after his execution. Since the practice had fallen into desuetude, the request had obvious political overtones, and the sheriffs pleaded with Newcastle that 'the Clamour against them for doing it would be very disagreeable'. Robert Alsop protested 'that he had always behaved with the greatest Moderation, and had the highest Opinion and Esteem for his Grace, and was much concerned that such a difficulty as this should be thrown upon him'.[79] On the day of the execution in fact, he refused to carry out the order without written confirmation, while his colleague judiciously absented himself.

In these circumstances, it was hardly surprising that the 1747 elections in the metropolis should be fought against the background of the Forty-Five. In Westminster, the Independent Electors, besieged by a torrent of anti-Jacobite propaganda and virulently censured for their refusal to support the subscriptions and loyalist associations, had great difficulty in finding suitable candidates to stand.[80] Indeed they quickly capitulated before the combined forces of the Court and Bedford House. In Middlesex, the Opposition committed political suicide by publicly disowning all subscribers. Even the support of the returning officers, Lord Mayor Benn, and several other aldermen, proved of little avail against two candidates representing 'the Protestant Interest against the Pretender and all his adherents'.[81]

Such a dramatic reversal of anti-ministerial fortunes since 1741 was less likely in the City where the Opposition party was firmly entrenched. However, the ministerial Whigs had carefully paved the way to win over the moderates. Pelham agreed to the repeal of the Aldermanic negative in March 1746, and, following another campaign by Sir John Barnard for the abolition of the closed structure of anticipatory finance, placated the smaller creditor in the City by raising the government loan of April 1747 by open subscription.[82] Together these actions isolated the radicals and left them vulnerable to the full force of anti-Jacobite propaganda. Henry Fielding portrayed the extremists as a group of malcontents who 'openly drew their Corks in the Pretender's favour' when the rebels reached Derby and contrasted Pelham's judicious foreign and economic policies with the spacious Patriot platform of his radical opponents.[83] Another writer reminded his readers that 'the too free and immoderate exercise of Liberty did not a little contribute to the fomenting and raising the late pernicious Rebellion', while the *General Evening Post* earmarked all 'enemies to associations and subscriptions' for vilification.[84]

The newspaper reports of the election suggest that the Patriots tried hard to settle their differences and present a united front to the electorate. The two leading radicals, Benn and Heathcote, were quickly dropped from the Opposition list.[85] So too was Edward Ironside, a Lombard Street banker who had signed the loyalist declaration of October 1745 but had failed to subscribe to the Guildhall fund. They were replaced, alongside Barnard, whose candidature transcended partisanship, by three moderate aldermen: Henry Marshal, the former MP for Agnondesham and sponsor of the loyalist address of September 1745; Robert Ladbroke, a distiller with considerable local influence in

Castle Baynard and Spitalfields; and Daniel Lambert, a familiar figure in City circles who had worked his way up from the ranks and had represented London in the previous parliament. The Half Moon Club pleaded that these candidates were preferable to those in the rival Merchants' list on account of their long standing connection with the corporation, a line which their opponents dubbed as 'the last Resource of a mad-Brain'd Party, who, seeing their Power and their Old Interest expiring together, are resolved to Die Hard'.[86] This strategy, the attempt by the Patriots to promote a moderate image and press the claims of seasoned politicians with strong local roots, proved unsuccessful. The current of anti-Jacobitism proved too strong.[87] Even the moderates failed to avoid the taint of treason and the charges of irresponsibility levelled at their more radical colleagues. The Merchants' list was returned in toto. It included Barnard, whose political reputation placed him in an unassailable position; Sir William Calvert, a renegade Patriot and avid supporter of the Guildhall subscription and the loyalist association; and finally two prominent City merchants, Slingsby Bethell and Stephen Theodore Janssen, whose Whig ancestry blended well with the political mood of Common Hall.[88] Although these candidates were hardly ministerial stalwarts, they were men whose allegiance to the Hanoverian crown was, in a moment of acute crisis, unquestioned. 'Both Westminster and Middlesex have elected Court candidates,' wrote Horace Walpole to Mann in early July, summing up the metropolitan results, 'and the City of London is taking the same step, the first time of many years that the latter two have been Whig.'[89]

The 1747 election thus fractured Patriot supremacy in the City. Pelham's timely concessions and the Jacobite bogey undermined their electoral popularity. Although they still dominated the Courts of Aldermen and Common Council, the contest was a signal reversal of their political fortunes. It did not, however, inaugurate a pro-ministerial landslide. Rather it stabilized the disposition of forces in the City, the Court party retaining control over wards which had remained conspicuously Whig in the period 1736–43 and winning a few converts from the opposition patriciate. At the same time there was an abatement of party strife, a trend which inhibited the growth of radicalism. It was for these reasons that George Heathcote resigned his aldermanship in January 1749 and retired to Bath a disillusioned man.[90]

Notwithstanding the electoral defeat of 1747 and the abandonment of the Tory-radical programme of reform, the Patriots had, in the twenty years which followed the City Elections Act, achieved some of their political objectives. Under their leadership, the City had played an important role in mobilizing public opinion against Walpole to a point where an assault on his parliamentary hegemony was possible. Indeed the strategies they adopted – the calculated appeal to the political nation by instruction, petition, and address, the use of the Press as a vital medium of communication, the experiments in political association – set important precedents for the future. John Wilkes built on foundations already laid. More important still, the Patriots had successfully resisted the attempt to undermine the City's autonomy and curtail its political freedom. London did not share Norwich's fate. The City continued to be the most formidable pocket of resistance to Whig oligarchy, a natural seed-bed for radical libertarianism notwithstanding the revival of Whig conservatism during the mid-forties, a community which Walpole's successors were frequently forced to accommodate and could never ignore. As such, it provided a source of leadership and inspiration for urban opinion outside the mainstream of institutionalized and gentry-dominated politics. This was the Patriots' ultimate legacy.

Notes

1. The City of London had the right to personally address the Crown; in addition, it was customary for the sheriffs to present City petitions at the bar of the Commons.
2. Alfred J. Henderson, *London and the National Government 1721–42* (North Carolina, 1945); Dame Lucy Sutherland, 'The City in Eighteenth Century Politics', in *Essays presented to Sir Lewis Namier* (ed. R. Pares and A. J. P. Taylor, London, 1956).
3. These conclusions are based on the poll books of 1710, 1713, 1722, 1727. The Guildhall Library has the best collection; see *A handlist of poll books and registers of electors in Guildhall Library* (Corporation of London, 1970), pp. 37–8. I have also located two copies of the Whig vote in 1713: *The poll for J. Ward, T. Scawen, Alderman R. Heyshaw, P. Godfrey 1713* (Brit. Lib., T. 1666 (18)); and *A List of the Poll for members of parliament for the City of London 1713* (Bodleian Lib., Oxford, Gough Lond. 204). For evidence of the resilience of party affiliations, see W. A. Speck and W. A. Gray, 'Londoners at the Polls under Anne and George I', *Guildhall Studies in London History*, i, no. 4 (April, 1975), pp. 253–62.
4. The *London Evening Post*, 9–11 May 1734, claimed Barber received 577 single votes and a great many others with Parsons alone. From the final figures it appears unlikely that Parsons collected more than 500 'flying' votes.
5. *An alphabetical List of the Livery 1733* in the British Library (1303 d. 12) notes the year of admittance and therefore gives us some idea of the turnover of the parliamentary electorate. See also T. C. Dale (ed.), *Index to the Liverymen of London in 1700 ... together with the names of those men who were in the Poll Book of 1710* (typescript, 1933). Between 1700 and 1710 nearly 4,000 new recruits joined the Livery, whose size remained at about 8,200.
6. See *An Essay on the Hard Case of the Retale Traders* (London, 1741); J. R. Kellett, 'The Breakdown of Guild and Corporation Control over the Handicraft and Retail Trade in London', *Econ. Hist. Rev.*, 2nd ser., x (1957–8), pp. 381–94; Sylvia Thrupp, *A Short History of the Worshipful Company of Bakers of London* (London, 1933), pp. 63–71; P. E.

Jones, *The Worshipful Company of Poulters of the City of London* (London, 1965), pp. 55–70; Oliver Warner, *The Innholders Company* (London), pp. 51–8; Arthur Adams, *The History of the Worshipful Company of Blacksmiths* (London, 1951), pp. 167–98; A. B. Robertson, 'The Open Market in the City of London in the Eighteenth Century', *East London Papers*, i, no. 2 (October 1958), pp. 15–22.

7. Guildhall MS. 9474; Corporation of London Record Office, (hereafter CLRO) Misc. MSS. 172.7 J. R. Kellett, 'The Breakdown of Guild and Corporation Control', *Econ. Hist. Rev.* (1957–8), pp. 381–94.

8. Valerie Pearl, *London and the Outbreak of the Puritan Revolution* (Oxford, 1961), p. 50; Arthur Smith, 'London and the Crown 1681–85' (unpublished Ph.D. thesis, Univ. of Wisconsin, 1967), p. 37. According to the 1733 Livery list there were 8,126 members of Common Hall, but 205 were disqualified from voting.

9. CLRO, Small MS. Box 30, No. 9; Misc. MS. 31.12; Brit. Lib., Hargrave MS. 139, f. 146 *et seq.*; *Hist. MSS. Comm.*, Portland, v, pp. 411–12, 438, 440.

10. Walter Mildmay, *The Method and Rule of Proceeding upon all Elections, Polls and Scrutinies at Common Hall and Wardmotes within the City of London*, ed. Henry Kent (London, 1841), pp. ccclxvi–ix; J. H. Plumb, *Sir Robert Walpole*, 2 vols. (London, 1956–60), ii. p. 109.

11. CLRO, MS. 120.1, ff. 30–1; Journals of Common Council, lvii, f. 103 v., 110; Sidney and Beatrice Webb, *English Local Government. From the Revolution to the Municipal Corporations Act*, 2 vols. (London, 1908), ii, p. 635.

12. *Hist. MSS. Comm.*, Portland, vii, p. 394, cited in Henderson, *London and the National Government*, p. 110.

13. The *Craftsman Extraordinary*, 9 October 1727.

14. The *Daily Journal*, 16 August 1727.

15. This is based on a survey of the voting behaviour of a random sample of 100 new liverymen (those that took the cloth after 1725).

16. *Hist. MSS. Comm.*, Carlisle MSS., p. 108.

17. These conclusions are derived from a detailed examination of the poll in conjunction with City directories, lists of merchants, and jury lists. See the *Daily Journal Extraordinary*, 9 April 1734 and the *Daily Post Extraordinary*, 9 April 1734.

18. See Richard Pares, *War and Trade in the West Indies 1739–63* (London, 1936), and also Jean O. McLachlan, *Trade and Peace with Old Spain 1667–1750* (Cambridge, 1940).

19. Brit. Lib., Add. MSS. 35909, ff. 82–3; the *London Evening Post*, 4–6, 23–28 February 1738.

20. *Journals of the House of Commons*, xxiii, pp. 54–5, 63–5, 94–6; *Cobbett's Parliamentary History*, x, col. 649.

21. Brit. Lib., Add. MSS. 32691, f. 343; The *Occasional Writer*, No. iv, 1738; The *Craftsman*, 25 March 1738; *Common Sense*, 17 February 1739; the *London Evening Post*, 22–24 February 1739; *The English Cotejo: or The Cruelties, Depredations and Illicit Trade Charged upon the English in a Spanish Libel lately published* (London, n.d.).

22. Richard Glover, *London: or, the Progress of Commerce* (London, 2nd edn., 1739), p. 27; the *London Evening Post*, 14–16 March, 30 March–1 April 1738; the *Historical Register*, xxiii (1738), pp. 183–5.

23. *A Reply to a Pamphlet entitled Popular Prejudicies against the Convention and Treaty with Spain Examined and Answer'd* (London, 1739), p. 9.

24. The *London Evening Post*, 8–10, 22–24 February 1739; *The Negotiators, or Don Diego brought to Reason* (London, 1739).

25. *Hist. MS. Comm.*, xiv, app. ix, p. 244; Thomas Gordon, *An Appeal to the Unprejudiced concerning the present Discontent occasion'd by the late Convention with Spain* (London, 1739).

26. CLRO, Journals of Common Council, lviii, ff. 121–2; the *Daily Gazetteer*, 2 March 1739. Printed lists of the Common Council and their respective trades were distributed to both Houses of Parliament on 6 March.

27. The *Daily Advertiser*, 24 September 1739.
28. CLRO, Book of Common Hall, vii, f. 277; the *Daily Post*, 27 September 1739; the *London Evening Post*, 25–27 September 1739; *A Narrative of what passed in the Common Hall of the Citizens of London Assembled for the Election of a Lord Mayor* (London, 1739).
29. *Hist. MSS. Comm.*, xiv, app. IX, p. 252; Brit. Lib., Add. MSS. 35406, f. 159.
30. CLRO, Small box 36, No. 21.
31. Stuart MS. 254/154, from a photostat of the original in the Royal Archives at Windsor by gracious permission of HM the Queen. (See also the microfilm series in Senate House, University of London.)
32. Godschall received 3,143 votes, Sir Edward Bellamy 1,311, and Micajah Perry 1,710. The original Court slate included Kenelm Faulkner, a Turkey merchant; Roger Drake, a West India merchant; William Baker, an American merchant and pro-ministerial alderman; and Perry, who had gravitated towards the Court party in October 1739, when Common Hall adopted more radical position under Heathcote's leadership. This list was abandoned in favour of one drawn up by Sir Joseph Hankey at Merchant Taylors' Hall. It included Perry and Bellamy, Sir John Bernard and Admiral Vernon, and was an obvious attempt to divide the Opposition and attract moderate elements who might have been alarmed by the increasingly radical temper of the Livery. See the *Daily Post*, 27 April 1741; the *Daily Gazetteer*, 29 April 1741; the *London Evening Post*, 30 April, 2 May, 9–12 May 1741. For full details of the voting, day by day, see *A Journal of the Shrievalty of Richard Hoare 1740–41* (London, 1815), pp. 79–84.
33. The Opposition had secured a temporary majority on the Court of Aldermen in 1737, following the victories of Daniel Lambert and Henry Marshall over two well known ministerialists, Peter Burrell, Sub-Governor of the South Sea Company, and William Selwin, in the wards of Tower and Farringdon Within. See Alfred Henderson, *London and the National Government*, pp. 168–9.
34. On 28 March 1740, the City pointedly congratulated the king on Vernon's victory at Porto Bello and declared their willingness to contribute to 'war so necessary for the protection of our long injured trade'. CLRO, Journals of Common Council, lviii, ff. 167–8.
35. In the final months of 1741, for example, the *Norwich Gazette* mentioned the London celebrations in favour of Vernon, Sir Robert Godschall's promotion to the Chair, and the political battles for seats on the Common Council.
36. *A Letter to Sir G----e C------n shewing Reasons for setting Him aside at the approaching Election* (London, 1739), p. 8; see also the *Craftsman*, 13 October 1739, and *The Liveryman: or Plain thoughts on Public Affairs* (London, 1740).
37. CLRO, Journals of Common Council, lviii, ff. 177–8, 225–6, 254–6; the *Daily Post*, 5 October 1739; *A Narrative of what passed in the Common Hall of the Citizens of London*, pp. 6–7; the *London Evening Post*, 12–14 May 1741; William Maitland, *The History of London from its foundations . . . to the present time*, 2 vols. (London, 1756), i. p. 619.
38. In January 1741 several wards demanded pledges from aldermanic candidates to support all efforts to repeal the aldermanic veto and also to refuse any place or pension from the government. See the *London Evening Post*, 1–3 January 1741. Although the Patriots espoused a delegatory theory of representation, they did not always do so in an unqualified manner. Sometimes they adhered to the views of Algernon Sidney, who defended the right and utility of instructions, but denied their mandatory character. See the *Champion*, 23 September and 8 November 1740; and the *Craftsman*, 17 March 1733 and 22 December 1739.
39. The instructions were printed in the *London Evening Post*. See also *Great Britain's Memorial* (London, 1741).
40. *Hist. MSS. Comm.*, Egmont Diary III, p. 192. The two aldermen were Humphrey Parsons and Sir Henry Marshall. Sir John Barnard, by contrast, called for Walpole's

removal before the general election. See *Cobbett's Parliamentary History*, xi, col. 1260.

41. On the Half-Moon Club, which met at Michael Martindale's tavern on Cheapside, see the *Daily Gazetteer*, 9 July, 4 October, 26 November 1740.

42. CLRO, Journals of Common Council, lviii, ff. 254–6; *The New Ministry* (London, 1742).

43. CLRO, Journals of Common Council, lviii, ff. 254–6; *Cobbett's Parliamentary History*, xii, cols. 1053–8.

44. M. Dorothy George, *English Political Caricature*, 2 vols. (Oxford, 1959), i, pp. 94–5; *The Yellow Sash, or H-----R BESHIT; Old England's Te Deum* (Brit. Lib., G 559/9); PRO, T.S. 11/982/3625. According to one servant of a Pater Noster Row bookseller, 11,000 copies of *A true Dialogue between Thomas Jones, a Trooper, lately returned from Germany, and John Smith, a Sergeant in the First Regiment of Foot-Guards* had been distributed throughout London.

45. CLRO, Journals of Common Council, lviii, f. 286; the *London Evening Post*, 15–17 March 1743.

46. Stuart MSS. 249/113^b and 251/30.

47. Brit. Lib., Add. MSS. 51417, f. 105.

48. John B. Owen, *The Rise of the Pelhams* (London, 1957), p. 213; *The Lord's Protest to which is added a list of the MPs who voted for and against continuing the Hanoverian troops in British pay Jan. 18 1743/4*.

49. CLRO, Journals of Common Council, lviii, ff. 284, 295–6, 302, 354–5, 361–2; John Almon, *The Debates and Proceedings of the British House of Commons 1743–6*, 2 vols. (London, 1764), ii. pp. 97–140.

50. Nicholas Rogers, 'Popular Disaffection in London during the Forty-Five', *The London Journal*, i, no. 1 (May 1975), pp. 23–4.

51. CLRO, Court of Lieutenancy Minute Book (1744–49), ff. 44–5; Rupert C. Jarvis, *Collected Papers on the Jacobite Risings*, 2 vols. (Manchester Univ. Press, 1971–2), ii. pp. 212–21.

52. The *London Gazette*, 10–14 September 1745. Many of the merchants signed another declaration expressing a willingness to accept Bank notes as legal tender. See the *London Evening Post*, 26–28 September, 28 September–1 October 1745.

53. Samuel Smith (ed.), *A List of the Subscribers to the Veterans Scheme* (London, 1748), pp. 1–2; the *Gentleman's Magazine*, xv (September 1745), p. 499; PRO, S.P. 36/67/169–72, 241, 36/69/76.

54. John Perceval, *Faction Detected. By the Evidence of Facts* (London, 2nd. edn., 1743); *The Desertion Discussed: by a Gentleman of Lincoln's Inn* (London, 1743); *The Groans of Britons at the Gloomy Prospect of the Present Precarious State of their Liberties and Properties, compared with what it has been* (London, 1743); *Public Discontent Accounted for, from the Conduct of our Ministers in the Cabinet and of our Generals in the Field* (London, 1743); *Opposition not Faction, or, the Rectitude of the Present Parliamentary Opposition to the Present Expensive Measures, Justified by Reason and Facts* (London, 1743). Egmont's pamphlet, which spawned at least seven editions within the space of a year, provoked replies devoted almost exclusively to foreign policy. The pamphlets cited here deal with the wider issues of political reform and Egmont's denunciation of the metropolitan radicals, with whom he was initially affiliated.

55. *Cobbett's Parliamentary History*, xiii, cols. 1337–42; Betty Kemp, *Sir Francis Dashwood. An Eighteenth-Century Independent* (London, 1967), pp. 21–9; *The Measures of the late Administration Examined*, with *an Enquiry into the Grounds of the present Revolution* (London, 1745). This pamphlet condemned the Septennial Act and the Riot Act, and also demanded the repeal of the Waltham Black, Smuggling, and Licensing Acts. It described the modest Place Bill of 1742 as an 'attempt to stop the Mouths of the People for a while, and to furnish the then new Ministry with a Pretense . . . of having done something for the advantage of the Publick'.

56. CLRO, Repertories of the Court of Aldermen, cxlix, ff. 386–7.

57. *A Selection from the Papers of the Earls of Marchmont in the possession of the Rt. Hon. Sir George Rose*, 3 vols. (London, 1831), ii. pp. 346–7.

58. James Heywood (Bridge) and Robert Bishop (Broad Street) has as on the committees responsible for the City instructions of February and October 1742. James Hodges (Bridge), a bookseller, had been on the February 1742 committee. Robert Henshaw (Aldersgate) an attorney, and Richard Sclater, a druggist and the deputy of Farringdon Without, were members of both committees on the aldermanic negative, 1743–5.

59. Rupert C. Jarvis, *Collected Papers on the Jacobite Risings*, i. pp. 97–119.

60. Brit. Lib., Add. MSS. 35598, ff. 47–8.

61. Add. MSS. 35598, f. 62; see also PRO, S.P. 36/69/198 and 36/70/62.

62. Theophilus Cibber, *The Association: or Liberty and Loyalty* (London, 1745), p. 4. Many of the associations were mentioned in the *London Gazette*. See also PRO, S.P. 44/186.

63. Add. MSS. 35598, f. 37; Sheffield City Library, Wentworth Woodhouse Muniments, M. 1, f. 309. I am indebted to Gordon Elliot of the University of Toronto for this reference.

64. John Debrett, *The History, Debates, Proceedings of both Houses of Parliament*, (London, 1792), ii, pp. 64–7. See also Colonel Martin, *A Plan for Establishing a National Militia in Great Britain, Ireland, And in all the British Dominions of America* (London, 1745), *The Counterpoise. Being Thoughts on a Militia and a Standing Army* (London, 1752), and Betty Kemp, *Sir Francis Dashwood*, pp. 25–7

65. Rupert C. Jarvis, *Collected Papers on the Jacobite Risings*, ii, p. 313.

66. P. C. Yorke, *Life of Lord Chancellor Hardwicke*, 2 vols. (Cambridge, 1913), i, p. 478; Chatsworth House, Derbyshire MS. 335/0.

67. Nicholas Rogers 'Popular Disaffection', *The London Journal*, i, no. 1 (May, 1975), pp. 5–27; many of the merchants who opposed the Spanish Convention rallied to the crown. See the list of petitioners, 23 February 1739, in the House of Lords Record Office, and the relevant lists for 1745 cited in 69 n.

68. Hardwicke confided to Herring on 12 October 1745, that he could not say 'the Association and Subscription in the City of London has made all the progress that one could wish'. Add. MSS. 35568, f. 93. See also J. J. Majende, *A Sermon Preach'd at the Cathedral Church of St. Paul, London, On Sunday Morning the 10th of November, 1745*, (London, 1745).

69. These comments are based on a detailed analysis of the subscription lists and the loyalist declaration. See Samuel Smith (ed.), *A List of the Subscribers to the Veterans Scheme* (London, 1748) and CLRO, Alchin Box D, no. 32.

70. Essex RO, D/DM Z 2.

71. A. A. Mitchell, 'London and the Forty-Five', *History Today*, xv, no. 10 (October 1965), pp. 719–26; see also Dr. Eveline Cruickshank's introduction on the Tory party in Romney Sedgwick (ed.), *History of Parliament 1715–45* (London, 1970), pp. 65–77; J. Colin, *Louis XV et Les Jacobits: Le projet de Débarquement en Angleterre de 1743–1744* (Paris, 1901), pp. 16–17; George Hilton Jones, *The Mainstream of Jacobitism* (Harvard, 1954), pp. 222–4.

72. PRO, S.P. 36/86/174 and 178, 36/85/334; James Browne, *A History of the Highlands and of the Highland Clans*, 3 vols. (Glasgow, 1840), pp. 432–7. The resident Jacobite agent in London appears to have been Dr. Peter Barry, a physician who lived in Craven Street, Westminster. During the Forty-Five Barry never talked of City politics and on one occasion (Stuart MS. 270/105) even confessed his ignorance of the political scene.

73. Stuart MS. 254/154. Balhady classified the City Opposition (with a few exceptions) as 'Jacobite-Patriot', a denomination which begged the question. Although his list gives us a good idea of the strength of the Opposition party on the Courts of Aldermen and Common Council, it is decidedly ambiguous on the question of dynastic loyalties.

The affiliations of some Common Councilmen, moreover, are wrongly ascribed. John Daye, the deputy of Cordwainer ward, for example, had voted for the Court candidates in 1727, had supported Selwin in 1734, and was a member of the executive committee of the Guildhall fund. Yet Balhady classified him as a 'Jacobite-Patriot'. In view of Balhady's flamboyant statements about the strength of Jacobitism in Britain – in May 1744 he even claimed that 'all the people of England (a few placemen & stockjobbers excepted)' were enthusiastic about the Pretender's return (Stuart MS. 257/55) – one cannot trust his optimistic calculations.

74. See, for example, Stuart MS. 269/191, where it is claimed that Heathcote had assured Sir Watkin Williams Wynne that the Jacobites would 'rise in the City of London' at the outbreak of the invasion provided they were supplied with arms. It should be noted, however, that Heathcote collaborated closely with the Earl of Marchmont during the rebellion, with a Scottish magnate whose allegiance to the Hanoverian succession was never seriously questioned. In December 1740, moreover, he had described the Pretender as 'a miserable fugitive that has not a friend in this kingdom', and three years later had informed Newcastle that he had been sent a pro-Jacobite manifesto. This circumstantial evidence at least throws some doubt on the reliability of Stuart reports. See *Cobbett's Parliamentary History*, xi, col. 978, and PRO, S.P. 36/60/131-7.

75. PRO, S.P. 36/86/164-5, 178-9; *An Appeal from the late David Morgan Esquire, Barrister at Law, to the Good People of England* (London, n.d.); *A Faithful Narrative of the wonderful and surprising Appearance of Counsellor Morgan's Ghost at the Meeting of the Independent Inhabitants of the City and Liberty of Westminster* (London, 1746); see also the comments on the crypto-Jacobitism of the Half-Moon Club in the *St. James Evening Post*, 2-4 April 1745.

76. *A Letter to A Tory Friend upon the Present Critical Situation of our Affairs* (London, 1746), p. 13.

77. David N. Mackay (ed.), *Trial of Simon, Lord Lovat of the '45* (Edinburgh and Glasgow, 1911), p. 127; P. C. Yorke, *Hardwicke*, i. pp. 583-4.

78. Journals of the House of Commons, xxv, p. 326; W. S. Lewis (ed.), *The Yale Edition of Horace Walpole's Correspondence*, 34 vols. (New Haven, 1937-70), xix, pp. 387-8.

79. PRO, S.P. 36/96/59/62.

80. Sir Thomas Dyke accepted the candidature of the Westminster Opposition after it had been refused by six others. See Salop RO, James Bonnell papers, 22 October 1747. I am indebted to Linda Colley of Darwin College, Cambridge, for this reference.

81. *Felix Farley's Bristol Journal*, 27 June 1747.

82. CLRO, Journals of Common Council, lix, ff. 13-14, 29-30; *Journals of the House of Commons*, xxv, pp. 62-3, 78, 92; P. G. M. Dickson, *The Financial Revolution in England* (London, 1967), pp. 223-7.

83. Henry Fielding, *A Dialogue between a Gentleman of London, Agent for two Court Candidates and an Honest Alderman of the Country Party* (London, 1747).

84. The *General Advertiser*, 19 June 1747; the *General Evening Post*, 30 June, 2 July 1747.

85. In late May and early June the Press believed George Heathcote would stand for the City. Lord Mayor William Benn was also cited as a possible candidate. At a general meeting of the Livery at Grocers's Hall, however, Barnard and Lambert were nominated on both lists, Janssen and Bethel completing the Merchants' slate, Henry Marshall and Edward Ironside the Patriot. Lambert eventually decided to stand for the Opposition alone and was replaced on the other by Sir William Calvert. See *Felix Farley's Bristol Journal*, 30 May 1747; the *London Evening Post*, 4-6 June 1747; and the *General Advertiser* for late June and July.

86. The *General Advertiser*, 7 July 1747.

87. See Henry Pelham's comments to Horace Walpole, 4 July 1747. Brit. Lib., Add. MSS. 9186, f. 105.

88. See the *General Evening Post*, 4–7 July 1747. Bethell was the great nephew of the Whig republican Slingsby Bethell, and Janssen, whose father had been associated with Robert Harley, was the grandson on his mother's side of the anti-Catholic crusader Henry Cornish, executed for his complicity in the Rye House Plot.

89. W. S. Lewis (ed.), *Horace Walpole's Correspondence*, xix, p. 425. Henry Pelham did not regard Janssen as a Court faithful, and Bethell had earlier joined anti-ministerial forces in opposing the Convention of El Pardo. See Add. MS. 19186, f. 105, and the petition of merchants 'trading to British Plantations in America', 23 February 1739, House of Lords Record Office.

90. William Maitland, *The History of London, op. cit.*, i. p. 670.

DAME LUCY SUTHERLAND

The City of London and the Opposition to Government, 1768–74[1]

In the Guildhall of the City of London, slightly scarred by the mischances of war, there stands a statue erected by the Corporation in 1772 to commemorate Alderman William Beckford, twice Lord Mayor and for sixteen years member of parliament for the City, who had died during his second mayoralty in 1770.[2] It depicts him life-size, in an oratorical attitude, and it bears as inscription the words which he was supposed to have addressed a few weeks before his death to his sovereign George III, when presenting a Remonstrance from the City of London arising out of the famous Middlesex Election dispute.[3] After assuring the King of the City's loyalty and its affliction under royal displeasure, he is there said to have continued:

> Permit me, Sir, to observe that whoever has already dared, or shall hereafter endeavour, by false insinuations and suggestions, to alienate your Majesty's affections from your loyal subjects in general, and from the City of London in particular, is an enemy to your Majesty's person and family, a violator of the public peace, and a betrayer of our happy Constitution, as it was established at the Glorious Revolution.[4]

The satisfaction of the City with the boldness of these words, and their belief in their value to posterity, was shared by others outside their walls. It was echoed by the great William Pitt, Lord Chatham (whose political follower Beckford was) who wrote in congratulation:

> The spirit of Old England spoke that never-to-be-forgotten day ... *true Lord Mayor of London*; that is *first* magistrate of the *first* City in the World! I mean to tell you only a plain truth, when I say, Your

Lordship's mayoralty will be revered till the constitution is destroyed and forgotten.[5]

Time has dealt less kindly with Beckford and his mayoralty than either his followers in the City or his leader in parliament expected. William Beckford was a man of some note in his day, and a very unusual figure among the sober ranks of the mercantile Lord Mayors of his time. He was the richest absentee West Indian sugar-planter of his generation, owning vast estates and many slaves in Jamaica (a somewhat embarrassing possession for a spokesman for English freedom),[6] was a big landowner also in Wiltshire,[7] where he exercised some political influence, had been since 1756 the devoted henchman of William Pitt[8] and – a vigorous, loquacious, and by no means unintelligent man – he was a prominent figure in parliamentary and City life. Nevertheless, his personal fame, such as it was, has been swallowed up in the notoriety of his son, the eccentric author of *Vathek*,[9] while his reputation in the City has been eclipsed by that of the picturesque demagogue John Wilkes, who may be considered his political successor there. Nor does the speech itself, or the occasion on which it was delivered, convey much to the posterity for which it has been preserved. It is a commentary on the fact that no age finds it easy to judge what about itself will be significant to the future that those wishing to honour Beckford should do so by commemorating an incident, in itself but a nine days' wonder but charged with the memories of past conflicts, while ignoring others of far greater interest in connection with the events of the time and the struggles of the future. Only a few weeks earlier, also in connection with the Middlesex dispute, the Lord Mayor had propounded to the Livery in Common Hall assembled what he called his 'Political Creed' – that 'the number of little paltry rotten boroughs', the placemen and pensioners in the House of Commons, and the corruption of electors and elected alike were ruining the state, and that to cure these evils there should be not only fewer pensioners and placemen (an old cry) but better public accounts and 'a more equal representation of the people'.[10]

For the importance of the career of Beckford as a leader in the City, and of his last mayoralty in particular, is to be sought in their relation to that ill-defined surge of opinion which we call eighteenth-century Radicalism, a movement interesting in itself, and of importance in relation to the nineteenth-century movement which succeeded it. The outburst of popular opinion which found expression during the Revolutionary Wars in the Corresponding Societies, and that earlier movement organized into the County Associations during the latter years of the American War of Independence, have received a good deal of attention from historians interested in the history of the Radical movement. The earlier crisis of 1769-70, associated with John Wilkes and the Middlesex Election, and in which Beckford was concerned, has aroused far less comment though Professor Butterfield has noted its significance[11] and it finds a place in Dr. Maccoby's comprehensive work.[12] Nevertheless, this earlier movement prepared the way for both the later outbursts of popular activity, and was accompanied by a remarkable ferment of opinion within the City and its surroundings – what we may call the metropolitan area – which left its mark upon the future.

The contention which I wish to advance is that a study of eighteenth-century Radicalism can best begin with an examination of what was actually going on in and around London at this time; that the origins of these events can be traced, in the City of London at least, as far back as 1756; and that the fact that they took place in the metropolis and found as yet little reflection in the country as a whole is the result of a circumstance of some importance: that in the metropolitan area, and at this time in the metropolitan area alone, there existed the predisposing conditions for the development of Radicalism as a political force – an organization adapted to political intervention and a sizeable body of persons, some of them at least with some education and independence of mind, who felt themselves ill-served by and were in consequence critical of their social and political environment.

All movements of public opinion are in their early stages ill-defined and inarticulate, and their characteristics are in consequence hard to isolate. These difficulties of identification are increased in the case of the eighteenth-century Radical movement by the fact that the organization of expressions of extra-parliamentary opinion had long been one of the recognized weapons of eighteenth-century political warfare; and that petitions and instructions to representatives and thanks to representatives both from the counties and the City of London were part of the stock-in-trade of parliamentary Oppositions of the period. It is not therefore safe to assume that such manifestations necessarily represent in themselves a movement of spontaneous popular opinion. We can be sure that such a movement is in being only when it can be shown that the initiative in organizing such manifestations has passed from the political groups in parliament to groups of persons outside the House. When, in addition, those taking part in such manifestations begin to display an increasingly critical attitude to existing institutions, and their political programmes to reflect this attitude, we can consider that something which may reasonably be called Radicalism has come into existence. This is, I think, precisely what we can see beginning to happen in the City of London in the last years of the reign of George II, gaining momentum in the first eight years of the new reign, and breaking into full expression in the metropolitan area in the general election of 1768 and the Middlesex Election dispute which succeeded it.

The City of London had a long tradition of corporate solidarity and also a long tradition of political activity in which this solidarity expressed itself. This is not to say, of course, that there were not differences of opinion among its inhabitants, and often active conflict within it. One of the most permanent of these divisions was one based on some sort of class conflict between a City aristocracy of wealth and office and the main body of what contemporaries called the 'middling' class of their fellow-citizens. But it is, nevertheless, justifiable to speak throughout the century of the political opinion of the City since, in times of stress, the climate of political thinking there was determined not by the prosperous aldermen, the directors of the great joint-stock companies, the rich merchants, and the thriving financiers of the London money market, nor by those whom they could carry with them (though in quiet and uncontentious times their influence was considerable). It was determined on the contrary by the lesser merchants, the tradesmen, the master-craftsmen, and the host of minor intermediaries who formed the majority in the popular organs of City government and who thronged the meetings and clubs where political opinion was formulated. And while the more prominent citizens tended for a number of reasons to give their political support to the Government of the day, the 'middling' citizens tended almost always in times of political controversy to find themselves in alliance with the parties in opposition.[13] It is paradoxical, but true to state, that throughout the first half of the eighteenth century there was no body of men more ready to be swayed by the catchwords of the old 'country' party as advanced by the opposition groups in parliament than these inhabitants of the nation's greatest city. Demands for the repeal of the Septennial Act, for place and pension bills and for the reduction of the standing army – all measures directed at the power of the Crown which the seventeenth-century constitutional struggles had taught Englishmen to suspect – were applauded as enthusiastically by the citizen in Common Council or Common Hall or in his tavern or coffee-house, as by any country squire on his grand jury or at the race-meeting. But the citizen can no more be called a Radical because he held these views than can the country squire. It was only when the City began to some extent to dissociate itself from the politics of Opposition as well as those of Government, to feel resentment at its place in a political system dominated by interests in many ways alien to it, that it can begin to be considered a focus of Radicalism as distinct from a centre of traditional anti-ministerialism.

The first clear signs of such a development seem to appear, like so many changes, as a result of war, and to have been the outcome of one of the rare occasions on which City opinion was ardently in support of, and not in opposition to, the Government. Between 1756 and 1768 its growth can be traced in three stages. In the first, during the great war ministry of William Pitt, when his unique personal supremacy depended on the support of public opinion as much outside as within the House, the City's sense of its political significance as a body was stimulated by the court which was paid to it and by its share in the exhilaration of victory. In the second stage, during the dissensions accompanying the peace settlement and the confusion following the break-up of the political system of the old reign, the City was again in opposition, and again acting in support of the opposition groups in parliament; but on such matters as its agitation against the peace terms, and its turbulent adherence to the cause of John Wilkes over the North Briton case and the issue of General Warrants, it displayed a degree of independence of action greater than it had shown on issues of national importance before. But the third stage, that between 1764 and 1768, was perhaps the most important of all, though during these years there was no issue in national politics which called the City into corporate action. For these were years of bad harvests, high cost of living, and industrial changes in the metropolitan area which caused a good deal of hardship and discontent and led to great and persistent labour unrest.[14] From 1764 onwards a strong undercurrent of economic malaise and social unrest is discernible beneath the surface of the life of the metropolis, and though until 1768 no major issue arose to transfer this discontent to the political field, there were already indications that such a transfer was imminent.

The development of these years can also be traced through the career as a City leader of William Beckford, for his entry into City politics in 1754 roughly coincided with it, and his actions did a good deal to further it. Before Beckford's time the political leaders to whom the City paid allegiance were themselves citizens first and foremost, and had risen to prominence through active participation in City government. Beckford, when he first stood for the City, was a man of some note and experience in parliamentary opposition but he had only two years before taken his freedom by redemption and been elected alderman,[15] and these steps were taken in preparation for his candidature.[16] He was the first politician of some experience outside the City to see its value as a backing for his personal power and the causes he wished to further, and, at first in self-interest, then with real zest, he worked his way through the offices of the City Corporation and increasingly identified himself with his constituents to consolidate his power. As Pitt's supporter he played the chief part in forging the links between the City and the great war minister;[17] as Lord Mayor in 1762–3 he led their opposition to the peace[18] and in and after his mayoralty he encouraged their support of John Wilkes, though there was even then no love lost between the two men.[19] And in his speeches and his actions he reflected the growing self-consciousness and dissatisfaction of his constitutents, and in doing so he began to earn the reputation of something of a demagogue in the House of Commons.[20] As early as 1761 he had extolled the 'middling classes of England' against 'Your Nobility, about 200£ men of quality' who 'receive more from the Public than they pay to it'.[21] In 1767 when he voted against a reduction in the land tax he did so, he claimed, because 'relief ought to be given to the poor man in preference to the opulent land-holder',[22] and in 1768 he voted, as he said, 'on principle' against the Nullum Tempus Act,[23] forced on the Government to secure landowners against the dormant claims of the Crown. In the light of this attitude, too, may be judged his tentative criticism of the existing political order. At his election in 1761 (though only seven years before he had spent great sums himself in borough elections) he told the City electors that 'our Constitution is deficient only in one point, and that is, that little, pitiful boroughs send members to parliament equal to great cities, and it is contrary to the maxim, that power should follow property',[24] and in 1768 he introduced a bill (repudiated energetically by Opposition and Government supporters alike) to impose an oath against bribery on parliamentary candidates at elections.[25] And, when he was preparing to fight a contested election for his City seat in the general election of that year, he claimed credit from his constituents for what he had said and done. If the situation in the metropolis and the attitude of the City leaders be taken into account, it seems indeed fairly clear that even had there been no re-emergence of John Wilkes, and no Middlesex Election to bring matters to a head, there would have been a recrudescence after 1768 of political activity in the City in alliance with the opposition groups in parliament, and that the City's share in this alliance would have been far from passive. As it was, the nature of the forces released by these new factors was quickly apparent. When in 1769 the ebullient Parson John Horne declared that 'Boroughs are, indeed, the deadly part of our Constitution',[26] when Beckford in 1770, during his second mayoralty, invited the opposition leaders to dine at Mansion House with the intention of springing on them a pledge to a programme of parliamentary reform;[27] and when these leaders, on their way to the dinner (having evaded the pledge), 'remarked that a great part of the populace had tickets in their hats on which was the following inscription: "Annual Parliaments. Equal Representation. Place and Pension Bill" ';[28] no one could doubt that a fully developed Radical movement within the City had come into existence.

It was, however, the almost unheralded, and quite uninvited, return of John Wilkes during the 1768 general election from exile in France (into which he had fled from justice four years before), and the renewal of his old claim to popularity during the excitement of a contested City election, which brought these forces into the open. His subsequent election for Middlesex, the muddle of his arrest, his sentence to imprisonment for his former offences, and his long contest from behind his prison walls with the Ministry and the majority of the House of Commons, brought about a surge of popular feeling under the pressure of which latent suspicions and hostilities became overt, and strange and unsuspected forces were suddenly released.

The impact of John Wilkes and his grievances on the political life of the nation in this, his second period of political activity, forms an odd interlude in the history of George III's reign. Historians have noted the constitutional precedents created by the Middlesex Election dispute, but have not found it easy to determine the importance of the episode in the politics of the time. It is, I think, only possible to do so with any accuracy if it is recognized, firstly, that the forces released by the excitement of his cause were those already taking shape within the metropolitan area, and that the ferment which prevailed there had only a transient effect outside its bounds; and, secondly, that the activities resulting from the ferment within the metropolitan area had little to do with Wilkes as a person or as a political leader, and arose only indirectly out of his grievances. To make clear why these propositions are correct it is necessary to analyse the character and career at this time of Wilkes himself, and the nature of the sentiments which he called forth, and the situation which was created within the metropolis by the outburst of these feelings.

John Wilkes was said to have observed some years later of one of his followers, 'He was a Wilkite, ... I never was',[29] and a recognition of the truth of this admission is the first step to an understanding of his career and what was going on at this time. To many of the issues which most deeply concerned the more thoughtful and intelligent of his followers Wilkes himself was profoundly indifferent, and the fervent loyalty of his less sophisticated followers also raised in him no more than a cynical acceptance. The qualities which brought him success as a demagogical political leader were: a strikingly original, if disreputable, personality, a great deal of assurance, a skill in exploiting the resources of the Press unparalleled up to that time (unlike most demagogues Wilkes was a poor public speaker),[30] and considerable success in those arts of political management which have in more recent times been associated with the office of a 'political boss'. His methods were those of inspired opportunism; his ends simple and purely personal. The gamble of his return from France in defiance of the law and his creditors was largely an enforced one, for his debts in France were too heavy for him to be able to remain there. His intention in this return was to make use of his old popularity and the excitement of a general election to raise, as a supporter frankly said, 'a storm ... under which you may get into port'.[31] The port he was making for was a seat in the House of Commons with the protection this would bring him from his creditors, and the improved bargaining power with an unfriendly Administration which the status might be expected to carry with it. After his failure in the City, and the check to his success at Middlesex, the extraordinary outburst of feeling which he evoked opened up an alternative course for him as soon as he should have served his prison sentence. From early in 1769 when (with still more than a year's sentence to run) he was elected an alderman of the City[32] in his absence, he set himself deliberately to the conquest of the City's corporate machine, seeing in it, no doubt, a new sphere of political power and a possible source of revenue when the financial bounty of his followers should be exhausted.[33] And so great was the popular support which he called forth that the very City leaders whom he was working to supplant, including Beckford himself, had to assist his rise in order to preserve their own popularity.[34] Though as time went on during this struggle he was obliged, in competition with those who had been his friends and became his rivals, to advance some programme of reform, in the years when metropolitan Radicalism was taking shape under the pressure of the forces his cause had released, he displayed not the slightest interest in its manifestations, and, indeed, deprecated any widening of the issue raised by the Middlesex Election[35] as likely to distract attention from his own grievances and person.

If then the Radicalism of these years owed nothing to Wilkes but was the outcome of the feelings aroused by his cause, it is necessary both to try to analyse the nature of this feeling and to determine how and by whom it was bent to Radical ends. Though every effort was made by propaganda in the Press to suggest that the personal popularity of Wilkes was strong throughout the kingdom, an examination of the evidence soon makes it clear that there was nothing in the nature of a vigorous and lasting Wilkite movement outside the metropolitan area. All the parliamentary opposition parties were both slow and reluctant to take up his cause against Administration (well-suited though it obviously was for opposition purposes), and when they did, they sought to isolate the cause of the electors of Middlesex from that of their chosen representative.[36] And that they were not merely politicians out of touch with public opinion but reflected the views of the politically active classes as a whole was shown clearly by the events of the petitioning movement of 1769–70.[37] It is true that in some parts of the country, and particularly in the commercial cities and great seaports and in some of the industrialized areas, there were signs of a sympathetic response to the clamorous exaltations of the metropolis, a response due no doubt to some similarities in their general conditions and attitude of mind;[38] but even here it was for the most part evanescent and it found at this time no organization to give it permanent force. And even the presence of the demagogue himself when he made a triumphal tour through the provinces after his release from prison did not succeed in giving the movement the vitality it was to show some years later.

The Wilkite movement was thus essentially, as the later Radical movements were not, a product of the metropolis. Here the personal devotion which he evoked was of a curious kind, impervious to disillusionment and discreditable revelations, and unaffected by the leader's unconcealed contempt for his followers. Edmund Burke, marvelling at his 'imprudence' and the fact that it did nothing to discredit him in the eyes of his fellows, remarked acutely that 'it may perhaps be ... some unusual and eccentric kind of wisdom'.[39] The devotion of the rank and file of these followers seems to have been compounded of appreciation of a personality so foreign to their own, sympathy for him as the victim (so they believed) of persecution by the great whose privileges they resented, and a delighted admiration of the insolence and imperturbability with which he defied and put out of countenance these persecutors. It would seem as if inarticulate resentment and dissatisfaction which had been piling up within the metropolitan area for years had suddenly found an outlet and a solace in identification with him and his cause. So new a phenomenon was this popular feeling that it has sometimes been suggested that it derived its strength from the emergence into political awareness of classes hitherto submerged, of the unorganized and ill-paid manual workers of the metropolis, and its wretched and degraded underworld. But, though the labour unrest of the recent years reached a climax about the time of the Middlesex Election and its accompanying disorders, there seems good reason to believe that it had little direct connection with the

Wilkite manifestations,[40] and the support of such allies would, in any case, have checked rather than assisted Wilkes's rise to power.

It is clear indeed that the backbone of Wilkes's support in the metropolis was precisely the same classes as that of the earlier popular leaders, what we should call its lower middle classes. In the City's Corporation it was the Common Hall, composed of the liverymen of the City Companies, which was always the bulwark of his power, and his voting strength there depended largely on the liverymen of the numerous lesser companies, many of which still retained to a considerable degree their old craft associations.[41] And outside the City, in other parts of the metropolis, the position was very similar. In Westminster, for instance, a list of twenty of his most active supporters drawn up in 1770 included the names of three apothecaries, two carpenters, a well-to-do poulterer, a stable-keeper, an engraver, a bookseller, an upholsterer, a coachmaker, and a working jeweller – as well as a baronet, two parsons (one of whom was respectable), a barrister, and a solicitor.[42]

But though the classes on which Wilkes's power ultimately rested were the same as those who supported his predecessors, the very strength of the feeling he elicited made fundamental changes in the movement which was coming into being. In the first place his influence extended over a wider area than that of any of his predecessors. London had long outgrown its ancient city boundaries and the city of Westminster, the borough of Southwark, much of the county of Middlesex, and even some of the county of Surrey were already becoming for all practical purposes part of the same great urban centre. But this expansion of the City had so far been reflected only very partially in a unity of political actions and ideas.[43] The strength of the City leaders of the past had depended on their control over the corporate organization of the ancient City, and they had only occasionally concerned themselves with stimulating the political opinion of the surrounding areas and never with giving it a permanent organization. Now, with all these areas united in a community of feeling, co-ordinated action could be planned and was in fact carried out. Not only were their corporate activities now synchronized, but a network of interrelated clubs and societies was created, through which enthusiasm could be maintained and the views of the various parts of the metropolis kept in line.[44] The famous Radical Quadrilateral, or even the Quintuple Alliance, of the future was thus foreshadowed. Wilkes has a claim to be considered at the same time the last of the old City leaders, whose strength rested on· their control over the Corporation, and the first of the new metropolitan popular leaders who relied on less tangible but more wide-flung support.

In the second place, and partly because the area over which his influence extended was thus enlarged, the cause of Wilkes attracted to him a type of supporter whose alliance earlier leaders had never enjoyed. These were the men, all of some education and some of considerable standing, who formed the nucleus of the Society of Supporters of the Bill of Rights, a society founded early in 1769 to buy off Wilkes's creditors, but which became in these earlier years the mainspring of the movement's policy. Few of these men were freemen of the City; but most of them had strong interests in the metropolitan area, and the greater number of them pursued their careers there. They were a highly diversified group of men, but they were all for one reason or another dissatisfied with the existing order; with few exceptions they were rather young, and a high proportion of them belonged to the rising professional classes (they tended to be the less prosperous and well-established members of the less socially regarded of these classes) for which, like the ordinary merchant and trading classes of the City, the existing political and social system made little provision.[45] And though, at first at any rate, most of them were warmly attached to the cause of Wilkes as a person, they were basically more concerned with the wider issues to which the Middlesex Election dispute gave rise. The most prominent among them were the able but erratic and misfit Parson John Horne (later to be known as Horne Tooke),[46] and two new and idealistic members of parliament, James Townsend[47] and John Sawbridge,[48] both of families with City antecedents, though they themselves had not hitherto interested themselves in its affairs. They were all in their thirties, were all to be prominent in Radical agitation for many years to come, and it was to a considerable degree through their influence that the fervour of the Wilkites was, in these early years, harnessed to Radical ends.

It might, however, be asked how it was that, with a leader like Wilkes himself indifferent or even hostile to the raising of such issues, they were able to bring about this result. The answer lies in the fact that until his release from prison in April 1770, Wilkes was not in a position to exercise leadership over the forces he had raised. The easy discipline of the King's Bench prison in which he was confined permitted him, it is true, to keep himself in the public eye and to fight his battle with the House of Commons, but he could neither take part in the corporate activities of the City, nor exercise a preponderant influence over the day-to-day activities of his supporters in the rest of the metropolis until he was able to be present in person. In the City it was in consequence William Beckford who, until his sudden death in June 1770, reaped the fruits of Wilkes's popularity, and between Beckford and these new and ardent recruits the links both of personal friendship and similarity of ideas were strong. In particular, both Townsend and Sawbridge adhered in parliament to the Chatham group of which Beckford was an old supporter.[49] And when in the summer of 1769 Beckford persuaded both of them to take up the freedom of the City, and arranged for them not only to be elected aldermen but also sheriffs for the year,[50] and when in November he himself was for the second time chosen Lord Mayor,[51] the control of the popular forces both in the City and in the metropolis as a whole was placed firmly in their united and friendly hands.

Since the alliance between Beckford and Wilkes was purely one of convenience – Beckford never joined the Supporters of the Bill of Rights and even in the two months between Wilkes's release from prison and Beckford's death it began to wear thin – Beckford had every reason to stress rather the general issues arising out of the demagogue's cause than his personal grievances. Moreover, the main issue which could be extracted from the Middlesex Election dispute, the threat to the rights of the electors from what might be considered a corrupt House of Commons, fitted in well with the tentative ideas about electoral and parliamentary reform which he had already been advancing. Thus the sympathies of the new recruits and the ideas of the old City leader were easily assimilated. In consequence it was during the short period between the rise of the Wilkite movement and the struggle of Wilkes himself to assume control of it, that the main contributions were made by the metropolis to the development of eighteenth-century Radicalism. In this period something in the nature of a programme of parliamentary reform was adumbrated; an attempt was made to set on foot a nation-wide agitation in support of their views, and (less important, but equally significant of the forces at work in the metropolis) a plot was laid to force a pledge of support for a reform programme on the leaders of the opposition groups in parliament.

The first of these contributions was that of the most permanent importance. It would seem to have been Beckford who took the lead here. The first step was taken at the beginning of 1769 when the metropolitan constituencies decided to send instructions to their representatives protesting against the actions of the House against Wilkes, and advancing other grievances. Both Middlesex and Westminster adopted and published their instructions before the City did, but it was the City's instructions, in the preparation of which Beckford was actively concerned, which first raised the issue of electoral and parliamentary reform.[52] The City representatives were instructed to work for shorter parliaments and a place and pension bill (both

echoes of the old Oppositions with which Beckford was familiar) and for
the imposition of the oath against bribery at elections which Beckford
had demanded in his abortive bill at the end of the last parliament. (A
further proposal advanced that voting might be by ballot is of more
uncertain origin, and does not occur again.) Further, throughout the
rest of 1769 Beckford began to dwell in his speeches in the House on the
'little paltry boroughs' he had complained of as early as 1761, and on
the undue influence which they gave to the aristocracy and to other
borough-owners.[53] And by 1770 he had produced the threefold
programme of reform – shorter parliaments, a place and pension bill,
and the more equal representation of the people, which he tried to force
on the unwilling parliamentary Opposition, and which obtained
widespread support in the metropolis. It was a programme based on the
assumption that representation and property were closely related, and
it was in no sense a demand for popular sovereignty, but it was (largely
for this reason) one which was to remain acceptable to most English
reformers for many years to come.

More immediately striking, however, though of less long-term
significance, were the attempts in these years to extend the movement
inside the metropolis to the nation as a whole. The course of these
attempts illustrates so well both the strength and the limitations of this
Radical movement of the metropolis in relation to the country as a
whole, that it is worth going into it in some detail. A first attempt made
by the City on its own at the time of the publication of its instructions to
its representatives was an almost complete failure.[54] Even in the
commercial centres where it was accustomed to stimulate common
action on commercial issues, it ran into unexpected difficulties, and in
the counties its contacts were too slight to bring forth a response.[55] A
second attempt in the summer of 1769 was made under more auspicious
circumstances, and met with more success. It did so because it was
undertaken in collaboration with the opposition groups in parliament.
As soon as the House of Commons had resolved on 15 April 1769 that,
Wilkes being incapable of sitting, Colonel Luttrell, the rival candidate,
be declared elected in his stead, a meeting of Middlesex Freeholders was
summoned, at which James Townsend announced 'the necessity of
seeking out some new remedy for a new grievance'.[56] Shortly afterwards
a deputation of the Livery of the City asked for a Common Hall for the
same purpose,[57] and it soon became known that the 'new remedy'
proposed by both Middlesex and the City was the presentation of
petitions to the Crown, which would not only demand redress of various
grievances, but (a definitely unorthodox departure) would also protest
to the King against the actions of the House of Commons. Early in May

it was rumoured that 'a petition of a very extraordinary kind is actually preparing, to be sent through every county in England in order to be signed by such freeholders … as may approve of its contents'.[58]

Before any petition was formally adopted, however, on the last day of the parliamentary session a dinner was held at the Thatched House Tavern, attended by the House of Commons members of all the opposition groups, at which it was agreed to take common action during the recess to stir up expressions of public opinion throughout the country in protest against the Middlesex Resolution.[59] All those metropolitan leaders who were also members of parliament were present; the toast of 'the City of London, not forgetting the Livery thereof'[60] was drunk, and though no statement was made about the means to be employed to voice the country's protest, it was obviously generally accepted that petitions to the Crown as proposed in Middlesex and London should be pressed on all counties and some of the larger boroughs, and that the leaders of metropolitan opinion and the parliamentary opposition groups should work alongside each other in the campaign.[61] There are even some signs of a definite 'deal' between the two groups of allies. All sections of the parliamentary Opposition shared, together with their dislike of Wilkes, a suspicion of the Radicalism of the metropolis. They were, in consequence, anxious to confine the petitions to the issue of the Middlesex Election alone.[62] It may therefore be of some significance that a circumstantial account appeared in the Press a few days before the Thatched House dinner of a meeting between George Grenville and William Dowdeswell, the leaders of the two main opposition groups in the House of Commons, with some persons in the City,[63] to discuss possible modifications in the terms of the Middlesex Petition; and it may also be noted that, though the petitions of Middlesex and the City ultimately came out in their original form, those from other parts of the metropolis, which were drawn up later, followed the pattern set by the rest of the country and confined themselves to the Middlesex issue.[64]

The popular leaders of the metropolis had thus succeeded in reaching an agreement with the parliamentary Opposition to work for a nation-wide expression of public opinion, and had imposed on them their own plan of action – though they may have done so at the cost of narrowing the issues on which the support of the nation was to be sought. In the implementing of the plan they also took an active part. In the county of Surrey[65] as well as throughout the metropolitan area it was they who made the running; they were also able to exert some influence over the commercial centres with which they were in contact, and individuals among them could help in stimulating opinion in counties further afield. It was reported in August that 'many of them are dispersed in different parts of the country endeavouring to stir up meetings of the freeholders...',[66] and Serjeant John Glynn in Cornwall and Exeter,[67] Beckford in Wiltshire and Somerset,[68] John Sawbridge in Kent,[69] and possibly one or two others elsewhere were active and prominent in this work.[70]

These activities mark, however, the extent of what they could do to further the progress of the campaign. The appeal was primarily to the counties, and by the very nature of the case, the chief part in arousing support in the counties had to be taken by the political leaders whom they trusted, and it is significant that almost without exception the influence exerted by individual metropolitan leaders in the counties arose from the fact that they were property owners there. More general efforts to exercise influence from the metropolis over the course of events were unsuccessful. An attempt by the Supporters of the Bill of Rights by circularizing the counties to encourage the setting up of permanent local organizations to correspond with, was very coldly received;[71] and the intervention of John Horne, Sir Robert Bernard, and others in the borough of Bedford to defeat the mayor favoured by the duke of Bedford,[72] did not (as it was confidently hoped) prove the beginning of a movement of revolt by boroughs against their patrons,[73] and would have been highly unpopular with their parliamentary allies if it had.

When the campaign had once been agreed on therefore the Radical forces in the metropolis could hope to play only a minor part in its course. Their influence was further weakened, moreover, by the open suspicion with which they were regarded by at least one section of the parliamentary Opposition and by large sections of public opinion throughout the country. While that part of the Opposition which followed the lead of Chatham and the Grenvilles were prepared to work amicably with them, this was by no means the case with the party supporting the marquess of Rockingham. The marquess himself for a long time resisted the proposal to promote a petition in his own county of Yorkshire, and did so largely because of his dislike of the metropolis and its motives. 'I *must say*', he wrote, 'that the thing which weighs most against adopting the mode of petitioning the King is, *where* the example was first set.'[74] And the course of the campaign showed that this suspicion was so widely shared by those whose signatures were being sought, that in many parts of the country the support of the metropolis was a hindrance rather than a help in the agitation. William Dowdeswell, the leader of the Rockinghams in the House of Commons, lamented from Worcestershire that 'Wilkes's character ... and the advantage which he necessarily must receive from the restitution made to the Public of its rights . . . have checkt this proceeding in most places,' and he added 'The injudicious list of grievances, which filled the first petitions, [i.e. those of Middlesex and London] still more disinclined the sober part of the People to signing petitions . . .'[75] While in Surrey the highly respectable Sir Anthony Abdy, battling in vain against the incursion of metropolitan organizers into the county, protested at 'the wild and warm proceedings of Messrs. Horne, Bellas etc. and others of the London Tavern, the generality of whose opinions and ideas I cannot agree or subscribe to'.[76]

The campaign as a whole had only a limited success. Only eighteen out of the forty English counties[77] and over a dozen of the larger boroughs[78] finally presented petitions, and these often took months to procure despite strenuous efforts on the part of those promoting them. Whether from suspicion of metropolitan Radicalism, or dislike of Wilkes or for other reasons there was little sign that the country gentry as a whole were anxious to make a protest even on the limited issue of the Middlesex Resolution. It was probably true that in most counties there were enough of what Rockingham called the 'young men' and 'the warm spirits'[79] to get a petition through a county meeting if they were given a lead by those whom they were accustomed to follow. It was also true that here and there they took the initiative without such a lead, or, as in Yorkshire itself, forced their leaders into action. In consequence in most counties where members of the parliamentary Opposition were influential petitions were set on foot. But when it came to circulating the petitions for signature the organizers often found a good deal of unwillingness to sign. 'It is amazing,' complained Dowdeswell, 'how in most places people of rank and fortune shrink from this measure; and with what deference all others below them wait for their leaders.'[80] And if there were unwillingness among the gentry, there was ignorance among the freeholders. There were indeed some signs of independent approval of the movement among the more substantial class of freeholder. John Robinson, suspiciously watching the progress of the Yorkshire petition from the neighbouring county of Westmorland, wrote, 'It gives me concern to find that the Quakers and Dissenters are so infatuated . . . as to sign and support it,'[81] and the notably independent freeholders of Kent, and apparently those of Essex,[82] supported petitions against the wishes of most of the local gentry. But in general the situation seems to have been much as Lord Temple described it in Buckinghamshire where he 'found the freeholders in general totally ignorant of the question, and but very little affected with it'.[83] The duke of Richmond also gave an admirable account of the position in an out-of-the-way county, that of Sussex, when explaining why, despite his personal sympathies, he did not organize a petition there. 'You will naturally say then, well why do not the effects appear? The reason is that from the distant situation of Sussex from London, ... from the weight of Government on account of the many dependants which so many Seaports occasion, from many of the leading men being in place or attached to Court; from the long habit in which the late Duke of Newcastle had brought the Whigs of approving all the measures of the old Court, the attachment of the Torys to the new Court, and from the natural indolence of men who do not feel the immediate effects of oppression. From all these causes, there was a supineness, that of itself would not stir, tho' they must and do see that things are not right. I could plainly see that there was discontent enough, if it was encouraged to do the business of a Petition, but I must have stirred it up, and in so doing I should have appear'd factious.'[84]

Nor was the response of the boroughs, even the more important ones, much more encouraging. Even in Bristol, though a petition was set going with enthusiasm, it hung fire so much that at one time doubts were felt whether it would ever be presented,[85] and at Liverpool a petition from a body of freemen was immediately offset by a counter-petition from the Corporation. In view of the conflicting interests among those sponsoring the petitions, and the evidence of widespread indifference and even dislike of the measure among those who were approached, it is not surprising that Administration, at first alarmed at the prospect of an outburst of public feeling on a nation-wide scale, ended by ignoring it altogether, nor that the movement petered out.

With the dying away of the agitations of these years, the bid which the Radical forces of the metropolis had made to enlist the country in their cause was virtually over. Beckford's attempts in 1770 to pledge the leaders of the Opposition to his programme of reform were easily evaded and were thus of comparatively little significance,[86] and the Remonstrances of the same year, in the course of which he won his posthumous statue from his fellow-citizens, called forth little response outside the metropolis. And with his death and the violent internal dissensions which accompanied the succession of Wilkes to power, the breach between the metropolis and the rest of the country was further widened. When in 1771 the Lord Mayor, Brass Crosby, was committed to the Tower by the House of Commons during the dispute between the City and the House over the printing of the Commons' Debates, the incident aroused in the country as a whole, as Edmund Burke mournfully observed,[87] little general comment or even surprise.

Nevertheless, the events of these years had a real importance in the history of eighteenth-century England. It was not without cause that

Christopher Wyvill, leader of the famous Yorkshire Association ten years later, printed as the introduction to his political papers the proceedings in Yorkshire in 1769–70,[88] and in the metropolis itself forces had been set at work which did not again die down. Moreover, the sketch of a programme of parliamentary reform had been drawn up which was to serve as the basis of the ideas of the majority of reformers for many years to come, and which might also serve as a starting-point for more revolutionary proposals. In 1771 when Wilkes and his friends felt obliged to advance proposals for reform they adopted Beckford's propositions *en bloc*,[89] but five years later, when Wilkes made his speech on reform in the new parliament in which he was permitted to sit, Beckford's 'more equal representation of the people' had developed into the principle 'that every free agent in this kingdom should ... be represented in parliament'.[90] And even when Wilkes spoke, Major Cartwright's famous pamphlet *Take Your Choice*, in which he advocated universal suffrage, was being shown round in manuscript in preparation for publication.[91]

Notes

1. No attempt has been made to bring up-to-date this lecture, delivered in 1959. For the convenience of readers, however, manuscript material since printed in the *Correspondence of Edmund Burke* is quoted from the printed instead of the MS. source.
2. William Beckford b. in Jamaica 1709, d. 21 June 1770. MP for Shaftesbury 1747–54 and London 1754–70. Lord Mayor 1762–3 and 1769–70. The statue, voted in 1770, was declared by his fellow-citizens, when displayed to them, to be an excellent likeness (*London Chronicle*, 11–13 June 1772, xxxi. 562).
3. The Remonstrance was presented on 23 May 1770.
4. The words engraved on the statue were those published in the Press. John Horne (Horne Tooke) claimed, probably correctly, to have written them up for the Press, and also to have suggested that the Lord Mayor should address the King. Much later he gave his support to the rumour that no such speech had been made. W. P. Treloar, who examined the matter in his *Wilkes and the City* (1917), pp. 98–100, was convinced that 'Beckford made no rejoinder ... or merely muttered a few indistinct words, and the speech was concocted afterwards.' The contemporary evidence is, however, quite clear. Richard Rigby wrote to the duke of Bedford on the same day, having just come from court, describing the incident and giving the gist of the words, adding 'This is the first attempt ever made to hold a colloquy with the King by any subject, and is indecent to the highest degree' (J. Russell, *The Correspondence of John, Fourth Duke of Bedford* (1846), iii. pp. 413–14). James Townsend, present as sheriff, wrote to Chatham, also on 23 May, that the Lord Mayor's speech 'greatly disconcerted the Court. He has promised to recollect what he said, and I fancy the substance will appear in the papers tomorrow' (W. S. Taylor and J. H. Pringle, *The Correspondence of William Pitt, Earl of Chatham* (1839), iii. p. 458). Beckford replying to Chatham's congratulations said that he spoke 'the language of truth, and with that humility and submission which becomes a subject speaking to his lawful king' (*Chatham Correspondence*, iii. p. 463).

5. *Chatham Correspondence*, iii. p. 462.
6. A rhyme was printed in the *Public Advertiser* on 18 November 1769:
   'For B[eck]f[ro]d he was chosen May'r
   A wight of high renown.
   To see a slave he could not bear,
   —Unless it were his own.'
7. He had purchased the estate of Fonthill, at Fonthill Giffard, Wilts., and greatly enlarged and beautified the house.
8. When he entered the House he supported the country party in opposition and was known as a Tory. After the death of the prince of Wales he gave his allegiance first to the duke of Bedford and then to Henry Fox, but when Pitt's abilities as a war leader became evident he attached himself enthusiastically and permanently to his new leader.
9. William Beckford, junior (1759–1844).
10. *London Chronicle*, 6–8 March 1770, xxvii. 225.
11. W. Butterfield, *George III, Lord North, and the People, 1779–80* (1949), pp. 181 *seq.*
12. S. Maccoby, *English Radicalism 1762–1785, the Origins* (1955).
13. I have treated this subject more fully in my 'The City of London in Eighteenth-century Politics', in *Essays Presented to Sir Lewis Namier*, (ed. R. Pares and A. J. P. Taylor, 1956).
14. The price of wheat reached a peak in the very bad year 1767, but was high (by comparison with the five years ending 1763) in the period 1764–8 inclusive, and the numbers of cattle and sheep brought to Smithfield market were also significantly lower in most of these years (T. S. Ashton, *An Economic History of England: The 18th Century* (1955), Tables I and VII, pp. 239 and 245). The first serious outburst of labour unrest in London was the riot in 1765 of the Spitalfield silk-weavers, automatically protected from French competition during the war. It was followed in the ensuing years by others, more or less serious, among the coal-heavers, sailors, weavers, tailors, hatters, and even (in 1771) by the cabinet-makers against the importation of foreign furniture by abuse of diplomatic privilege. An official return made in 1772 to the City of the number of death sentences passed at the Old Bailey showed an increase from fourteen in 1760 to ninety-one in 1770 (*London Chronicle*, 3–5 November 1772, xxxii. 440).
15. He became a freeman of the Ironmongers' Company, and was alderman for Billingsgate Ward.
16. He was supported by the Tory interest in the City, in particular it would seem by Alderman William Benn, a notable City politician of the time. After his election he thanked the electors for the trust they placed in him despite 'the short time I have had the honour of being known to you, and the prejudices that have been injuriously raised against me' (*Public Advertiser*, 8 May 1754).
17. There is considerable evidence of this in the printed *Chatham Correspondence* and in the unpublished Pitt MSS. in the Public Record Office.
18. He opposed the Preliminaries of the Peace of Paris in the House in November 1762 and in 1763 when the Court of Aldermen, not daring to summon the Common Council, voted an address, refused to accompany them to present it (Court of Aldermen, Repertory Book 167, pp. 280 *seq.*; Brit. Mus. Add. MS. 32948, f. 269: T. Walpole to Newcastle, 12 May 1763).
19. Wilkes attacked Beckford savagely in the *North Briton*, though when writing to Lord Temple, who thought well of Beckford, he tried to blame the hostility shown on Charles Churchill (W. J. Smith, *The Grenville Papers* (1852), ii. p. 59). Reports made to the Secretary of State on Wilkes's movements reported on 8 November 1763 a visit of Wilkes to the Lord Mayor Beckford at his house (*ibid.*, ii. p. 158), and on 19 December 1763 Beckford wrote him a friendly letter promising assistance (Brit. Mus.

Add. MS. 30867, f. 242). On 17 February 1764 Beckford spoke and voted in the House
· against General Warrants (Parliamentary MS. Diary of James Harris).

20. He was called 'The scavenger to throw dirt upon government' (MS. Parliamentary
Diary of James Harris, 16 November 1763) and 'the Dr. Lucas of the English House of
Commons' (*Hist. MS. Com.* Emly MSS., 8th Rept., Pt. I, Sect. I, 190 b, 7 March
1765).

21. Brit. Mus. Add. MS. 38334, ff. 29 *seq.* Apparently an attempt at a verbatim report of
Beckford's speech on the Address on 13 November 1761.

22. So he claimed in 1768 (*Public Advertiser*, 22 March 1768). As he was at this time still a
supporter of the Administration set up by Chatham there may well, however, be
other reasons.

23. H. Cavendish, *Debates of the House of Commons during the Thirteenth Parliament of Great
Britain* (1841), i. p. 241.

24. *London Evening Post*, 4–7 April 1761, quoted *Memoirs of William Beckford* (1859), i. p.
33.

25. J. Brooke, *The Chatham Administration, 1766–1768* (1956), p. 337, n. 4. Sir Roger
Newdigate welcomed the proposal as likely to reduce competion for seats from
'Nabobs' and other monied rivals of the landed interests. Cf. H. Walpole, *Memoirs of
the Reign of King George III* (ed. D. Le Marchant, 1845), iii. pp. 157–60.

26. He expanded this statement with the condition 'if they are to be the instruments of
forcing through those barriers which the Wisdom of our Ancestors has placed
between the hereditary and elective legislators of England' (*Public Advertiser*, 8
September 1769).

27. A. Stephens, *Memoirs of John Horne Tooke* (1813), i. pp. 387–8. Horne's account of
this incident is supported by a letter from Chatham (*Chatham Correspondence*, iii. p. 431,
n. 1).

28. *London Chronicle*, 24–27 March 1770, xxvii. 296.

29. He was alleged to have said this to George III of Serjeant John Glynn. The story was
widely reported, see H. Bleackley, *Life of John Wilkes* (1917), p. 376.

30. He had a weak voice and was unable to sway large assemblies, e.g. the large and
contentious meeting at Westminster Hall on 31 October 1770, at which Wilkes
completely lost control of proceedings. He himself referred to his 'weak and bad voice'
(*London Chronicle*, 8–10 November 1770, xxviii. 456).

31. Brit. Mus. Add. MS. 30869, f. 175: H. Cotes to J. Wilkes, 15 December 1767. Some
time before 16 June 1767 Wilkes had suggested to his friends that he might stand for
the City (*ibid.*, f. 131: Heaton Wilkes to J. Wilkes, 16 June 1769). They were uniformly
discouraging. He nevertheless persisted, and on 6 October 1767 a letter from him to
Arthur Beardmore, a City politician, was printed in the *St. James's Chronicle*. Cotes
thought Westminster more hopeful.

32. He was on 2 January 1769 elected alderman of the ward of Farringdon Without. His
eligibility for election was challenged, but legal action was not taken, and after his
release from prison he was sworn in. The question is fully treated in Teloar, *op. cit.*, pp.
70 *seq.*

33. As early as 1770 it seems clear that he was trying to get profitable jobs in the City for
friends and relatives in the proceeds of which he might share (*Public Advertiser*, 27 May
1771 *seq.*). In 1779, after a three years' struggle, he achieved the climax of his personal
ambition, the highly lucrative position of City Chamberlain.

34. Camden congratulated Beckford on Wilkes's failure to be elected for the City (Letter
of 28 March 1768 in the Hamilton MSS.), though during the election Beckford and the
other popular candidate Barlow Trecothick had treated Wilkes 'with much civility'
(Walpole, *Memoirs of the Reign of King George II, op. cit.*, iii. p. 185) and supported
Wilkes's candidature for Middlesex, and for election as alderman.

35. *Public Advertiser*, 22 May 1771. H. Cotes in a letter to John Horne said that the breach

between Horne and Wilkes really began over the Middlesex petition of 1769, which Wilkes had wished to be confined entirely to the rights of the electors of that county.

36. Edmund Burke wrote to his friend Charles O'Hara on 9 June 1768: 'The plan of our party was . . . not to provoke Administration into any violent measure upon this subject . . . besides we had not the least desire of taking up that gentleman's cause as personally favourable to him' (printed R. J. S. Hoffman, *Edmund Burke, New York Agent* (Philadelphia, 1956), p. 434).

37. See below, pp. 42–6.

38. The response in different parts of the country varied greatly and can only be understood in relation to local conditions. One of the most interesting accounts in the Press was a letter in the *London Chronicle*, 10–12 May 1770, xxvii, 452, from one signing himself 'Viator' whose business, he said, took him much about the kingdom. 'There is scarce an inn, shop, or private house, into which I enter, but the pleasure of conversation, and the regular despatch of business, are hindered by discourse and altercations about Wilkes, Grievances and Middlesex Election.' He adds that he was in Worcestershire when Wilkes was released from prison and that in some places he passed through on 17 and 18 April no business could be done, that Worcester itself was a scene of confusion, but that in Kidderminster the 'Vicar of the Parish, the Bailiff of the Borough, the Master-weavers and principal inhabitants' had managed to prevent riotous behaviour by 'journeymen-weavers, their apprentices and others of the vulgar'. In Bristol there was in 1769 a considerable body of discontent, described by Richard Champion in his MS. Letter Book (in the possession of Miss P. Rawlins, of Denbigh, N. Wales) as having 'a great and formidable appearance, and a real strength'. The local friends of Wilkes 'took advantage of the times to head' it but behaved 'with such a wildness of popularity and so little attention to common sense' that they 'frightened away many worthy men'. At Plymouth there were riotous rejoicings when the news was received in June 1769 that John Sawbridge and James Townsend had been elected sheriffs. The crowd changed the name of HM ship *Barrington* to *Liberty*, and burned jack-boots and an effigy of Bute. They were said to be led by an 'eminent attorney' (*Gentleman's Magazine*, 1769, p. 361).

39. E. Burke to C. O'Hara, 19 November 1773 (Hoffman, *op. cit.*, p. 551).

40. See G. F. E. Rudé, 'Wilkes and Liberty, 1768–69', *Guildhall Miscellany*, July 1957 and 'The London "Mob" of the Eighteenth Century' *Historical Journal* ii, i (1956), pp. 1–18. There was much unrest among the merchant seamen in the Thames-side just at the time of the riots accompanying Wilkes's election for Middlesex, but even his enemies made no attempt to suggest he did anything to exacerbate these disorders. Rockingham, reporting to the duke of Newcastle on 10 May 1768 the dispersal of the mob which had collected outside the House of Lords, said that the Justices returning reported that the crowds were 'much diminished but . . . that they [*sic*] were still some who cried Wilkes and Liberty and some who cried that bread and beer were too dear and that it was as well to be hanged as starved' (Brit. Mus. Add. MS. 32990, f. 36v).

41. J. R. Kellett, 'The Breakdown of Gild and Corporation Control over the Handicraft and Retail Trade in London', *Economic History Review*, April 1958, pp. 381 *seq.*

42. List of the signatories to the Westminster Remonstrance, with their occupations, inserted by 'Sly-boots' in the *Public Advertiser*, 7 April 1770.

43. L. B. Namier, *Structure of Politics at the Accession of George III* (2nd edn., 1957), pp. 65 *seq.*

44. Wilkes was an honorary member of a wide variety of convivial clubs, most of which had some political significance. The most important of the societies primarily political in their purpose were, besides the Supporters of the Bill of Rights, who met at the London Tavern, the Sons of Freedom who met at Appleby's tavern in Westminster, the Society which met at the Standard Tavern, Lincoln's Inn Fields, and the long-established Society of the Antigallicans whose annual meeting was said

in 1771 to be 'the most numerous meeting of the year of the Middlesex Freeholders' (*Public Advertiser*, 25 April 1771). The annual May Feast at Southwark was also this year used for political ends (*ibid.*, 29 May 1771).

45. In the earlier years of the Society several country gentlemen were members, Sir Francis Blake Delaval, Bt., of Seaton Delaval, Northumberland, 1754–68 MP for Andover, Sir Robert Bernard, Bt., of Brampton, Hunts., who was returned by the popular interest for Westminster in 1770 and held the seat till 1774, a young Welsh gentleman Robert Jones of Fonmor Castle, nr. Cardiff, and Hill Street, Berkeley Square, 'a gentleman of good character, but not esteemed to be a man of very extensive literature and knowledge' (Brit. Mus. Add. MS. 35632, f. 49: John Vernon to 2nd Lord Hardwicke, 12 June 1769), and Lord Mountmorres, the younger brother of the patriotic Irish peer Lord Charlemont. They each seem to have had different private reasons for their allegiance, to have been concerned chiefly with the activities in Westminster, and to have detached themselves from the movement after the split within the Society in 1771. Another highly individualistic supporter, and one who remained personally attached to Wilkes throughout, was old Dr. Thomas Wilson, Prebendary of Westminster, an ardent admirer of the republican historian Mrs. Catherine Macaulay, sister of John Sawbridge. Among the legal supporters were Serjeant John Glynn, MP for Middlesex 1768–79, Wilkes's counsel, two young barristers William Adair and Robert Morris, a Welshman; the attorneys Charles Martin and John Reynolds (the latter Wilkes's attorney), George Bellas, Proctor of the Admiralty Court, Arthur Beardmore, and John Boddington. Sir Joseph Mawbey, Bt., brewer and distiller, MP for Southwark 1761–74, represented the older type of popular leader.

46. 1736–1812. For him see A. Stephens, *Memoirs of John Horne Tooke*, 2 vols., (1813).

47. 1737–87. Son of Chauncy Townsend, merchant and contractor. MP for West Looe 1767–74 and for Calne 1782–7. Took up his freedom by patrimony 1769, alderman 1769, sheriff 1769–70, Lord Mayor 1772–3 (see W. P. Courtney, 'James Townsend, M.P.', *Notes and Queries*, 11th Series, v, 2–4).

48. *c.* 1732–95. MP for Hythe 1768–74, for London 1774–95. Took up his freedom by redemption in 1769. Alderman 1769, sheriff 1769–70, Lord Mayor 1775–6.

49. In 1771 Townsend called Beckford 'my intimate confidential friend' (*London Chronicle*, 10–12 October 1771, xxx, 360).

50. John Horne in a letter signed 'Roberto' in *The Gazetteer*, 25 September 1771, described Beckford's initiative in this matter.

51. Beckford's nomination was organized by James Townsend. Beckford wrote to Shelburne, 24 October 1769, 'Our friend Townsend has, by his encouragement, brought this about' (Bowood MSS.). When his name was put forward with that of Trecothick, the hostile majority in the Court of aldermen, believing his protestations that he would not stand, elected him in order to force on another election. When Beckford permitted the Livery to persuade him to change his mind, they considered this a disreputable trick.

52. The Middlesex freeholders met to agree on instructions to their representatives on 12 January; those of Westminster on 25 January. The City instructions were agreed on 10 February 1769. For Beckford's part in this, see *Public Advertiser*, 11 February 1769.

53. On 29 February 1769 he stated, 'The fact is, a number of great men are got together to parcel out every thing, without regard to the people' (Cavendish *Debates*, i, p. 150). On 1 March 1769 he stated, 'We should cut off the small paltry boroughs' (*ibid.*, i, 281) and the next day he spoke of MPs whose seats were obtained by 'bribing some paltry borough' (*ibid.*, i, 304).

54. The *London Chronicle*, 2–4 February 1769, xxv, 114, reported that Essex was said to be considering instructions and that Bristol 'and the capital places in the kingdom, are impatiently waiting the sense of the City of London' to draw up their instructions. In

all between 31 January and 9 February the paper reported four cities – Norwich, Exeter, London, Bristol – and six counties – Devon, Middlesex, Essex, Wiltshire, Hampshire, and Berkshire – as awaiting the London lead. Copies of the London instructions were sent by post to all parts of the kingdom 'with a view to animate other Counties and Boroughs to follow the example' (*London Chronicle*, 9–11 February 1769, xxv, 144). Bristol sent instructions. For their reaction see W. R. Savadge, 'The West Country and American Mainland Colonies 1703–1783, with special reference to the Merchants of Bristol', unpublished thesis, Oxford University.

55. Its chief effect was to stimulate a crop of loyal addresses to the Crown, organized by the supporters of Administration. They were duly printed in the *London Gazette* between the beginning of February until the end of May 1769.

56. *London Chronicle*, 15–18 April 1769, xxv, 366.

57. The calling of a Common Hall was first demanded on 27 April 1769, the day on which the Middlesex petition was passed, but owing to obstruction the petition from London was not presented until 5 July 1769.

58. *London Chronicle*, 11–13 May 1769, xxv, 456. There was a precedent. The petition of the City to the Crown against the Cider Tax in 1764 was said in the House to be 'the first instance of a petition to the King against Parliament' (MS. Parliamentary Diary of James Harris, 16 March 1764).

59. The dinner was held on 9 May 1769. A list of the seventy-two members of the Opposition in the House of Commons present is included in the *Chatham Correspondence*, iii. pp. 359–60, n. 1.

60. *London Chronicle*, 11–13 May 1769, xxv, 450.

61. There was no formal agreement on the steps to be taken.

62. The marques of Rockingham suspected the followers of Grenville and Chatham of a desire to introduce radical matters into the petition. He wrote to Burke about the proposed Buckinghamshire petition expression gloomy suspicions of the attitude of Lord Temple and his supporters. 'Lord Temple will try to include all the matters mentioned in the City and Livery Petition, he will do it politically as a compliment to them and I even should scarce be surprised – if annual or triennial Parliaments were recommended' (*Correspondence of Edmund Burke* ed. T. Copeland vol. ii, ed. L. S. Sutherland, p. 48. Rockingham to E. Burke, 17 July 1769). But in fact Temple Grenville fully accepted the desirability of confining the petition 'to the principal point, and to express themselves upon that with vigour and decency' (*ibid.*, T. Whately to E. Burke, 23 August 1769).

63. *London Chronicle*, 4–6 May 1769, xxv, 430.

64. The Westminster Petition was, however, the first to call for the disolution of parliament, a point on which they were later followed by the Yorkshire Petition.

65. See p. 45 below. An account of the popular activities in Surrey at this time was published by Sir Joseph Mawbey under the title of 'Surriensis' in the *Gentleman's Magazine*, 1788, pp. 1052–53.

66. Brit. Mus. Add. MS. 35632, f. 51; John Vernon to the 2nd Lord Hardwicke, 16 August 1769.

67. He was a freeholder in Cornwall and was Recorder of Exeter. At the Cornish meeting of Freeholders at Bodmin on 6 October 1769 he spoke an hour. At Exeter at a meeting at Guildhall in the same month he attended as Recorder and made an excellent speech (Wilkes MSS., Brit. Mus. Add. MS. 30870, f. 213: [unsigned] Exeter, 24 October 1769).

68. Beckford attended the Wiltshire meeting at Devizes on 16 August 1769 with Lord Temple who was visiting him, and spoke. The duke of Grafton considered the petition largely the work of 'our old friends Popham and Beckford' (*Autobiography and Political Correspondence of Augustus Henry, third Duke of Grafton*, ed. W. R. Anson (1898), p. 239). He was unable to attend the meeting at Wells in October to pass the petition from

Somerset, but he sent a letter giving 'my sentiments freely and a copy of the chief grievance', which he authorized his correspondent to make public if necessary (Bowood MSS.: W. Beckford to Shelburne, 24 October 1769).

69. In Kent a petition was, after a good deal of difficulty, stirred up despite the opposition of the gentry. John Sawbridge was among those active in furthering it. *Chatham Correspondence*, iii. p. 365: J. Calcraft to Chatham, 25 November 1769. Walpole, *Memoirs*, iii. p. 393: 'Sawbridge and Calcraft obtained ... a petition from the county of Kent, though all the magistrates shrunk from it, two gentlemen only appearing there and they dissenting.'

70. Horace Walpole reported that Sir Joseph Mawbey and Calcraft, assisted by Sir Robert Bernard, also took the lead in obtaining the Essex petition (*ibid.*, iii. p. 400) without the support of the gentry.

71. The Supporters of the Bill of Rights at a meeting on 31 May agreed to despatch a circular 'invoking the friends of Liberty throughout the whole British Empire to concur in promoting the Constitutional Purposes for which this Society was established'. Two complementary letters were sent out. Copies, dated 20 July, are reproduced in the *London Chronicle*, 17–20 February 1770, xxvii, 174–5. Dowdeswell, who received a copy, decided not to reply (*Burke Correspondence*, ii. 53–4. W. Dowdeswell to E. Burke, 10 August 1769). Walpole reported that it received little response (*Memoirs*, iii. p. 372).

72. For this incident see *Public Advertiser*, 6 September 1769, seq.

73. A good deal of propaganda was put out in the Press to encourage it, and an unsuccessful attempt was made to repeat the operation against the duke of Grafton at Thetford (*Public Advertiser*, 20 September 1769). On 11 October the same paper reported that such was the feeling throughout the Corporations of the kingdom that at their annual elections of officers they 'seem determined to make choice of those gentlemen only whose conduct has proved them to be steady friends to their Country' – an obvious piece of propaganda quite unrelated to fact.

74. *Burke Correspondence*, ii. 64. Rockingham to E. Burke, 1, 3 September 1769.

75. *Ibid.*, ii, 70. W. Dowdeswell to E. Burke, 5 September 1769.

76. FitzWilliam MSS. (Sheffield): Sir Anthony Abdy to Sir George Colebrooke (copy), 1 July 1769.

77. Middlesex, Surrey, Devonshire, Cornwall, Wiltshire, Somersetshire, Gloucestershire, Buckinghamshire, Yorkshire, Essex, Worcestershire, Derbyshire, Cumberland, Herefordshire, Kent, Dorset, Northumberland, Durham.

78. It is not always easy to be certain which of the petitions discussed in the boroughs were actually delivered, particularly in the case of those which came late in the movement, when the arrangements for publicity were uncertain. The following seem, however, certainly to have been presented: Westminster, Southwark, Canterbury, Exeter, Bristol, Liverpool, Berwick-on-Tweed, Worcester, Durham, Newcastle-upon-Tyne, Coventry, Wells, and Hereford. The official *Gazette*, which so carefully included all the earlier loyal addresses, ignored the petitions completely.

79. *Burke Corr.*, ii. 62. Rockingham to E. Burke, 1–3 September 1769.

80. *Ibid.*, ii. 70. W. Dowdeswell to E. Burke, 5 September 1769.

81. Brit. Mus. Add. MS. 38206, f. 149. J. Robinson to C. Jenkinson, 3 November 1769.

82. See above.

83. *Burke Corr.*, ii. 76. E. Burke to Rockingham, 9 September 1769.

84. *Ibid.*, ii. 67. Richmond to E. Burke, 2 September 1769.

85. Add. MS. 30870, f. 190: J. Green (of Wine Street, Bristol) to J. Wilkes, 16 September 1769.

86. See p. 41 above. Besides the attempt to pledge the Opposition leaders into a programme of reform, they also tried to trick Chatham into pledging his support of

triennial parliaments (*Chatham Correspondence*, iii. p. 464 n. 1). He rejected the idea, though on 1 May 1771 he declared himself converted to it.

87. He wrote to Charles O'Hara, 2 April 1711 (printed Hoffman, *op. cit.*, p. 488): 'The people of the City have habituated themselves to *play* with violent measures. A Mayor of London sent to the Tower in his year of office, would at any other time have been a very dangerous symptom. It is now no indifferent one; but not what it would have been formerly.'

88. C. Wyvill, *Political Papers, chiefly respecting the Attempt of the County of York and other Considerable Districts, ... to effect a Reformation of the Parliament of Great-Britain*, n.d., York, i, xi *seq.*

89. The Bill of Rights Society first adopted this programme at a meeting on 11 June 1771 (*Public Advertiser*, 13 June 1771).

90. *Parliamentary History*, xviii, 1295.

91. F. D. Cartwright, *The Life and Correspondence of Major Cartwright* (1826), i. p. 95.

PAUL LANGFORD

London and the American Revolution

One of the more interesting features of colonial radicalism in the years before and during the American Revolution, at any rate in retrospect, is its ardent faith in the existence across the Atlantic of a substantial body of sympathy and support. Precise estimates of the dimensions of this body varied enormously, but most of those who opposed the exercise of imperial authority in the thirteen colonies regarded the government's policies as a sinister conspiracy on the part of a ruling clique of placemen. Even those who were realistic enough or knowledgeable enough to accept that those policies had a significant measure of approval both in and out of Parliament, considered that there were none the less in Britain a great many friends who offered succour and sympathy. Prominent among such friends, it was commonly considered, were the citizens of the imperial capital itself. The amicable disposition of London and Londoners was indeed a source of continuing consolation and reassurance to the many colonists who between the Stamp Act of 1765 and the shedding of blood at Lexington and Concord just a decade later found the mother country's policies in general increasingly baffling and disturbing. The debt was indeed formally recognized by the Congress in the summer of 1775, in an official communication of thanks to the Lord Mayor of London.[1]

> The City of London, my Lord, having, in all ages, proved itself the patron of liberty and the support of just government, against lawless tyranny and oppression, cannot fail to make us deeply sensible of the powerful aid our cause must receive from such advocates: a cause, my Lord, worthy the support of the first city in the world, as it involves the fate of a great continent and threatens to shake the foundations of a flourishing and, until lately a happy empire.

Understandably Americans were more inclined to emphasize the extent of London's enthusiasm for their cause than to identify its sources or constituents. To a great extent the passion for American liberty which was associated with the metropolis was indistinguishable from the general ferment produced by the growth of metropolitan radicalism in the 1760s and 1770s. The significance of this ferment is now well known, particularly as regards its implications for the development of radical politics in America. Wilkes's battle with government and Parliament over general warrants in the early 1760s and over electoral rights in the late 1760s, the corresponding movements in favour of constitutional reform which sprang up both in London and the provinces, above all the explosion of radical politics which occurred in and around the capital between 1768 and 1771, all filled a deep and sensitive need for Americans desperately seeking allies against the alleged tyranny of the administration. It was particularly important for the colonists that English patriots should reciprocate colonial concern for the preservation of the mother country's liberties, by expressing their own interest in the maintenance of America's liberties. Fortunately this reciprocity was apparently forthcoming. The allegedly consistent support for the colonial cause which came from the radical groups of the capital was a welcome reinforcement to the psychology of those in the colonies who sought to push America along the road to resistance and eventually revolution.

The great martyr of the new radicalism seemed especially anxious to cultivate good relations with the sons of liberty. In the colonies Wilkes achieved a celebrity even greater than that of William Pitt, and made every effort to maintain it. The famous donation of £1,500 which the Assembly of South Carolina made for his assistance, was merely part of widespread, if elsewhere somewhat less generous, sympathy in the south.[2] More important still was the correspondence with Bostonians, which proved particularly fruitful of quotable remarks, much repeated in public and in the Press. 'I hold Magna Charta to be in full force in America as in Europe,' Wilkes gratifyingly announced, adding, with more enthusiasm than knowledge of his subject, that he regarded North America as 'a territory containing near four hundred and fifty thousand inhabitants, which has never hitherto produced a single Jacobite.' On the other side prominent Boston politicians assured their champion in London that 'the fate of Wilkes and America must stand or fall together', and demonstrated their fidelity to his cause by christening their children after Wilkes and dispatching portraits of the new-born sons of liberty across the Atlantic.[3] Like most English radicals Wilkes did not deign actually to set foot in America, but visiting Americans were appropriately impressed by his concern for the cause. 'John Wilkes speaks very warmly of America and highly applauds their proceedings,' it was reported home, in a refrain much repeated by colonial newspapers.[4] Nor were his compatriots wanting in this respect. Typical was the report in the *New York Journal* in April 1769, asserting that 'All Mr. Wilkes's friends are friends to America. Some of them talk of seeking a shelter from arbitrary power in those peaceful desarts. Mrs. Macaulay, the celebrated female historian, talks of ending her days on the banks of the Ohio.'[5] Indeed Mrs. Macaulay achieved considerable fame in America. Like her male comrades she became involved in correspondence with colonial radicals, as 'the Patriot of the Age and a warm friend to America', not without beneficial effects for her book sales – the publisher who assured Boston readers that Mrs. Macaulay's *History of England* 'is recommended to every Son and Daughter of Liberty in North America', knew when he was on to a good thing.[6] Such contacts as these were not significantly affected by the factious strife which developed among the London radicals in the early 1770s. Despite the bitter quarrel between the Horne and Wilkes wings of the 'Supporters of the Bill of Rights', and despite the effective retirement of Robert Morris, who as Secretary of the Society had taken particular interest in good relations with colonial connections, correspondence with American patriots, and communications with visiting Americans continued to be close and amicable.[7]

More important, however, than the unofficial activities of the radical agitators of the metropolis, was encouragement offered to the American cause by official or semi-official institutions. As Wilkes himself boasted in the House of Commons in March 1776, 'The capital of our country has repeatedly declared, by various public acts, its abhorrence of the present unnatural civil war, begun on principles subversive of our constitution.'[8] Enormously divisive, factious, and complicated though City politics were in this period, Americans encountered a most reassuring readiness to support their struggle against imperial authority. The official organ of municipal government, for example, the Lord Mayor, Aldermen, and Common Councilmen, sitting in Common Council, expressed strong and influential support for America's opposition to government. Initially, like almost every other potential ally of that opposition, it seemed regrettably slow to take up the cudgels, quite missing for example, the immediate significance of the Stamp Act; but later it became a vociferous champion of colonial liberties. Particularly in the key period 1774–6, when the empire was drifting towards civil war, a whole series of petitions and addresses to King, Lords, and Commons, expressed the capital's indignation at the policies which were being pursued towards the colonies. By 1775 indeed Americans were able to learn that the Common Council had virtually declared itself an ally of the rebellious colonies, resolving 'That the present Situation of our public affairs, in consequence of the severe Proceedings against the American Colonies, is so exceedingly alarming, that it is the Duty of this Court, to use every possible Endeavour to prevent all further Oppression, and to obtain Relief to so numerous and valuable a Part of our Fellow-Subjects.'[9] The Restraining Acts, and above all the Coercive Acts were

> not only contrary to many of the fundamental Principles of the *English Constitution*, and most essential Rights of the Subject, but also apparently inconsistent with natural Justice and Equity, and we are therefore of Opinion, that our Fellow Subjects, the *Americans*, are justified in every constitutional Opposition to the said Acts.[10]

If anything more encouraging still from the colonial viewpoint, were the frequently expressed sentiments of the London Livery, the fundamental democracy of the capital, comprising as it did those who as members of the City companies, were entitled to vote in elections. Even at the time of the Middlesex Election crisis, the Livery, acting formally in Common Hall for the purpose of petitioning the crown, were capable of inserting American grievances into their remonstrances, and later they were still more active, for instance drawing up instructions for the London MPS, in 1774, which included the repeal of the offending American legislation of that year. In the following year they were no less emphatic, declaring in April 1775 their total support for America's resistance, and two months later publicly thanking Lord Effingham for resigning his army commission rather than fight in America.[11] Most striking of all perhaps was the 'Address to the Electors of Great Britain' which was approved at a Livery meeting in September 1775. According to this address the now virtually inevitable war against the colonies was a war not for trade or dominion but for the arbitrary power of the crown, an indefensible exertion of the royal prerogative backed by illegal claims to taxation, and an illegal standing army of foreign troops. Observed closely and eagerly by colonists resident in or visiting London, voraciously reported and read in the colonial press, such activities, supported as they were by many other informal bodies of London citizens in political action, ranging from the Middlesex electors to the London North America merchants,[12] understandably convinced the colonies that at least in London they had a sincere and powerful champion.

Even so this impression, substantiated though it seemed, was in some respects misleading. For one thing it is clear that a good deal of the enthusiasm generated for America owed more to political calculation than that inherent zeal for principles of liberty which the colonists thought they detected. Wilkes himself was a charlatan and far from representative of the many sincere radicals and dissenters who supported him, but it is not without significance that he viewed the American Revolution primarily as a source of political mileage. His most frenetic activity on America's behalf occurred in 1775–6 when a severe shortage of domestic political issues helped not a little to impel him as Lord Mayor in that year, to direct the attention of Londoners to colonial questions. In 1769–71, during the crisis associated with the Middlesex Election, the Printers' case and allied controversies, he had contented himself with kind words and encouraging compliments rather than effective deeds. Though at that time he had hotly denied John Horne's charge that his sympathies for America were bogus, it is obvious in retrospect that Horne was right. In 1765, for example, when Wilkes's brother Heaton had suggested the possibility of seeking service in North America, he hastened to dispel any illusions on this score.

> You are mistaken as to my ideas of America. I am too well inform'd of what passes there by some gentlemen I have seen, and there is a spirit little short of rebellion in several of the Colonies. If I am to be an exile from my native Kingdom, it shall not be in the new world; so far as I can command.[13]

Wilkes's insincerity and opportunism are too well known to make his record worth dwelling on, but they are not altogether irrelevant to the general tendency both of the capital and other sections of the political nation more or less permanently in opposition to government. In this respect indeed, the colonists quite misunderstood the significance of London's evolution in these years. From their vantage point it seemed that the metropolis had suddenly, during the early years of George III, taken a novel and radical stance against the crown and in defence of British and colonial liberties. As the *New York Journal* observed, 'There has been a strange turn in the city within these few years. It was almost wholly in the hands of the tories, but now it has got into the hands of the whigs.'[14] This was a most unhelpful way to describe the political evolution of the metropolis in the 1760s. For it was the party labels, themselves not a very useful guide to the politics of the eighteenth century, which had changed at the accession of George III, not the fundamental motors of London politics; the basic truth was that a natural tendency of the latter was opposition to the ministers of the day, a tendency which had largely prevailed at least since the 1730s, and which was thereafter broken only occasionally, notably during the patriotic reaction associated with Pitt's wartime administration. There were exceptions of course, particularly among the financial and mercantile oligarchs who tended to be attached to the great Whig interests or at any rate to work with the Treasury in its everyday financial operations. But the tone which normally coloured the political life of the City under George II, especially insofar as municipal and parliamentary elections were concerned, was that of the great mass of small businessmen and craftsmen. Precisely because they tended to be hostile to the alliance of government and great interests, they were known to others and indeed to some extent among themselves as 'Tories', a term which in their case meant little more than hostility to the establishment at court and in the City, in short the metropolitan equivalent of 'country' opposition to the court.

After 1760, when so many of the Tory country gentlemen joined the court, and those who went into opposition to George III raised anew the banner of anti-monarchist Whiggism, these City interests naturally began to describe themselves as Whigs. But the truth was that they were naturally and temperamentally opposed to government, government which relied on the great merchants and financiers of the city to finance its operations, government which represented the supremacy of placemen and courtiers, government which was carried on in the heart of a vast and constantly expanding industrial agglomeration completely out of sympathy with the existing structures and values of politics. In this context the men who dabbled in City politics in the 1760s, men like Beckford, Pitt and Wilkes himself, not to say the many lesser radicals involved, all found it easy to enlist powerful forces of social and political discontent. Sorting out the precise concerns and ideological assumptions of these forces is not easy.[15] But what is clear is that any issue which offered an opportunity to strike at government in the 1760s and 1770s, was eagerly grasped. Many of the issues naturally involved the City itself, either peripherally as in the Wilkesite agitations over general warrants and the Middlesex Election, or very directly as in the case of the bitter dispute between the municipal authorities and the House of Commons over the Printers' affair of 1771. Others like the cider tax, introduced by the Bute Administration in 1763 and repealed in 1766, thanks largely to the bitter resentment aroused in the classic cider growing region of the West Country, had little to do with London as such and were clearly exploited for their political value. In some respects America as a great political issue fell more naturally into the second category than the first – a useful stick with which to beat government when more promising weapons were not to hand. It is to some extent this which explains the uneven quality of London's campaigning for America's ends. In the 1760s, with a plethora of likely constitutional issues, America appeared at best tacked on to other grievances. But in 1774–6, when the City radicals were badly short of political material, and when North had engineered a remarkable degree of political consensus in Parliament and in the country, America became a more useful weapon. The ebullient observation of one American journalist was in this respect more significant than he knew. 'The City of London, which is in full Opposition to the Measures of Administration, unite the Cause of America with their own.'[16] It is assuming a great deal to assume that administration's American policy was itself a fundamentally unacceptable policy in London.

This is not to say that there was any kind of contradiction between opposition to government as a general principle and opposition to the claims of Parliament over the colonies. On the contrary the colonists basked in the knowledge, or at least the belief, that their particular case was merely a part of the general case to be made against Whitehall and Westminster in the early years of George III's reign. Even this, however, can be questioned. There are strong indications that while the growth of resistance in America was to some extent convenient for London's politicians, it was also embarrassing in respect of the doctrines on which it was based. This is clearly implied for example, by the apparent reluctance of the protest movements involved in the Middlesex election crisis, to take a firm stance in support of America's opposition to the Townshend duties. Thus the Middlesex freeholders' instructions to their MPs in December 1768, important because they represent the first attempt by the Wilkesites to draw up a coherent and systematic programme, quite failed to take note of colonial problems, though the net was cast wide for other material.[17] The maintenance of trial by jury, inquiries into the St. George's Fields' Massacre and related riots, and indeed into the state of justice in Middlesex generally, even an investigation of East Indian affairs, all were included in the demands of the electors, but without any mention whatever of America.

Superficially more helpful from the colonial vantage point were the great metropolitan petitions provoked by the House of Commons' expulsion of Wilkes in 1769, the petition of the Middlesex electors to the king in May[18] and the petition of the London Livery in June. It was a source of great encouragement to Americans that these two petitions, unlike the petitions of the same period from other parts of the country, specifically referred to their own grievances as well as to the more predictable aspects of the Middlesex election affair itself. Yet these references to America, much cried up across the Atlantic, were largely incidental to the main concerns of the petitioners, and exceedingly restrained in the language they employed. The Middlesex petition itself, signed by 1,565 freeholders who were 'supposed to be possessed of above two thirds of the property in the county', consisted of thirty-four clauses, of which no less than thirty-three were concerned exclusively with domestic grievances.[19] These covered every conceivable cause for concern in the policies of administration since the accession of George III and apart from the central issue of the Middlesex election, ranged from specific complaints about general warrants, the St. George's Fields' Massacre and the alleged peculation of Lord Holland as Paymaster-General, to generalized charges of 'irreligion and immorality, so eminently discountenanced by your Majesty's royal example, encouraged by administration both by example and precept'. Yet only one clause, the thirty-fourth, mentioned America and that somewhat enigmatically. 'The same Discretion has been extended by the same evil Counsellors to your Majesty's Dominions in America, and has produced to our suffering Fellow Subjects of that Part of the World, Grievances and Apprehensions similar to those of which we complain at home.'

Not surprisingly in view of this rather restricted and imprecise espousal of the American case, reports in the colonial newspapers tended to refer to the petition in appropriately vague terms, relying rather on the nearly contemporaneous petition of the London Livery for specifics. Yet even this was almost entirely occupied with the domestic Wilkesite grievances and contained only one somewhat cryptic paragraph concerning America, as the victim of the same wicked ministers who had treated the Middlesex electors so abominably. 'They have established numberless unconstitutional regulations and taxations in our colonies.'[20] This sounded like the central issue of concern to the colonies, the sovereignty of Parliament in matters of taxation. But the specific matters raised quickly destroy this implication. 'They have caused a revenue to be raised in some of them by prerogative. They have appointed Civil-law Judges to try revenue causes, and to be paid from out of the condemnation money.' This reference to the allegedly unconstitutional and unparliamentary powers of the Vice-Admiralty courts was doubtless gratifying to American opponents of the ministry, but it scarcely represented a serious attempt to take up the fundamental grievances of the colonists. 1769 was the year in which American opposition to Parliamentary taxes on the grounds explained in detail by John Dickinson, that it was the principle of taxation not the method of taxation, which was totally unacceptable, was finally made crystal clear to Englishmen. Nobody could doubt once the non-importation movement of 1768–70 had re-opened the basic constitutional issue closed for a while in 1766, that it was Parliament's sovereignty that was in question. Yet the London Livery like the Middlesex petitioners betrayed no anxiety to come to grips with this issue. Denial of Parliament's right to tax the colonies, was something which Americans assumed all true Englishmen must accept; in practice even those Englishmen who were ready to speak out on America's behalf tended to avoid doing so. This lack of enthusiasm for the constitutional arguments advanced in America actually emerges from every display of interest in colonial affairs which the American journals so avidly seized upon as a prominent feature of the Wilkesite agitation of 1769. The fourteen instructions to the City MPs, drawn up in February 1769 by the Livery, included only one relating to America, and that merely a pious hope that the trade and manufacturing interests of London would be safeguarded, and that differences between the mother country and colonies would soon be resolved. The twelve instructions from the constituents of Southwark to their representatives in Parliament included an almost identical clause.[21] Electors who were certainly not afraid to berate Parliament for its violent and unconstitutional attacks on the rights of the British electorate, showed little anxiety to do so for its violent and unconstitutional attacks on the rights of America.

More satisfying from the American viewpoint were the official and unofficial demonstrations of solidarity forthcoming in the two years leading up to the Declaration of Independence. The Livery instructions for the general election of 1774, drawn up by Wilkes and his friends to test the acceptability of Parliamentary candidates, specifically required pledges of support for the repeal of the North Administration's programme following the Boston Tea party, in particular the Boston Port Act, the Massachusetts Bay Regulating Act, the Massachusetts Bay Justice Act, and the Quebec Act.[22] 'The passing of such Acts will be of the utmost importance for the security of our excellent constitution, and the restoration of the rights and liberties of our fellow-subjects.' As was the case with the Whig opposition the final decision of government to introduce authentic coercive measures, which could be opposed without espousing America's denial of Parliamentary sovereignty, went far towards resolving the dilemma of those who had no desire to encourage the notion of colonial independence, and made possible somewhat less vague and half-hearted support for America than had previously been the case. Thus the slide to war and the ministry's continuing determination to take stern measures, particularly the

Restraining Acts of 1775, provoked a campaign of London remonstrances on the subject of American policy. Even so it would be a mistake to make too much of these demands for repeal of the ministerial measures of 1774–5. In the instructions of 1774 for instance, they were tacked on to the end of a long list of demands, which included the restoration of what was described as 'Revolution' government, the introduction of short Parliaments, bills to exclude placemen from the House of Commons, measures for the protection of electoral rights and even a degree of Parliamentary reform.

Still more important in this as in subsequent demonstrations, the chief concern of the politically articulate in the metropolis seems to have revolved around the Quebec Act rather than the more specifically American legislation of 1774. In fact the only official protest from the capital was directed exclusively against this measure, not strictly one of the Coercive Acts at all. The Common Council petitioned the House of Commons against the Quebec Bill in strong terms at the beginning of June 1774, went on to petition the crown against giving royal assent to the bill two weeks later, and conducted a vigorous correspondence with the Protestant English settlers in Canada, leading to formal instructions to the City's MPs in February 1775 in favour of repeal.[23] The Quebec Act was even more objectionable in America than in England, but not for quite the same reasons. The colonists saw it as a sinister portent of what was to come if the ministry had its way in North America generally, with implications for the continued existence of English law, the English system of elected representative assemblies, and the capacity of the colonies to expand into the west. But in England, even the opposition elements in the City seem to have seen it as essentially an isolated measure, reprehensible not for its American implications, but for its intrinsic denial of British traditions. The strengthening of popery by the recognition of the Roman Catholic church in Canada, the damage done to the English common law tradition by the apparent intention of administration to prevent the introduction of trial by jury into Canada, and the uncongenial maintenance of a French executive system of government, all deeply alarmed some Englishmen but not for their bearing on the colonial situation. There was nothing surprising about such alarm. The issues of the Quebec Act, for example, appealed far more to strong anti-papist and anti-gallic emotions in England, than did the colonial claims of immunity from Parliamentary control. Americans would have preferred a little more concern with their own plight.

No less important than the question mark over fundamental sympathy towards America on the score of the Quebec Act, are the precise and to some extent mysterious circumstances in which the various demonstrations of metropolitan opinion evolved. It is not possible, of course, to be certain of such circumstances, since the relevant records are exiguous in the extreme. It must also be stressed that the evident existence of a clear bias or influence in the process of opinion-making does not necessarily invalidate the result. A spontaneous political protest is not merely a very rare phenomenon, it is virtually inconceivable. Almost every eighteenth century petition, address, instruction, or resolution had its origin in the particular activities of politically inspired individuals, and this obvious and undeniable fact does not alter the equally obvious fact that a significant body of assent, perhaps even enthusiasm, was required to turn such manipulation into an effective movement. Even so it is important to identify the actual influences at work, and in the case of the metropolitan expressions of opinion on American affairs, it has to be admitted that these influences were far from impartial. It is obvious for example, that in the City of London proper, the configurations of concern with America closely follow the erratic fortunes of the party most dedicated to the manufacturing of issues likely to exacerbate relations between the capital and the government, the Wilkesites themselves. Despite his success with the Middlesex electors and the political populace of the metropolitan region, Wilkes did not gain an easy or rapid ascendancy in the City itself. Before first contesting Middlesex he had been humiliatingly defeated in the City's parliamentary election, and even after the resounding success of the Middlesex elections, he did not have his own way entirely. Elected Alderman for Farringdon Without (not without difficulties being made by the Court of Aldermen) in January 1769, and Sheriff in July 1771, he nonetheless found it no easy task to gain the driving seat in City politics.

There were many other politicians who did not necessarily submit willingly to Wilkes's leadership, whatever lip-service they paid to his cause. Beckford before his death in 1770, Trecothick and Oliver, and Shelburne's radical friends, Townshend and Sawbridge, to name only the most prominent, did not make things easy, nor did their friends among the magnates, notably the Rockingham Whigs and the Shelburne–Chatham group, whose interference in City politics reached new heights in the wake of the Middlesex elections. Both in the Society of the Supporters of the Bill of Rights, which was shattered by Horne's bitter personal attack on Wilkes himself, and in City elections, where Wilkesite candidates in the early 1770s were constantly opposed by such as Sawbridge and Townshend, the feuding of the radical groups worked against the obvious radical interest, much to the delight of its enemies.

It was such feuding which with the help of the City's elaborate electoral procedures prevented Wilkes from becoming Lord Mayor in 1772 and 1773, though on each occasion he managed, by the slenderest of margins, to top the poll in the Livery. Only in October 1774 did Wilkes finally obtain the prize he wanted, and then by dint of using the techniques which had been used against him previously, and in the face of bitter opposition from rivals such as Richard Oliver. But once he was chief magistrate of the capital Wilkes expected to achieve great things. 1775 was designed to be the Wilkesite annus mirabilis.

1775 also happened to be a critical year for Anglo-American relations, and Wilkes was clearly intent on using the opportunities presented. It was the Wilkesites who in the set of instructions designed for the acceptance of parliamentary candidates in London in 1774, had had America inserted, albeit somewhat obliquely, in the programme of the Livery. But 1775 saw a more important series of démarches. For the first time under Wilkes's Lord Mayoralty, the City went some way towards endorsing America's position in principle and demanding extensive concessions by Parliament. The Common Council's resolutions of February 1775 declared solidly against the Quebec Act, the Coercive Acts, and also the threatened (and eventually successful Restraining Bills of 1775.[24] There quickly followed petitions both to Lords and Commons against the Restraining legislation. More compelling still, and far more interesting for its clear and unequivocal support of America's ideological cause, indeed the only such support to come from London, was the Common Hall address, remonstrance and petition to the Crown in April 1775, described by George III as a 'new dish of insolence from the Livery of London' and 'this fresh insolence from the Shop that has fabricated so many'.[25] Asserting that 'no Part of the Dominions can be taxed without being represented', itself a most untypical endorsement of the colonies' challenge to Parliamentary sovereignty in matters of taxation, the petitioners went on to identify a whole list of grievances:

We have seen the sacred Security of Representation in their Assemblies wrested from them; the Trial by Jury abolished; and the odious Powers of Excise extended to all Cases of Revenue; the Sanctuary of their Houses laid open to Violation at the Will and Pleasure of every Officer and Servant in the Customs; the Dispensation of Justice corrupted, by rendering their Judges dependent, for their Seats and Salaries, on the Will of the Crown; Liberty and Life rendered precarious, by subjecting them to be dragged over the Ocean, and tried for Treason or Felony here, where the Distance, making it impossible for the most Guiltless to maintain his Innocence, must deliver him up a Victim to ministerial Vengeance; Soldiers and others, in *America*, have been instigated to shed the Blood of the People by establishing a Mode of Trial which holds out Impunity for such Murder; the Capital of *New England* has been punished with unexampled Rigour, untried and unheard; involving the Innocent and the Suspected in one common and inhuman Calamity; chartered Rights have been taken away without any Forfeiture proved, in order to deprive the People of every legal Exertion against Tyranny of their rulers; the *Habeas Corpus* Act and Trial by Jury have been suppressed, and *French* despotic Government, with the Roman Catholic Religion, have been established by Law, over an extensive Part of your Majesty's Dominions in *America*; dutiful Petitions for Redress of these Grievances, from all your Majesty's *American* Subjects have been fruitless.

The petition went on to liken the American Revolution to the Revolution of 1688, to compare George III obliquely with James II, and to demand the dismissal of the crown's ministers. The remaining months of Wilkes's Lord Mayoralty saw further petitions for the dissolution of Parliament, on the grounds of its total failure to reconcile the colonies to the mother country, and for the extension of royal mercy towards the colonies, an Address to the Electors of Great Britain condemning the American war and the court's rejection of the Olive Branch Petition, and the receipt of Congress's offical letter of thanks, which Wilkes read to Livery on his last public appearance as Lord Mayor.[26] Thereafter, during the war there were few protests by the City against the measures of government;[27] it is not without significance that during Wilkes's period of office as Lord Mayor, the City did far more and went much further to express its enthusiasm for colonial liberty, than during the rest of the Revolutionary period put together.

This is not to claim that the power of the Wilkesites was the only influence tending to push the City into asserting strong views on American questions. No less important, though partly related, were the activities of colonial agitators. There was, naturally, in the capital a body of businessmen with clear interests in the affairs of America, if only through their own trading affairs; but much more significant in this context were the Americans who visited England in the late 1760s and early 1770s and gravitated naturally to the commercial and dissenting radical groups in the metropolis. Most of them did so by instinct and the desire for social ease. But a few actually threw themselves into domestic politics, as in a sense the celebrated Franklin did, or even into specifically metropolitan politics. Outstanding among the latter were the Lee brothers. Arthur Lee was actually in London, as a law student, from 1766, and put his undoubted energies and irascible temperament to the service of his country and connections. Though he made few serious attempts at political office, he laid claim to a large share of the credit for London's campaigns on America's behalf, partly by dint of his journalistic propaganda both in the British and colonial press, partly by his backstage activities among the radical groups in the capital. His own letters to family and friends in Virginia, present him simultaneously as the manipulator of metropolitan opinion, and as the observer and reporter of mounting pro-American feeling in London. He was of course, as great a braggart as a trouble-maker, and not to be taken entirely seriously all the time. But the influence which he attributed to himself in 1769 for instance, is not altogether to be discounted. He claimed in particular that the single reference to America in the Middlesex petition of that year, feeble and half-hearted though it was, was his own exclusive work, carried out, moreover, in the face of considerable hostility.

> I procured the introduction of the grievances of America into the famous Middlesex Petition. This was not effected but with great trouble and difficulty even in the following words. 'The same *discretion* has been extended by the same evil counsellors, to your Majesty's dominions in America, and has produced to our suffering fellow subjects in that part of the world, *grievances*, and *apprehensions* similar to those of which we complain of at home.' The subject was novel, supported only by myself, almost a stranger, and appeared to many of the leading men to be foreign to their purpose.[28]

This account of the origins of the first clear signal of support from the London populace for America is circumstantially plausible and perfectly consistent with the general reluctance of petitioners in this period to become involved in colonial problems. Indeed Lee's reports are additional testimony to this reluctance. According to his own evidence, he worked hard to get American grievances included in the manifestos of the Society of Supporters of the Bill of Rights, and generally to acquire sympathy in England for his compatriots. As he confessed, his object was to mix 'popular subjects here with that of America ... and by that means to gain a more easy ear to the discussion of American grievances'.[29]

This was also plainly the object of William Lee, Arthur's brother.

William indeed played a more prominent role, partly because he was heavily engaged as a merchant in the North America trade, partly because he met with some success in standing for elective offices. Though he failed to get into Parliament for the large metropolitan borough of Southwark, where he was soundly beaten by a government supporter and a radical without American connections,[30] he was elected Sheriff of London in 1773 (with that other dynamic and radical American, Stephen Sayre) and even Alderman in 1775, significantly in time to take a public lead during Wilkes's Lord Mayoralty. It is difficult to believe that he did not draw up the one really detailed outline of colonial grievances, signed by the Lord Mayor on behalf of the Livery in April 1775, for he attended its delivery to the king with Wilkes himself, and certainly he did much to bring American matters before the City. Like Arthur, when he boasted of his activities in this respect, he also admitted the extraordinary difficulty of arousing authentic interest in American rather than English concerns. Thus he explained his part in the City's protests against the Quebec Act.[31]

> I take to myself no small share of merit, from sounding the first alarm, and raising up the opposition to it in the House of Commons and the City, by keeping a continual fire in the papers. The principles of this act are abominable beyond expression; but what hurts me most is the ministerial plan openly avowed, to make use of the Canadians to enslave all America, which may possibly be accomplished in a few years, if the act is not repealed, as you will be hemmed up between two fires, the Canadians on your back from Hudson's Bay to the Mississippi, and ships of war on your coast. The people here, however, will not make any opposition to the act on this ground.

Not all those involved in the 'stimulating' of London opinion were Americans. The Common Council petition of March 1776, which exists in draft form among the Shelburne papers, was certainly drawn up in part by Richard Price, though it is possible that much of it was the work of Arthur Lee, who among his many useful contacts numbered Lord Shelburne.[32] There is nothing surprising about these pieces of evidence, though it is likely that they represent the tip of the iceberg. Factious groups and individual politicians were all accustomed to dabble in the politics of the metropolis and employ its weight for their own purposes, and if they obtained the consent of those to whom they applied, it would scarcely be fair to complain that the result was totally unrepresentative. But it is difficult to resist the impression, nonetheless, that the specific declarations of support so approved in the colonies were generally the work of anything but spontaneous feeling, and that in many cases Londoners themselves were more concerned to belabour ministers than to adopt the controversial principles of the colonists.

Manipulation and manoeuvring are not the only points to be made in qualification of the notion that London's pro-American demonstrations were spontaneous and unambiguous; it is also the case that there existed in the metropolis a somewhat forgotten, but nonetheless substantial body of opinion which clearly concurred with the feelings of hostility generally entertained in the country at large. It is worth noting for example, that there occurred in 1775 at least two London addresses which entirely contradicted the remonstrances and petitions of the City and endorsed a policy of coercion in America. Over a hundred jurors of the Tower Hamlets addressed the crown in favour of strong measures, and well over a thousand signatures of Liverymen were collected for a similar address representing the City at large.[33] Even in the capital's official ruling body, the Common Council, there was far more support for the government's position, both in general and on the question of America, than enthusiasts on the other side claimed. In this connection it is most important to bear in mind the clear and extremely significant distinction between the Common Council on the one hand and the Common Hall on the other. The former was in some measure the sovereign body in the City, and comprised the Lord Mayor, Aldermen, and Common Councillors, in short the properly elected representatives of London. Both the Lord Mayor and the Court of Aldermen had extensive powers in their own right, but with the Common Councilmen they could claim more or less complete authority.

Common Halls, which were composed of the entire body of the Livery, or so many of them as were present, were the City's constituent body acting together for electoral purposes, and normally their function was severely restricted. But it was obvious that from the point of view of radical agitators, a Common Hall had potentially vast political value; it could not unfairly claim to represent the most democratic body in the capital, it had few irksome procedures or officials likely to interfere with political manipulation, and it was peculiarly open to the arts of demagogy and the techniques of organization. Early in the Middlesex election dispute, in May 1769, the Wilkesite radicals had grasped its significance, and had attempted to force the summons of a Common Hall, which legally required the assent of the Lord Mayor. Five hundred Liverymen had met at the Half Moon, the tavern where so much unofficial City business was conducted in the eighteenth century, and formally requested such a summons, only to have the request turned down by the Common Council. Fortunately for the agitators, the Livery was due to meet on Midsummer Day for the election of sheriffs, and a noisy and well attended meeting, to the visible chagrin of the Lord Mayor and Recorder, took the opportunity to carry a petition, the important petition of June 1769 against the House of Commons' conduct.[34] Subsequent use of the Livery in Common Hall assembled, as a vehicle for the transmission of political pressure depended on the complaisance of Lord Mayors, or the coincidence of another election meeting. But when such complaisance or coincidence did occur, the results could be spectacular. During Wilkes's Lord Mayoralty (Wilkes himself having made a point when elected, of promising to call a Common Hall 'whenever called upon'), it was the Common Hall which produced by far the most violent demonstrations of metropolitan opinion, especially on America. For example, the lengthy and detailed critique of Britain's American policies presented to the crown in April 1775 came not from the Common Council but from the Common Hall. The distinction was a most important one, as the court and its friends recognized. In fact the government reacted strongly to Wilkes's intensive and novel use of the Common Hall in 1775. Traditionally the crown received the addresses, petitions, and remonstrances of London, formally and officially, that is with the king on his throne and the officers of the City in attendance for a reply. But the petition of April 1775 produced a claim from the court that in future such procedure would be followed only if the communication in question came from the 'body corporate of the City', that is the Court of Common Council. As George III privately observed to Lord North, 'this will bring this affair into proper order and at least make a distinction between the Livery and Common Council, and prevent my sitting in future to hear myself insulted'.[36] The Livery or rather their radical leaders, chose to interpret this manoeuvre as a fundamental attack on the liberties of the City and deployed some interesting arguments in the process. It was urged for instance, that the true body corporate of the City was the entire citizenry consisting of freemen, livery, aldermen, common councillors, and officers, and that consequently 'The full Body Corporate never assemble, nor could they act legally together as one great aggregate Body.'[37] But neither this, nor the legal arguments adduced from precedent and provided by the lawyer friends of the Wilkesites, nor the Livery's alarming demands for impeachment of the ministers who had advised the crown not to receive their petitions on the throne, moved the king; such petitions were subsequently received at the king's public levee, with none of the formality and pomp which the City regarded as essential.

If the Livery and the municipal corporation had been of a similar mind, none of this would matter very much, and the tendency of historians to treat the political activities of Common Council as indistinguishable from those of Common Hall, would be of little consequence. But that it does matter at least for an understanding of the City's attitudes towards the American Revolution is clearly indicated by the records of the Common Council. The only really positive statements of support for America came from the Livery. By contrast the petitions and addresses that came from the Common Council were the ones which prudently avoided impugning the validity of Parliamentary authority. The conscious tailoring of protests needed to make them acceptable to the Common Council's conservative prejudices is clear for example, in the case of the petition of which a draft has survived, that of March 1776. In the form originally drafted, it was a devastating assault on the government's position. Its extravagant and intemperate tone suggested the language of Charles I's opponents rather than George III's, and with its specific request to the crown to 'dismiss from your Service those Advisers whose ignorance and lack of power have brought us to that dreadful precipice on which we are now standing', it trespassed on exceedingly dangerous ground.[38] But none of this was adopted in the event. Instead the Common Council's petition to the king consisted of the milder paragraphs of the draft, lamenting the civil war about to afflict the empire, and begging the crown to make plain its terms of reconciliation with the colonies before actually proceeding to arms. The substantive contents of the draft were almost entirely dropped in the process of finding a form of words, which would procure the assent of the City's official representative body.

The explanation of the difficulty experienced in driving through Common Council a more extensive set of demands becomes clearer when it is realized that a large number of its members were, if not enthusiastic supporters of government in all its policies, at any rate somewhat reluctant critics. Debates of Common Council were rarely recorded, but the report, defective though it must in part be, of a debate of July 1775, makes this evident. The debate is all the more interesting in that it preceded one of the more important City addresses on America, that of July 1775, which came at a time when a measure of conciliation seemed still possible and before the war situation had escalated beyond control. It arose from a communication of the New York General Committee of Association, listing America's grievances, and asking for London's official support. The result was a bitter dispute, with the voicing of sentiments which would have surprised and dismayed those who considered London to be strongly pro-American.[39] Thus the debate was begun by Deputy Poole, who 'observed that the dispute was between Administration and America, consequently that the court had very little right to interfere, and the more particularly, as it was only an association of the people of New York; that it was an opposition of the Americans to all order and good government; that it was wholly with the Americans to relieve themselves, by complying with the just and reasonable demands of government'. Issue was joined on fundamental constitutional issues, including the question of whether colonial charters exempted Americans from Parliamentary authority, and the status of the Declaratory Act of 1766. Alderman Harley, well-known as one of the City MPs and a strong supporter of administration, read the Declaratory Act and accused both his opponents in the debate, and their American allies, of directly denying the validity of the act, a denial which William Lee eagerly took up. Lee had only recently been elected Alderman for Aldgate Ward after a somewhat humiliating defeat in Vintry, and made a strong speech of denunciation against Parliament's assertion of its rights, observing 'that the act could not give a right which did not exist; that Parliament had no right *then*, nor had they *now*, to make such an act'. Such strong language, far from persuading the Common Council utterly divided it, and those who had proposed firm action were compelled to back down and accept an adjournment.

The next day, when debate was resumed, there was a further wrangle over 'the law construction of the present state of the Americans' opposition to government', with the City's legal expert, deeply embarrassed by the difficulties of deciding whether Americans were still full citizens of the empire or traitors and rebels. 'The Recorder could not refuse speaking, when plainly called upon; but gave such an opinion as left the Court as uninformed as they were before the question was put.' In the event the meeting approved an address to the Crown, asking for the suspension of hostilities. But it was carried by the intriguingly narrow majority of 74 votes to 59, with the Aldermen evenly divided, and the Common Councilmen, who tended to be more opposition-minded than their superiors, showing 66 in favour and 51 against. Moreover, the wording of the address was extremely moderate. There was no attempt to assert the constitutional or legal validity of the Americans' demands, merely a plea on behalf of the colonists as a people anxious 'to remain firm in all duteous obedience to the constitutional authority of this kingdom', and a request for cessation of actual hostilities in order to enhance the prospects of reconciliation. Such language was quite different from that adopted by the Livery on American matters, and almost pleased the ministers. As George III himself observed, 'the Address and Petition of the Common Council is certainly the most decent and moderate in words that has been for some time fabricated on that Side Temple bar'.[40] Still more significant, when an attempt was made later on to send a copy of the address to the General Committee of Association in New York, and effectively to open a regular correspondence with a revolutionary organization, the motion was lost in full Common Council by 69 to 56 votes. In a body regarded as perpetually opposed to government, under pressure both from Lord Mayor above and Livery below to adopt vigorous measures, it is interesting that an actual majority was not prepared to engage in a public correspondence with those whom so many of its members and electors alleged to be the victims of tyranny.

The ultimate demonstration, though in these circumstances a somewhat superfluous one, that London was not quite of the mind pictured in the colonies, is provided by the evident fact that when the crunch came, when Britain and America finally moved into an irretrievable war posture, even radical Londoners manifested no really serious disposition to action rather than talk. The colonists were encouraged to believe that there would actually be insurrection in the imperial metropolis if North and his colleagues dared to proceed to extreme measures. The *Maryland Gazette*, for example, was much heartened to hear of an organization describing itself as the London Association, a mysterious society which planned to raise help for the Americans in the capital, and which might even be imitated in provincial centres.[41] The danger in London was admittedly taken seriously at least by one minister. Lord Barrington, the Secretary at War, warned his colleagues in January 1776, that

London is of all places in the island the most attentively to be watched, on account of the many actively desperate and ill-affected people who are in it. I need not say how little the magistracy of the City is to be trusted, or how much to be feared...

If an insurrection in London should be attended with the least success, or even to continue unquelled for any time ... it is highly probable, there would also be risings in many parts of the kingdom. The present apparent quiet should not make it forgotten, that there is a very levelling spirit among the people.[42]

Yet this example of ministerial alarm was based more on generalized fear of social disruption and tension, than a reasonable belief in the readiness of English mobs to take up the American cause. In any event there was little need for concern. The London Association turned out to be bogus, and the worst that was unearthed was the odd attempt by

Americans resident in London to spirit potential supporters out of the country, and more particularly an extraordinary plot against the person of the king by none other than Stephen Sayre, himself one of those colonists who had actively engaged in metropolitan politics to the extent of becoming Sheriff. The ministry endeavoured to make something of this alleged conspiracy to capture George III, seize the Tower of London, and spearhead a general insurrection, but their materials proved inadequate.[43] As North's brother remarked when Sayre's affair came before Parliament, 'Nothing new has yet come out in Mr. Sayre's business and I believe there is little or nothing to come. I fancy it will be found to have proceeded not further than two or three very infamous and treasonable conversations between 2 or 3 crazy Patriots – but it is very right that it should be sifted and examined until the whole is known.'[44] The farce ended in appropriate manner with Sayre successfully suing the ministry for the warrant of arrest which had been issued against him, and all talk of rising ceased, not to be repeated thereafter. In the conservative reaction which occurred in London in the mid-1770s not even the cause of Wilkesite radicalism was to prosper, and that of America ceased to be even a matter of serious comment or interest. At its height the reaction destroyed Wilkes's attempt to obtain the office of City Chamberlain, threatened to enlist the City's organs of government in the ministerial camp, and almost extended to the raising of recruits by special subscription for service in America, on the pattern adopted in provincial cities in 1778. Any hope that the Declaration of Independence would prove the signal for metropolitan insurrection and that the imperial civil war would turn into an English civil war proved wide of the mark.

In the last analysis a definitive profile of London's stance on America is out of the question. Even so certain things are clear. The impression gained in many quarters, and especially in the thirteen colonies themselves, that the capital was totally committed to support for the principles of America's resistance, was deeply misleading. Such declarations of support as were forthcoming, were organized by interested parties, carried in the face of substantial opposition, and expressed in terms of moderation which side-stepped the main issue, as colonists would have seen it. Above all America was essentially an incidental rider to the radical politics of London in these years, and hardly central or even integral to it. What ultimate difference this makes is admittedly debatable. The basic fact was that London did much that was spectacular but little that was effective in the politics of the 1760s and 1770s. Earlier in the eighteenth century it had grown accustomed to leading popular and provincial opposition to the government, in such celebrated affairs as the Sacheverell trial, the excise crisis, the Spanish depredations, the Pittite agitations. But under George III, it was, in domestic matters, far more radical than the voice of the provinces, and on some issues like the Peace Preliminaries of 1762, and the resistance of America itself, it was quite unable to gain real support there. Thus George III reflected on the irritating habit of the greatest corporation in the country he ruled, before one threatened petition in 1775:

> ... if the Common Council can on Friday be prevented from taking any step with regard to the Rebellion in America it would be desirable, but the comfort is by the absurd Steps taken by that Body if they act otherwise it will not be of much effect; I have no doubt but the Nation at large sees the conduct of America in its true light.[45]

Far more important perhaps was London's role in American eyes. There every scrap of evidence that Englishmen were in sympathy with their cause was snapped up and cherished by radical colonists at least until 1776, when such comfort ceased to be really necessary.[46] Had Americans grasped or been taught to grasp the true position in London, which provided so much of this evidence, it is at least conceivable that they would have seen the policies of administration in a somewhat different light.

Notes

1. *Addresses, Remonstrances, and Petitions, Commencing the 24th of June, 1769, Presented to the King and Parliament, from the Court of Common Council, and the Livery in Common Hall assembled, with his Majesty's Answers: Likewise the Speech to the King, made by the late Mr. Alderman Beckford, When Lord Mayor of the City of London* (London, 1778), pp. 115–17. This, an official publication, issued by order of the Common Council, was based on the minutes of Common Council and Common Hall. It is used here in preference to the manuscript originals of the latter, which are to be found in the City of London Record Office, and also to the unofficial publication, *City Petitions, Addresses, and Remonstrances, etc. etc. etc.* (London, 1778), John Wilkes's copy of which is preserved in the Guildhall Library.
2. For a recent discussion of this and other expressions of sympathy, see P. Maier, *From Resistance to Revolution: Colonial Radicals and the Development of American Opposition to Britain, 1765–1776* (London, 1973), pp. 203–4.
3. 'John Wilkes and Boston', *Mass. Hist. Soc. Proc.*, xlvii (1913–14), 190–216.
4. *Boston Chronicle*, 10 April 1769.
5. *New York Journal*, 27 April 1769.
6. Sterling Library (Yale), Bromfield Collection, H. Bromfield to E. and C. Dilly, 29 January 1770, July 1770; *Boston Gazette*, 4 September 1769.
7. On Morris, whose circular letter had inspired the South Carolina grant to Wilkes, see J. E. Ross, ed., *Radical Adventurer: The Diaries of Robert Morris, 1772–74* (London, 1971).

8. *The Speeches of John Wilkes* (London, 1777, 2 vols.), i. 104.

9. *Addresses, Remonstrances, and Petitions*, p. 65.

10. *Ibid.*, pp. 67–8.

11. I. R. Christie, *Myth and Reality in Late-Eighteenth-Century British Politics and Other Papers* (London, 1970), p. 247; *Addresses, Remonstrances, and Petitions*, pp. 79–83; *London Magazine*, 1776, p. 377.

12. The activities of the merchants, which are better considered in relation to those of the business community in general, than in terms of their specifically metropolitan aspects, are not treated here.

13. William L. Clements Library, Wilkes MSS. I, f. 91.

14. 24 August 1769.

15. Of particular value in this context see L. S. Sutherland, 'The City of London in Eighteenth Century Politics', in R. Pares and A. J. P. Taylor, eds., *Essays presented to Sir Lewis Namier* (London, 1956), and G. Rudé, *Wilkes and Liberty* (Oxford, 1962).

16. *Pennsylvania Chronicle*, 24 September 1770.

17. *English Liberty: Being a Collection of Interesting Tracts, From the Year 1762 to 1769* (London, n.d., 2 vols.), ii. 240.

18. Technically this was the second Middlesex petition; the first, limited to the election issue as such, had been presented to the Commons in April.

19. *London Magazine*, 1769, pp. 276, 227–9.

20. *Ibid.*, p. 386.

21. *New York Journal*, 27 April 1769. An illustrated broadsheet of the London instructions is at Guildhall Library, Fo. pam. 2089.

22. *Gentleman's Magazine*, 1774, p. 444. The last of the Coercive Acts, the Quartering Act, was not mentioned.

23. *Addresses, Remonstrances, and Petitions*, pp. 45–64.

24. *Ibid.*

25. Sir J. Fortescue, ed., *The Correspondence of King George the Third, from 1760 to December 1783* (London, 1927–8), iii. 200, 201.

26. *Addresses, Remonstrances, and Petitions*, pp. 79–83, 103–26; *London Magazine*, 1775, pp. 542–3.

27. They consisted largely of two further addresses on the subject of the war, in March 1776 and March 1778, and the ostentatious grant of the City's freedom to Richard Price, the radical pamphleteer, for his defence of America. (*Addresses, Remonstrances, and Petitions*, pp. 127–51).

28. R. H. Lee, *Life of Arthur Lee* (Boston, 1829), pp. 245–6.

29. Lee Family Papers (Microfilm), to R. H. Lee, 11 June 1771; R. H. Lee, *Life of Arthur Lee*, p. 193.

30. See Sir L. Namier and J. Brooke, *The History of Parliament: the House of Commons, 1754–1790* (London, 1964), i. 387. Generally America seems to have figured little in London's parliamentary elections. The only authenticated case of consequence is that of Barlow Trecothick, the London merchant of American birth, whose candidature for the City in 1768 aroused some opposition. One broadsheet described him as a 'Gentleman zealously attached, both by Nature and Education to *Boston* Principles, and *Bostonian* Maxims; a strenuous Promoter of *Faction* and *Disobedience* to the Mother Country; and, upon all Occasions a fast Friend to the interests of *America*, and opposed to those of Old England.' (Bodleian Library, Gough London 115; see also Guildhall Library, 5276/51/6.) According to the Duke of Newcastle, the opposition to Trecothick gained 'great strength from his actions as a friend to the Colonies, in opposition to the trade of Great Britain, which however untrue . . . has . . . weight in popular elections'. (British Museum, Add. MS. 32987, f. 325.) In the event Trecothick squeezed into fourth place in the poll.

31. W. C. Ford, ed., *Letters of William Lee, 1766–1783* (New York, 1891, 3 vols.), pp. 91–2.

32. W. L. Clements Library, Shelburne MSS, vol. 88, ff. 36–47.
33. *London Gazette*, 24 October, 28 October 1775.
34. *Addresses, Remonstrances, and Petitions*, pp. 5–9. For a graphic account of this meeting, see L. S. Sutherland, ed., *The Correspondence of Edmund Burke* (Cambridge, 1960), ii. 32–5.
35. H. Bleackley, *Life of John Wilkes* (London, 1917), p. 283.
36. *Correspondence of George III*, iii. 201.
37. *Addresses, Remonstrances, and Petitions*, p. 97. The king's reaction was not the only problem raised by the radicals' use of Common Hall. In 1769 Sir James Hodges, the Town Clerk, had refused to sign the Livery's controversial petition of June, and in so doing had initiated a dispute about the responsibilities of municipal officials. Moreover, in 1770 three conservative companies, the Goldsmiths, Grocers, and Weavers, had declined to receive summonses to extraordinary, non-electoral meetings of Common Hall, and were vindicated in their action by judicial decision (on appeal) in 1775. See City of London Record Office, Misc. MSS. 5–16, for Hodges' defence of his conduct in 1769, and P.D. 42–4 (Alderman Plumbe's Case) for the legal arguments employed on behalf of the companies.
38. Shelburne MSS, vol. 88, ff. 36–47.
39. *London Chronicle*, 8 July 1775.
40. *Correspondence of George III*, iii. 233.
41. 23 November 1775.
42. Shute Barrington, *Political Life of William Wildman Viscount Barrington* (London, 1814), 153–7.
43. P. Maier, *op. cit.*, pp. 259–60.
44. E. Hughes, 'Lord North's Correspondence, 1766–83', *Eng. Hist. Rev.*, lxii (1947), 227.
45. *Correspondence of George III*, iii. 233.
46. See P. Maier, *op. cit.*, chap. viii.

J. ANN HONE

Radicalism in London, 1796–1802:
Convergences and Continuities

The early 1790s, a time of extraordinary political and ideological ferment, have received over the years the attention of numerous historians. Our knowledge of British provincial radicalism remains patchy.[1] The course of London radicalism has been charted better. Undoubtedly there is still much we do not know. Possibly some of what we do know is misleading, since most historians have had to rely heavily on the papers accumulated, more or less for their benefit, by the radical tailor, Francis Place.[2] But the general outline is clear.

In 1788, London radicals met to celebrate the centenary of the Glorious Revolution with little or no expectation that the energy of the movements of the 1760s, the 1770s and early 1780s would recur soon. By late 1791, old reform societies, such as the London Constitutional Whigs and the Society for Constitutional Information (sci), had been aroused from what Major Cartwright called their 'slumbers' by the heady news from France.[3] By early 1792, new societies were proliferating, some like the London Corresponding Society (lcs), representing a novel phenomenon, the politically awakened artisan.[4] These societies were stimulated by Paine's *Rights of Man*, the first part of which appeared in February 1791; the second in February 1792. The Society of Friends of the People, which mainly comprised young Whig mps, was also formed early in 1792. It rejected Paine's doctrines. But, like the other societies old and new, it emphasized that political change was the panacea for present ills. The theoretical support for this belief was culled from Locke, Burgh, Price, and Priestley among others and was strengthened, at least temporarily, by the French Revolution. 'The change of government in France,' wrote Joel Barlow in 1792, 'is a renovation of society.'[5]

Almost from the start, the Government showed that its tolerance was to be limited. The Proclamation against seditious libels was published on 21 May 1792. It was aimed chiefly at the cheap edition of the *Rights of Man*, approximately 200,000 copies of which were in circulation by 1793.[6] Paine fled to what he mistook as the safety of France.[7] Other exponents of extreme views, including Thomas Spence, an advocate of communal land ownership, and William Hodgson, a prolific deist propagandist, were imprisoned. The Scottish courts dealt with the LCS delegates to the British Convention at Edinburgh with a savagery unmatched in England. But in May 1794, with the war against France into its second year, the English Government arrested twelve leading members of the SCI and the LCS, charged them with treason and suspended the Habeas Corpus Act.[8]

These were stringent measures. They alarmed members of the Society of Friends of the People, although disgust with the tone and direction of the radical movement and the defeat of Grey's motion for moderate parliamentary reformation had rendered the Society inactive for some months.[9] The more 'democratic' societies were forced to protest their innocence and their 'constitutional' aims. Support declined for Paine's emphasis on innovation, for his assertion that, 'Every generation is, and must be competent to all the purposes which its occasions require.'[10] The rhetoric of the restoration of lost rights, the appeal of the golden age of Alfred, and the Saxon 'constitution' came into its own.[11] Many of the societies lost members, some collapsed. In the event, however, the Government could hardly regard its harshness as successful. The Treason Trials in November 1794 were a fiasco. After three consecutive acquittals, the other prisoners were released.[12] In 1795, in the context of a growing anti-war sentiment and severe grain shortages – there were bread riots in July and August[13] – the LCS revived and increased its membership. In June, thousands of Londoners, if not the 100,000 claimed, attended the LCS general meeting in St. George's Field and cheered the speakers' demands for universal suffrage and annual parliaments. An even greater crowd attended the LCS meeting 'in a field near Copenhagen House' on 26 October. But, three days later, the 'marble or bullet' which broke a window of the state coach carrying George III to open parliament gave the Government an opening for the introduction of more effective curbs on the dissemination of radical propaganda.[14]

The Treasonable Practices and Seditious Meetings acts became law on 18 December 1795. Historians disagree about the necessity or justification for these two acts, as they do about earlier and later repressive measures. But even those historians who, like E. P. Thompson and G. A. Williams, point to the efforts made by the LCS in

1796 to renew propaganda and membership drives and to re-establish links with the provinces, do not seriously overturn the general acceptance of the winter of 1795–6 as the beginning of the end of the radical movement's momentum.[15] Some historians take the story through to the banning of the popular societies in July 1799, stressing that what activity there was up to then must be viewed as the preserve of a handful of plebeian conspirators. Even then, with few exceptions, the examination is cursory; attention has moved to the 1807 Westminster election and the revival of the campaign for parliamentary reform.[16]

Of course, it is not possible to deny the adverse effect of the Two Acts or of the preventive and punitive measures enacted in 1797–9. The Two Acts made it treasonable to incite hatred or contempt of King, Constitution, or Government with written or spoken words. Meetings of over fifty persons were banned unless approved by a magistrate. As a result popular lecturers, such as John Thelwall, were forced to desist. Participants at debating clubs like the Westminster Forum were prosecuted. The perils of publication increased. The LCS's attempt to revive connections with certain provincial corresponding societies, by sending John Binns and John Gale Jones on a 'missionary' tour, was frustrated. The two deputies were arrested in Birmingham on 11 March 1796. And the events in St. Pancras Fields on 31 July 1797 proved that the organizers of protest meetings faced the certain disruption of the proceedings and arrest.[17] In 1798 and 1799, as further restrictions on the Press and the banning of the LCS and United English and Irish societies were added to the already impressive list of sanctions against protest,[18] defeat and retreat were prevalent. Many radicals felt that nothing now could be effected in England. Some migrated to France or to the United States of America.[19] An increasing number questioned the wisdom of the entertainment and pursuit of grand visions of 'man's' immediate amelioration. By 1800 there were few men or women with intellectual pretensions who were inclined to challenge Dr. Samuel Parr's condemnation of the concept of Universal Benevolence as dangerous, unnatural and productive only of 'airy projects, eager hopes, tumultuous efforts and galling disappointments'.[20] Events in France, initially so conducive to a belief in the efficacy of 'man-mending' schemes, also contributed to this disillusionment and for some people Napoleon's seizure of power on 10 November 1799 (18 Brumaire) served to confirm fears already held.[21]

However, there are degrees of and limits to disruption. There has been an over-emphasis both on what ended in the winter of 1795–6 and on the defeats and retreats of metropolitan radicalism at the end of the century. The desertions or quasi desertions of such men as Robert

Southey, William Godwin, Dr. Parr and Coleridge, have been taken to represent too much.[22] In addition, there has been an uncritical acceptance of radical historiography. Thomas Hardy and Francis Place, who wrote the accounts of the radicalism of the 1790s and early years of the nineteenth century from which the notion of cessation followed by revival is primarily derived, had good reasons for emphasizing the effectiveness of Pitt's repressive measures.[23] Participants in an ideological war, they were concerned to brand Pitt as tyrant and to distance themselves and the LCS from 1796–1802, years when in the eyes of many Britons, radical activity was synonymous with conspiracy.

The question of conspiracy is by no means exhausted. Recent studies make it increasingly difficult to accept the view of 'Whig' and 'Labour' historians that only a few 'cranks and fools' engaged in seditious activity.[24] It is impossible to agree with Charles James Fox's assertion that innocent men were confined in dungeons on account of

> insurrections and rebellions which ... *never did exist* but in the imagination of *a set of men who raise such reports* that they may the more easily depress the cause of freedom.[25]

But it is not the intention to pursue the question here. Any discussion of conspiracy should not be divorced from a rigorous investigation of the peculiar problems of evidence confronting the historian, and such an examination is beyond the scope of this essay.[26] Besides, the historiographical distortion with which we are concerned is not to be corrected only by focusing on the continuity and extent of seditious activity from 1796 to 1802. This essay draws attention to the important associations formed after 1795, to the survival of legitimate radical activities and to the continuity of radical personnel, during the years which bridged the end of one century and the beginning of another. And if it is accepted that 1796–1802, far from seeing stasis except for a few wild insurrectionists, saw continuous activity by radicals in a situation which pushed them into closer alignments and associations, it will be realized also that this provides a new dimension to the questions of reformism and sedition.

In 1796 and 1797 many London radicals remained hopeful and energetic. The LCS reorganized itself to conform with the new laws.[27] It embarked on an ambitious publishing venture, its *Moral and Political Magazine*.[28] And with such splendid rhetoric as:

> They have lopped the tree of liberty to a stump, but have not killed it.

The juices have concentrated themselves in the root, and are preparing to shoot forth with tenfold vigour, luxuriance and verdure.

it tried to cheer and exhort its provincial connections.[29]

It was also clear early in 1796 that John Horne Tooke, the former parson of Brentford and active Wilkite, his friends and members of the LCS were continuing to promote the radical cause together. Whether the LCS was an original conception of the shoemaker, Thomas Hardy, is problematical. But from its formation in January 1792, the LCS was, to a large extent, guided in thought and action by Horne Tooke and by other members of the SCI.[30] This association was disrupted by the arrests of May 1794; by the subsequent collapse of the SCI and by Horne Tooke's illness following his trial and acquittal in November 1794.[31] However, by early 1796, if not before, Tooke's Wimbledon House was again a meeting place for London's radicals. Here, every Sunday, 'a motley assemblage ... men of rank and mechanics' dined together.[32] Important introductions were effected. In 1796 Sir Francis Burdett and Tooke met this way, Burdett being brought to Wimbledon by William Maxwell (of Carriden) and Robert Cutlar Fergusson, both themselves relative newcomers to London radical politics and members of the LCS.[33]

In May 1796, Tooke stood for Westminster at the general election. His platform utilized the current issues of war, distress, taxation, and the Two Acts in such a way as to ensure for his canvass the active co-operation of a man like William Sturch. Sturch, an ironmonger and a Unitarian, had threatened resignation from the SCI in December 1792 and had resigned a year later.[34] He now re-established himself in Westminster, remaining prominent in its political activities for the next twenty-five years. Tooke was proposed by Felix Vaughan, the talented young barrister and author of the LCS's *Address to the other societies of Great Britain*.[35] He was seconded by Sutton Sharpe, brother-in-law of Samuel Rogers, the poet. Other former members of the SCI, who showed their support, included the rich 'Colonel' Bosville; Jeremiah Joyce, a Unitarian preacher and fellow sufferer in 1794; and the apothecary, Michael Pearson, Tooke's 'steady and uniform accomplice and comforter' for 'forty long years'.[36] LCS support included that of Hardy; Thelwall; Gale Jones; the glass cutter, Samuel Brooks; the watch-case maker, P. T. Lemaitre; and William Frend, mathematician and ex-fellow of Jesus College, Cambridge.[37] George Puller, a currier and formerly chairman of the London Constitutional Whigs,[38] was active too. Like the others, he was to have long standing connections with metropolitan radical politics.[39]

A post election occasion for a further public display of the continuing association between members of the SCI and the LCS was the second anniversary of the 1794 acquittals. Five hundred men dined together at the Crown and Anchor tavern, Strand, on 5 November 1796, presided over by William Bosville, and addressed by Thelwall and Earl 'Citizen' Stanhope, among others. Toasts to Horne Tooke and reaffirmations of his election rhetoric, 'security for the future, and justice for the past' figured prominently.[40]

Of more importance for London radicalism was the possibility which existed in 1796 of a wider association still, one between Horne Tooke, his supporters in the popular societies and the Foxites. During 1796 it was clear that an association of this nature (though neither Tooke nor Fox was directly involved), had formed in the City of London. Here, a renewal of radical activity had been accompanied by the burying of quarrels generated by Fox's coalition with Lord North and the 1784 election.[41] At the election for the four City MPs, H. C. Combe, the brewer friend of Fox and Sheridan was returned. This was a triumph for the 'true Whigs' and evidence that the parliamentary opposition was regaining a foothold at least in territory once predominantly its own.[42] But the 'popular' vote was for Combe *and* William Pickett, an ex-Pittite, reformer, now standing as an independent on the most radical platform. Pickett was not returned, but he won nearly 3,000 votes. Combe and Pickett were voted for by men like J. T. Rutt, Abraham Thorn and Sturch whose reform interests dated to the 1780s and by LCS members including the publisher, D. I. Eaton and the shoemaker, Samuel Miller.[43] In addition, Combe and Pickett were the choice of many of those liverymen most prominent in reactivating Common Hall as a source of opposition to the Government. Some of these men, for example the draper, Robert Waithman and the Unitarians, Samuel Goodbehere and Samuel Thorp, were 'Whigs' – in later years affirming loyalty to Foxite principles.[44] Others, including George Billinge; the Unitarian and wine merchant, Joseph Holden; the silver refiner, Robert Albion Cox, and the hatter, Richard Sharp, had then, or developed later, closer associations with Horne Tooke and Burdett.[45]

The election for two members to represent the borough of Southwark also provided evidence of harmony among reformers. The Foxite, George Tierney was the 'Patriot' furthering 'truth'.[46] On Tierney's eventual victory in December – he successfully challenged the June decision – Thomas Hardy requested the LCS publicly to thank him and 'the worthy electors of the borough'. Anti-radical propagandists depicted Tierney as Horne Tooke's puppet.[48]

This, like the rumours of a coalition between the LCS and the Whig

Club and an alliance between Horne Tooke and Fox during the Westminster election, was not true.[49] However, in this latter case there was at least substance to the imputations. Fox and Horne Tooke had contested the seat in 1790. Then their enmity had embarrassed mutual friends like Samuel Rogers.[50] Now, although Tooke made it clear that he stood as an independent, and that he, unlike Fox, had suffered in the cause of liberty, he declared that he could 'work with Mr Fox'.[51] At a post election celebration of the 'triumph' of almost 3,000 votes cast for Tooke, compared with Fox's 5,160 and the Tory candidate's 4,810, Tooke was tactful. His committee had emphasized the need for radical parliamentary reformation. Tooke stressed the inviolability of the principles of justice and liberty, principles which he said must stand above individuals and parties. When the question of Fox's equivocation on parliamentary reform was raised by a member of the LCS, Tooke replied, 'I think the best and hope the best of Mr Fox.'[52]

In his move towards Fox, Horne Tooke was probably influenced by Bosville who had easy relationships with Fox and several Foxite MPs, and by Sir Francis Burdett, for whom Fox was then and for some years to come,

The wonder of the age, whose mind is so superior to the times in which he lives, whose abilities and integrity will adorn the page of History when his opponents shall have sunk into everlasting oblivion.[53]

Above all Tooke was driven by his desire for union among all friends to freedom.

It was the need for unity which Tooke stressed at the dinner meeting at the Crown and Anchor on 18 May 1797. Here, before 1,000 'friends to parliamentary reform', among whom were Foxite MPs, Tooke's friends and 'aides', and members of the LCS, and in the context of a widespread clamour for peace, dismissal of the King's Ministers, and an anticipated Foxite motion for parliamentary reform, Tooke argued for the acceptance of the resolution for a 'full, fair and free representation of the people'. To insist on the substitution of 'equal personal' for 'free' was, he said, to emulate the folly of starving men who, when presented with a dinner, began to 'debate about the bill of fare'. Unity must be their foremost consideration – the emphasis also of Burdett, Fergusson, and Maxwell. It was Fergusson who made it clear that if Fox would pledge himself not to accept office without Reform, the suffrage provisions of the expected Foxite Motion would be acceptable, at least for the time being.[54] A little over a week later, household suffrage was publicly supported by several of Tooke's closest allies, including Bosville, Robert Knight, E. B. Clive, the Earl of Oxford, and William Scott, the brother-in-law of Lord Oxford.[55]

Officially the LCS was opposed to the acceptance of anything less than universal suffrage and annual parliaments. This had been reasserted at the end of 1795 and again during 1796. Fox had been acclaimed by Thelwall and John Richter, a prominent member of the LCS, for the lead he gave to the national campaign against the introduction of the Treason and Sedition Bills.[56] But the Whig Club's plan for a general association to bring about the repeal of the Two Acts, a plan thought by Fox to be the best 'that has offered or is likely to offer of uniting the different descriptions of persons who are hostile to the present Ministry',[57] was rebuffed by the LCS. Fox might believe that the only course remaining to the shattered Whig party – stabilized after the desertions to Pitt in 1794 at about fifty-five – was to 'go further towards agreeing with the democratic or popular party than at any former period'.[58] But without a statement on Reform, let alone a commitment to universal suffrage and annual parliaments, his sincerity and intentions remained suspect. Following the general election, the LCS reassured the provincial societies that the reports of a coalition with the Whig Club were false and warned of the dangers of 'partial reform'.[59] Now, it denounced the household suffrage provisions of the Foxite motion, introduced by Grey on 26 May 1797.[60]

However, even in 1796, there were members of the LCS who, like Gale Jones saw the reasonableness of working for and accepting something 'less objectionable' than radical reform.[61] At the dinner on 18 May 1797, Tooke persuaded the Irishman, John Binns and the hatter, Richard Hodgson – both LCS members – that their objections to the resolution served no good purpose.[62] And on 31 July, at the public meeting organized by the LCS and before its disruption by the magistrates, Hodgson questioned the LCS's continuing denunciation of those who did not support universal suffrage and annual parliaments. He urged the exercise of

> the most extensive toleration towards those persons who differ from us in opinion as to the necessary degree of reform, provided only that we are assured of their sincerity.[63]

During the rest of 1797, reasons for thinking the Foxites the sincere friends of the people accumulated. After the convincing defeat of the Foxite motions for Parliamentary Reform in both Houses, Fox and most of his party seceded from Parliament as he had threatened. The subsequent indecision experienced by some of them during the summer recess was kept to themselves.[64] The Foxite Dr. Parr stood by John Binns during his trial at Warwick in August for sedition. The talents of Sir Samuel Romilly and Felix Vaughan ensured his acquittal.[65] On the question of the war, the Foxites were as fierce as members of the LCS, and unlike those MPs who had strengthened the demand for peace and the parliamentary opposition to Pitt in the first half of 1797,[66] they continued to denounce an 'unjust' war. In addition, Fox and the Whig Club embraced the 'cause of liberty all over the world' as ardently as the LCS. At Fox's suggestion, the Whig Club moved in June 1797 to present the Polish patriot, General Koscuisko, with a sword. The gesture was intended to show 'that England still supports freedom and liberty'.[67] More importantly, in view of the LCS's feelings towards, if not affiliation with, the United Irishmen, Fox in 1797 made clear his opposition to the course of action being adopted by the British Government with respect to the deteriorating situation in Ireland. For so long as he remained in Parliament, Fox spoke against the imposition of martial law and against the other harsh methods being used in Ireland.[68]

Any final doubts about Fox's sincerity were removed by his outspoken speech to the Westminster electors on 10 October. On this occasion, Fox spoke up for those members of the LCS arrested at their meeting in St. Pancras Fields on 31 July. He defended their right to discuss universal suffrage. He went much farther when, in a similar vein to recent declarations by Fergusson, Burdett, and the LCS, he claimed that only 'a radical reform', 'an entire and complete change of system' could save the country. His assertion that popular convulsion and the possibility of invasion were lesser evils than quiet submission to tyranny closely paralleled the LCS's rhetoric of blood and death rather than enslavement. It was equally ambiguous.[69] From the LCS Fox received a letter of approbation. His frankness, firmness, and integrity were praised. On the question of the suffrage the LCS stressed a continuing difference of opinion but agreed to differ, conceding that Fox's stand was the result of 'weighty consideration'.[70]

By the beginning of 1798 the rumours of the association of Horne Tooke, the LCS, Fox, and the Whig Club, current since their efforts against the Treason and Sedition Bills and reinforced by the general election, appeared to have foundation. There was agreement in public among these most vocal opponents of Pitt's Administration on the major issues of the day. They were unanimous in denunciation of the war and of the Government's handling of the Irish situation. They were united in their opposition to the Assessed Tax Bill. The Government's financial difficulties stemmed, they argued, from its corruption, profligacy, the expense of an unjust war, and the oppression of Ireland.

The Foxites were to the fore in organizing the parish meetings which, as in the preceding May,[71] could circumvent the restrictions on public meetings and in this case, the illegality of petitions against a money bill.[72] The LCS savaged Pitt in print, and it is probable that the United Parochial Committees which met at the Crown and Anchor Tavern on 2 January 1798, comprised members of the Society as well as Whig Club members.[73] Sturch and Thomas Wishart, best described perhaps as radical-Foxites but closely associated with Horne Tooke and the LCS, chaired the parish meetings of St. Clement Danes and St. Martin-in-the-Fields respectively, a foretaste of their future parochial and political Westminster activity.[74] Three weeks after the meeting of the United Committees, the Crown and Anchor was filled to overflowing as, for the first time, Horne Tooke and members of the LCS joined in the annual celebration of Fox's birthday. The evening provided an impressive display of 'union' and defiance, the Duke of Norfolk toasting 'Our Sovereign the Majesty of the People' and comparing the 2,000 present to the number who 'rallied round one honest man, Mr. Washington, to support their liberties.'[75]

Whatever the promise of the evening of 24 January 1798, it was not to be repeated for some time. Within weeks, what Place called Pitt's 'Reign of Terror' was underway.[76] Beginning with the dismissal of the Duke of Norfolk from the Lord Lieutenancy of Yorkshire and his Colonelcy of the Militia, and including Fox's removal from membership of the Privy Council – a mild rebuke evidently compared to what Pitt at one stage contemplated – the Foxites were subjected to a series of reprimands and punishments.[77] Public distrust of the Foxites was increased by their defence of the United Irishman, Arthur O'Connor who, on 28 February, was arrested with James O'Coigley, John Binns, and several others on the point of sailing to France. In May, O'Coigley was convicted of treason.[78] O'Connor, although acquitted then, had by early August confessed to treasonable intentions.[79] As support for the Foxites continued to decline, they greatly modified their public behaviour. It was, after all, no part of true Whiggery to fly in the face of the people's will.[80]

The Tookeites and more especially the LCS had incurred even greater suspicion and were hit harder. Robert Fergusson was imprisoned for his part in the attempted rescue of O'Connor from a second arrest on 26 May.[81] Burdett escaped indictment for the same offence only, so it was said, because his father-in-law, Thomas Coutts, was banker to the King.[82] In March and April, forty-seven members of the LCS were arrested – further arrests followed in 1799.[83] Public reaction to the arrests and to the suspension of the Habeas Corpus Act on 20 April was, on the whole, muted. Financial crises, two serious naval mutinies, invasion scares, and actual landings (however feeble) in Ireland and England, ensured a receptive mood for official pronouncements of conspiracy and gratitude for timely action.[84]

From late 1798 onwards, however, this national solidarity was subjected to the strains of severe dearth, war weariness, and military disasters. The number of issues potentially embarrassing to the Government increased. And some of these issues were developed, albeit with varying success, by metropolitan radicals who, though they might, like Horne Tooke, counsel patience against the certain return to favour of their political principles, were at the same time alert for 'the proper time ... when truth may be useful'.[85]

In the City of London, there were forums where, as in parliament, or on the hustings, protest still could be voiced more or less with impunity. The revival of radicalism at the Guildhall, noticed in 1795–6, continued to be confined mainly to Common Hall; the Common council and Court of Aldermen remained pro-Government.[86] But in 1798–1800, the radical liverymen won some notable victories, including resolutions for peace and for an inquiry into the disastrous Helder expedition. A four year struggle with the Court of Aldermen ended triumphantly in September 1799 with H. C. Combe's election as Lord Mayor.[87] Early in 1800, the Society of the Independent Livery of London was formed.[88] Its members included Robert Waithman, Thomas Hardy, Joseph Holden, Abraham Thorn, George Billinge, R. L. Percy – later secretary to the Westminster election committees – and T. L. Rogers, an Oxford Street boot and shoe warehouseman who worked with the Earl of Oxford and William Bosville in the reform campaign of May 1797 and who was to be the first secretary of the Middlesex Freeholders' Club.[89]

Through the monthly meetings of this group, through support for the Middlesex county meeting in October 1800, at which Henry Clifford, a lawyer and a Tookeite, played a dominant part,[90] and in their leadership of the campaign to repeal the income tax, these men and others were involved in attempts to organize a national petitioning movement for peace and the removal of ministers.[91] They were active in the promotion of the radical orthodoxy that war was the real cause of the scarcity and high food prices and they worked for co-ordinated metropolitan radical action.[92] Their attempt to secure additional parliamentary representation for the Independent Livery failed. Combe was returned at the top of the poll for the four City MPs at the general election in 1802. But Benjamin Travers and Robert Waithman, who stood specifically as representatives of the Independent Livery and who pledged themselves to obey the wishes of their constituents, fared poorly. Travers conceded defeat early in the contest. Waithman had trouble in obtaining a hearing and did not stand a poll.[93] This was an indication of the continuing strength of government support in the City and partial vindication of Fox's pessimism regarding the efforts of the Livery.[94] However, it is clear that the Independent Livery did not see themselves solely as a Guildhall pressure group and it is doubtful whether they shared Fox's concept of the Corporation as the spearhead of opposition.[95] Holden, Percy, Rogers, Billinge, and Thorn were among the group of Middlesex freeholders who invited Sir Francis Burdett to contest Middlesex at this general election.[96]

There were good reasons for choosing Burdett and for focusing on Middlesex. Most radicals were content that this time Fox should be the 'popular' as well as the Whig candidate for Westminster. John Graham, who stood as an independent, received little support.[97] Horne Tooke was particularly grateful to Fox for the latter's stand against Lord Temple's bill.[98] This bill had been passed in May 1801. It excluded men in holy orders from the House of Commons and was aimed at Tooke, who had unexpectedly entered the House in February 1801 as member for Old Sarum, a seat in the gift of Lord Camelford, Pitt's radical if not revolutionary cousin.[99] Burdett was Tooke's protégé and his successor now that Tooke's own parliamentary ambitions were ended. Most importantly, Burdett had played a prominent part in the development of the Coldbath Fields prison issue, an issue with perceived potential in the contest for Middlesex.

The issue had developed, like many other radical issues, through a combination of chance happenings and deliberate efforts. When the LCS members were arrested in April 1798, money for them and their families was raised by the usual procedure, a committee, among whose members were William Frend, Place, and Hardy.[100] Donations were received from the Foxites, Charles Grey, Samuel Whitbread, and Lord Holland, and Burdett, Horne Tooke, Bosville, R. A. Cox, and E. B. Clive, among others.[101] And the prisoners had assurances from Tooke 'that anything that may be necessary in the law way will be provided gratis';[102] an important consideration given that the defence of Hardy, Tooke, and Thelwall in 1794 had cost between £3,000 and £4,000.[103] But lack of any trials – 1794 and the conviction of O'Coigley only in May 1798 were contributing factors – removed a proven way of arousing feeling against the Government. It was some months before the means were found by which the imprisonment of so many of London's radicals and the iniquity of the Government could be publicized.

In December, however, Burdett raised, in the House of Commons, the question of conditions in Coldbath Field prison, Clerkenwell, the place of confinement of some of the LCS prisoners and of the Irishman, Colonel Despard. It is not clear whether the initial moves were made by the prisoners or by Horne Tooke and Burdett. When, during the debate on the continued suspension of the Habeas Corpus Act, Burdett combined censure of the ministers with details of the condition of the inmates of the 'English Bastille', he had already paid several visits to the prison and was in possession of the LCS prisoners' accounts of their experiences.[104] Assured that 'a system of the grossest Tyranny' existed at the prison, Burdett gave notice of his intention to move for an inquiry.

Although the Habeas Corpus Act was resuspended almost unopposed – the Foxites, as a group of course, were not attending parliament – there was enough explosive in Burdett's charges to force the Government to take up, and attempt to take over, the Coldbath Fields issue. It succeeded at first. The January Middlesex Quarter Sessions, presided over by William Mainwaring, MP for Middlesex, and the Parliamentary Select Committee, appointed at government instigation the day before Burdett's motion was due, dismissed Burdett's allegations as 'absurd and unfounded'.[105] But in focusing on this prison, the radicals had a sound cause. Even when allowances are made for the political bias of the prisoners and their defenders and it is recognized that much of what they complained about, as for example, solitary confinement, was in keeping with the most advanced penology of the day,[106] it remains that Thomas Aris, the governor of the prison, was a rogue. The conditions at the prison could not be concealed indefinitely. Indeed, it was John Nares, a Middlesex magistrate, who ensured that charges against Aris continued to be presented at the Quarter Sessions after communication between Burdett and the prisoners had been made virtually impossible.[107]

In July 1800, Burdett, armed with information from recently released prisoners, the latest findings of the Quarter Sessions, and with the parliamentary support of Sheridan,[108] again raised the question of the condition and management of Coldbath Fields prison. He mentioned the maltreatment of the Manchester United Englishman, William Cheetham and the mutineer, James Johnston. More importantly, since they were devoid of Jacobin overtones, he referred to the cases of Peter Chenu, a compositor committed for assault who died five weeks later, and of Mary Rich, a girl of thirteen imprisoned by mistake and subsequently raped. Although many MPs probably shared William Windham's conviction that even 'under the best superintendence ... a prison must necessarily be a scene of woe', few shared Mainwaring's judgement that Mary Rich was better off in jail since her home conditions were appalling.[109] And many shared a national concern for, and pride in, English prison reform. Coldbath Fields prison, only six years old and built in the vanguard of this movement,[110] seemed to merit their attention. Burdett's motion on 22 July for an address to the King requesting a commission of inquiry was passed.

The Parliamentary Select Committee, the debates and the Quarter Sessions ensured that the radicals' campaign received some publicity. Further publicity was obtained in various ways. The issue's development was followed closely by the metropolitan radical journal, the *Monthly Magazine*, the latest and highly successful venture of Richard Phillips, former editor of Leicester's fiercy *Herald*.[111] J. S. Jordan and John Smith published, in pamphlet form, Burdett's speeches of July 1800.[112] Both men had connections with the LCS and Horne Tooke dating from the early 1790s; Jordan published the *Rights of Man*. Both men had personal experience of Coldbath Fields prison; Smith for publishing, in 1795, the LCS's *Summary of the Duties of Citizenship*[113] and Jordan for publishing, in 1798, Gilbert Wakefield's *Reply to some parts of the Bishop of Landaff's [sic] Address*.[114] Cruder but effective publicity was obtained when the former United Irishman, Patrick Duffin who, during his confinement in Coldbath Fields and afterwards, supplied Horne Tooke with information for Burdett's parliamentary use,[115] brought the dying Johnston on his release from prison to Jordan's Fleet Street shop. Here, Jordan and Duffin, with the approval of the unfortunate sailor weighed him, recorded his five stone weight loss and displayed him labelled 'a man brought to death's door under the management of Mr Aris' outside the shop and before a large crowd.[116]

The riots which occurred within the prison and in the surrounding fields on the evening of 14 August 1800, may have been largely spontaneous – bread riots erupted in London in September – and the publicity gained fortuitous.[117] But the cries of 'Murder, Murder!', 'We are dying of starvation', 'pull down the Bastille!' set up by men inside the prison and outside among the crowd, referred directly to the Johnston case and to the earlier but fundamental question of the brutal imprisonment of innocent men – innocent because unconvicted.[118] This latter indictment of the Government was made again by Fox at the crowded gathering for his election anniversary dinner on 10 October.[119] While the Report from the commissioners inquiring into the condition of the prison, which was presented in November with its criticisms of the infrequent meals, underweight bread, damp cells, and irregularities in the book-keeping and punishment records, could be and was taken as vindicating Burdett's campaign.[120]

The reach of radical propaganda was greatly extended by the development of the Coldbath Fields prison issue. In July 1802, Burdett could and did oppose William Mainwaring on the Brentford hustings, not only as the champion of justice and the advocate of 'No Bastille', but also as the defender of 'Bread and Plenty'. Burdett's supporters provided a mummery of jailers and whips, sanctimonious magistrates, and shackled emaciated men, evocative of the grimness of 1800 as well as of the prison.[121] Mainwaring was identified with Pitt and his Ministers against whom Burdett and the Foxite, Charles Sturt, had moved a motion of impeachment for their wastage of 'oceans of blood', and 'millions of treasure', of their wanton suspension of the Habeas Corpus Act and their indiscriminate arrests of persons subsequently 'immured in the prison of Coldbath Fields'.[122] Mainwaring was attacked as the defender of 'that new system of police, of secret imprisonment and secret torture'.[123] That Addington had replaced Pitt as Prime Minister in March 1801, that peace had been negotiated in October, and that by 1802 most of the repressive legislation had expired and the State prisoners been released,[124] served to strengthen rather than weaken Burdett's campaign.

On 28 July 1802, Sir Francis was returned behind George Byng, the Whig candidate, and ahead of Mainwaring, the former Tory member.[125] In part, Burdett owed his victory to the Foxites. Indeed, his closeness to the Whigs in 1802 was to be used against him in later more acrimonious times for the 'friends to reform'.[126] Foxites who appeared publicly to promote 'Byng and Burdett', or who voted for both, included Fox, Tom Sheridan, the 6th Duke of Bedford, Lord William Russell, Thomas Erskine, Philip Francis, the Earl of Thanet, Lord Derby, Dr. Parr, Denis O'Brien, Peter Moore, and the Duke and Duchess of Devonshire.[127]

Burdett's return also owed something to the diligence of his agents and legal advisors, among whom were John Frost, John Augustus Bonney, and Robert Fergusson. Frost was a former member of the SCI and of the LCS. He had been imprisoned in 1792 and subsequently struck off the roll of attorneys.[128] Bonney had been articled to Frost. He too was a former member of the SCI and probably of the LCS. In 1794, he had been arrested for treason together with Horne Tooke, Thelwall, Hardy, Joyce, and the other seven 'apostles'.[129] By 1802, Bonney was an experienced promoter of the radical cause, having, among other things, assisted in the defence of Paine, D. I. Eaton, John Binns, Arthur O'Connor, and Thomas Thompson, another United Irishman and one of those involved in the unsuccessful attempt to 'spring' O'Connor on 26 May 1798.[130] Unlike Frost, who was to fall out soon with his colleagues, Bonney continued to be active in Middlesex and Westminster radical politics until his death in 1813.[131]

Other 'democrats', including John Gale Jones, Patrick Duffin, William Dickie – foreman of the Middlesex Traverse Jury which had reported unfavourably on Coldbath Fields prison in July 1800 – and Peter Finnerty, formerly the printer of O'Connor's Dublin *Press*, worked publicly to secure Mainwaring's defeat.[132] However, in the end, this was secured by the votes of 300 Isleworth millowners whose dubious freeholder status was ignored by the sheriffs, the radical liverymen, R. A. Cox, and William Rawlins. Rawlins, an upholsterer had voted, like Cox, for Pickett and Combe in 1796. For their partisanship in 1802, Cox and Rawlins eventually received short jail sentences.[133]

Not surprisingly, the Middlesex contest was rumbustious, reminiscent of the bravura days of 'Wilkes and liberty'. It aroused national interest and provoked extravagant praise and denunciation from participants and observers. It was one of several singled out for condemnation by anti-Jacobin propagandists. To them, an attack on the conductors of one of His Majesty's prisons was symbolic of an attack on all institutions and evidence of a revived republican and revolutionary zeal.[134] On the other hand, Burdett and his supporters emphasized that his immense mob following was evidence of a revived spirit of 'rational and legal liberty'.[135] At his moment of triumph, Sir Francis offered his opponents the consolation that the lesson to be drawn from his victory was,

> that the people of England may get rid of the odious system upon which the late Administration acted ... by quiet, peaceable and constitutional means.[136]

The fears of those who detected the spirit, if not the presence of O'Connor in Burdett's campaign, were heightened by the rush of Burdettites and Foxites to Paris as soon as the election was over.[137] The exposure of the Despard plot in November did nothing to weaken the Government's belief that Burdett's victory had given more encouragement to what it considered 'a disaffected party' than anything that had 'been done for many years'.[138] However, in the long run it was the radicals' emphasis that gained greater currency. Whether this was due to better propaganda during the election and after the arrest of the 'unfortunate Colonel Despard', or to the recognition and assimilation of the truth, is another question.

Burdett's election was a triumph for Horne Tooke who, although he had close associations with the City and with Westminster, probably knew Middlesex best, a legacy of his days as the parson of Brentford and Wilkes's campaign manager. The Middlesex contest in 1802, had therefore, varied and strong links with the past. But since Burdett's return was petitioned against by Mainwaring,[139] the contest also marked the beginning of the struggle to obtain for Burdett a secure and 'popular' seat. This struggle was to absorb much radical energy in the next five years and eventually to re-focus attention on Westminster. It was also a struggle conducted with decreasing, and finally no Whig support.[140]

The 1802 election for Middlesex serves then as a convenient reminder that few, if any, dates or events can be treated in isolation from preceding and succeeding developments. The period 1796–1802 can be viewed as an entity to the extent that it encompasses the time of greatest fears of insurrection and invasion and some of the most repressive legislation ever passed in Britain. It was also a period marked by displays of rare unanimity among those hostile to the Government and to 'things as they are'. But otherwise, in so far as London radicalism is concerned, these years represent only time in the lives of men who, for various reasons, including economic and psychological ones, sought to challenge the status quo.[141] Faced with repressive and punitive measures many of these men lowered their expectations of the scope and speed of change. However, using what means were to hand, they continued to promote what they saw as the cause of 'Truth and Virtue'. Few of these men began their radical careers in 1796. Most of them continued after 1802 to seek ways 'to eradicate gross abuses and renovate the original compact between the governors and governed', which was Thomas Hardy, declared, 'the constant study and unwearied labour of good men in all ages'.[142]

Notes

1. But see R. W. Davis, *Political change and continuity 1760–1885: a Buckinghamshire study* (Newton Abbot, 1972); David J. V. Jones, *Before Rebecca: popular protests in Wales, 1793–1835* (London, 1973); R. S. Neale, 'Class and ideology in a provincial city: Bath 1800–1850' in *Class and Ideology in the Nineteenth Century* (London, 1972); A. Temple Patterson, *Radical Leicester: a history of Leicester 1780–1850* (Leicester, 1954); M. I. Thomis, *Politics and Society in Nottingham 1785–1835* (Oxford, 1969).
2. E.g. Brit. Mus. Addit. MSS. 27808, 27811, 27812, 27813, 27815, 27816, 27837, 35142, 35143.
3. Cartwright, *A Letter to the Duke of Newcastle* (London, 1792), p. 88. See also P. A. Brown, *The French Revolution in English History* (3rd impression, London 1965), chs. 2, 3.

4. See E. P. Thompson, *The Making of the English Working Class* (Pelican edn., Harmondsworth, 1968), ch. 1; G. A. Williams, *Artisans and Sans-Culottes* (London, 1968).

5. Barlow, *Advice to the Privileged Orders in the Several States of Europe* (London, 1792), p. 2; and see E. C. Black *The Association: British Extraparliamentary Political Organization 1769–1793* (Cambridge, Mass., 1963), chs. 5, 6; W. P. Hall, *British Radicalism 1791–1797* (New York, 1912), section i, ch. 5; W. A. L. Seaman, 'British Democratic Societies in the Period of the French Revolution' (London Univ. Ph.D thesis 1954), chs. 1, 3.

6. R. K. Webb, *The British Working Class Reader 1790–1848: Literacy and Social Tension* (London, 1955), p. 38.

7. For a recent biography of Paine, see Audrey Williamson, *Thomas Paine* (London, 1973).

8. Brown, *The French Revolution in English History*, chs. 4–6; S. Maccoby, *English Radicalism 1786–1832* (London, 1955), pp. 56–79, 147; Thompson, *The Making ... Class*, pp. 134–45, 151–2; G. S. Veitch, *The Genesis of Parliamentary Reform* (Reprint, London, 1964), pp. 273–4.

9. H. W. C. Davis, *The Age of Grey and Peel* (Reprint, Oxford, 1967), pp. 100–2; Seaman, *op. cit.*, pp. 14–16.

10. *Rights of Man: Part I* (Penguin edn., Harmondsworth, 1969), p. 64.

11. Thompson, *The Making ... Class*, p. 133; and see C. Hill, 'The Norman Yoke' in *Puritanism and Revolution* (Panther edn., London, 1968), pp. 58–125; E. J. Hobsbawm, 'The Social Functions of the Past: Some Questions', *Past and Present*, lv (1972), pp. 3–17.

12. Brown, *The French Revolution in English History*, ch. 6.

13. See Maccoby, *English Radicalism*, p. 90; and see W. M. Stern, 'The Bread Crisis in Britain, 1795–96', *Economica* xxxi (1964), pp. 168–87.

14. Maccoby, *English Radicalism*, pp. 90–5; Thompson, *The Making ... Class*, pp. 153–8.

15. Thompson, *ibid.*, pp. 161–3, 181–2; Williams, *Artisans and Sans-Culottes*, pp. 102–5.

16. E.g. G. D. H. Cole and A. W. Filson, *British Working Class Movements: select documents 1789–1875* (London, 1967), ch. 3; Henry Collins, 'The London Corresponding Society' in *Democracy and the Labour Movement*, ed. John Saville (London, 1954), pp. 103–34; Davis, *The Age of Grey and Peel*, chs. 4, 5; Hall, *British Radicalism 1791–7*; Seaman, 'British Democratic Societies'; Veitch, *Genesis of Parliamentary Reform*, pp. 341–4.

17. Brown, *The French Revolution in English History*, pp. 152–3; Thompson, *The Making ... Class*, pp. 158–62; Veitch, *Genesis of Parliamentary Reform*, pp. 334–5.

18. See Maccoby, *English Radicalism*, pp. 128–33.

19. E.g. R. B. Aspland, *Memoir of the life, works and correspondence of the Rev. Robert Aspland of Hackney* (London, 1850), p. 74: Aspland to his parents, 21 September 1799; *Recollections of the life of John Binns ... written by himself* (Philadelphia, 1854), p. 164; PRO, Privy Council Papers 1/3535: A. Galloway to R. Hodgson, 24 December 1801.

20. Samuel Parr, *A Spital Sermon, preached at Christ Church upon Easter Tuesday 15 April 1800* (London, 1801), p. 8; see also *Memoirs of the late Thomas Holcroft written by himself*, ed. W. Hazlitt (London, 1816), iii. 64–5; Hazlitt, 'William Goodwin' in *Spirit of the Age* (Everyman edn., London, 1928), pp. 182–94; *Monthly Magazine* January 1799, pp. 9–14: 'The Enquirer' no. xvi, 'In what degree is the future melioration of the State of Mankind probable?'

21. E.g. A. Cobban, *The Debate on the French Revolution 1789–1820* (London, 1970), p. 376: Robert Southey to John May, 26 June 1797; *Political Papers, comprising the correspondence of several distinguished persons ... with the editor, the Rev. Christopher Wyvill* (York, 1804), vi. 42: Wyvill to Fox, 10 November 1799; Brit. Mus. Addit. MSS 51650 (Holland House Papers), ff. 65–6: W. Roscoe to Lord Holland, 25 December 1799.

22. See above n. 20; and see *A Letter to William Smith Esq. M.P. from Robert Southey Esq.* (2nd edn., London 1817), pp. 20–1; H. N. Brailsford, *Shelley, Godwin and their circle* (London, [1945]), pp. 154–7; Thompson, *The Making . . . Class*, pp. 180–1, 196, 200.

23. See esp. Brit. Mus. Addit. MSS. 27808 (Place Papers), written 1824; Brit. Mus. Addit. MSS. 27818 (Place Papers), Hardy's correspondence; *Memoir of Thomas Hardy, founder of and secretary to the L.C.S. . . . written by himself* (London, 1832); and see *The Autobiography of Francis Place*, ed. Mary Thale (Cambridge, 1972).

24. E.g. Marianne Elliot, 'The United Irishmen and France, 1793–1806' (Oxford Univ. D. Phil. thesis 1975); J. L. Baxter and F. K. Donnelly, 'The Revolutionary "Underground" in the West Riding: Myth or Reality?' *Past and Present*, lxiv (1974), 124–35; Thompson, *The Making . . . Class*, pp. 182–92, 515 ff. See also A. W. Smith, 'Irish Rebels and English Radicals 1798–1820', *Past and Present*, viii (1955), pp. 78–85.

25. *The Celebrated Speech of . . . Fox, with the Proceedings of the Meeting at the Shakespeare Tavern . . . 10 October 1800* (4th edn., [1800]), pp. 28–9.

26. But see J. Ann Hone, 'The Ways and Means of London Radicalism, 1796–1821' (Oxford Univ. D. Phil. thesis 1975), ch. 2: 'The Case for Conspiracy'.

27. See *Articles for Future Regulations for the L.C.S., recommended by the Executive Committee, 12 December 1795* printed sheet, copy in Brit. Mus. Addit. MSS. 27817 (Place Papers), f. 41.

28. See Brit. Mus. Addit. MSS. 27815: LCS correspondence, 1796.

29 *Ibid.*, f. 130: LCS to the Perth Society, n.d. [September/October 1796].

30. See Brit. Mus. Addit. MSS. 27818, esp. ff. 560, 647; *Memoir of Thomas Hardy*; PRO, Treasury Solicitors Papers, series 11, vol. 951, files 3494–5; vol. 952, part 9496: confiscated papers of Hardy, John Richter, Tooke; *Trial of John Horne Tooke for High Treason 17–22 November 1794* 2 vols. (London, 1795), *passim*.

31. See PRO T.S. 11. 951/3494–5; T.S. 11. 952/9496; T.S. 11. 959/3505 pt. ii; *Trial of Horne Tooke*, esp. i. 35; W. E. Saxton, 'The political importance of the Westminster Committee of the early nineteenth century, with special reference to the years 1807–22' (Edinburgh Univ. Ph.D. thesis 1958), vol. i. sect. i. 18–22.

32. Alexander Stephens, *Memoirs of John Horne Tooke* (London, 1813), ii. 295–6.

33. See M. W. Patterson, *Sir Francis Burdett and His Times* (London, 1931), i. 117; Stephens, *Horne Tooke*, ii. 306; Brit. Mus. Addit. MSS. 27818, f. 614: Hardy to Andrew Wilson, 18 November 1826, draft.

34. PRO T.S. 11. 952/3496: Sturch to D. Adams, 11 December [1792]; T.S. 11. 953/3497: same to same, 2 December 1793.

35. Dated 29 November 1792. For Vaughan's authorship, see *Memoir of Hardy*, p. 24.

36. Horne Tooke, *The Diversions of Purley: part ii* (London, 1805), p. 193.

37. See Frida Knight, *University Rebel: The Life of William Frend 1757–1841* (London, 1971), for Frend's career and radical activities. For the election, (27 May–13 June), see *Jordan's Complete Collection of all the Addresses and Speeches . . . at the late . . . contest for Westminster* (3rd edn., London, 1796); *Speeches . . . addressed to the Electors of . . . Westminster* (2nd edn., London, 1796); *The Westminster Election . . . 1796*; W. H. Reid, *Memoirs of the Public Life of John Horne Tooke* (London, 1812), pp. 72–137; Stephens, *Horne Tooke*, ii. 165–229.

38. N. Hans 'Franklin, Jefferson and the English Radicals at the end of the eighteenth century', *Proceedings of the American Philosophical Society*, xcviii (1954), p. 420.

39. See Hone, 'The Ways and Means of London Radicalism' *op. cit.*; J. M. Main, 'Radical Westminster, 1807–1820', *Historical Studies, Australia and New Zealand*, xii (1966), 186–204; Saxton, 'The Political Importance of the Westminster Committee of the early nineteenth century', *op. cit.*

40. Brit. Mus. Addit. MSS. 27817, f. 44. Stewards for the dinner included SCI members: A. Blake, W. Bosville, Thomas Brand, John Chatfield, J. T. Rutt, John Satchell,

Christopher Hull; LCS members: W. Frend, Samuel Miller, Jonathon Panther, Robert Fergusson, J. Savage.

41. For these quarrels, see Black, *The Association*, esp. pp. 105–15, 196, 214–15.

42. See Lucy S. Sutherland (q.v.) and G. Rudé, 'Collusion and Convergence in eighteenth century English Political Action' in *Paris and London in the 18th Century* (Fontana edn., London, 1970), pp. 319–40, for the use made of the City by the parliamentary opposition during much of the eighteenth century.

43. Corporation of London, Guildhall Library, *The Poll for Members to serve in Parliament for the City of London 1796* [London, 1796].

44. See J. R. Dinwiddy, '"The Patriotic Linen Draper", Robert Waithman and the Revival of Radicalism in the City of London, 1795–1818,' *Bulletin of the Institute of Historical Research*, xlvi (1973), 72–94. For Goodbehere and Thorp, see *Monthly Repository* November, December 1818, pp. 723, 773–4, December 1822, p. 722.

45. See *D.B.N.* for Sharp; and see below p. 89 for Billinge, Holden and Cox.

46. Hector Campbell, *The Names of those Patriots in the Parish of St. John, that supported Mr. Tierney* (London, 1796), esp. pp. 7–8.

47. Brit. Mus. Addit. MSS. 145: general committee, 29 December 1796.

48. E.g. *A Political Eclogue. Citizen H. Txxxe, Citizen Txxrnxy, R. B. Esq.* (London, 1797).

49. Brit. Mus. Addit. MSS. 27815, f. 130: LCS to Perth Society n.d. [September/October 1796]; M. Dorothy George, *Catalogue of Political and Personal Satires* (London, 1942), vii. no. 8813; and see Marilyn McBriar, 'Burke, Paine and Fox as interpretors of the French Revolution' (Melbourne Univ. MA thesis 1971), p. 204, for a discussion of this point.

50. *Recollections of the Table-Talk of Samuel Rogers*, ed. M. Bishop (London, 1952), p. 56.

51. Stephens, *Horne Tooke*, ii. 170–200: speech, 28 May 1796.

52. Reid, *Horne Tooke*, pp. 131–6: speech at Crown and Anchor Tavern, 28 June 1796.

53. Patterson, *Burdett*, i. 52: Burdett to Thomas Coutts, n.d. [ca. 1793–6].

54. *Courier*, 19 May 1797.

55. *Peace and Reform Meeting of the Householders of the Parish of St. Mary-le-bone . . . 30 May 1797* [London, 1797].

56. E.g. *Speech of John Thelwall at the Second Meeting of the LCS . . . 12 November 1795* (London, 1795), esp. pp. i–ii.

57. Arundel Castle Archives, Howard letters 1760–1816 I, letters addressed to 10th and 11th Dukes of Norfolk: Fox to Norfolk, 28 December 1795; and see *Declaration of and Form of Association recommended by the Whig Club* ([London], 1796), esp. pp. 2, 11.

58. *Memorials and Correspondence of C. J. Fox*, ed. Lord John Russell (London, 1853), iii. 135–6: Fox to Holland, Wed. 1796; and see L. G. Mitchell, *C. J. Fox and the Disintegration of the Whig Party 1782–94* (Oxford, 1971), for the trials and tribulations of the Whigs.

59. Brit. Mus. Addit. MSS. 27815, f. 130.

60. *'Thoughts on Mr. Grey's Plan of Reform' in a Circular Letter to the Popular Societies of Great Britain and Ireland* (London, 1797).

61. Jones, *Sketch of a Political Tour through Rochester, Chatham, Maidstone, etc.* (London, 1796), pp. 90–1, 97.

62. *Courier*, 19 May 1797.

63. *Narrative of the Proceedings at the General Meeting of the L.C.S., held . . . 31 July 1797, in a Field near the Veterinary College, St. Pancras* (London, 1797), p. 9.

64. E.g. Brit. Mus. Addit. MSS. 51660 (Holland House Papers), f. 7: 5th Duke of Bedford to Lord Holland, 25 September 1797; Bedford County Record Office, Whitbread Papers, W1/866: C. Grey to Samuel Whitbread, 16 October 1797.

65. Binns, *Recollections*, pp. 72–7.

66. See *The Later Correspondence of George III*, ed. A. Aspinall (London, 1963), ii. xxi–xxix, for the activities of the 'central Party' and the 'armed neutrality'.

67. *Morning Chronicle*, 7 June 1797: account of Whig Club, 6 June 1797.
68. Loren Reid, *Charles James Fox: A Man for the People* (London, 1969), pp. 325–6, 328.
69. *Speeches of C. J. Fox and Erskine . . . at the Shakespeare Tavern . . . 10 Oct 1797* (London, 1797), esp. pp. 9–12, 16; and see *Narrative of the Proceedings . . . 31 July 1797*, pp. 12, 27–30.
70. Brit. Mus. Addit. MSS. 27815, ff. 186–7: Robert Dawre, president, executive committee to Fox, 10 November 1797.
71. *Peace and Reform. Meeting of Parish of St. Mary-le-bone 30 May 1797*.
72. *Memoirs of the Whig Party during my time by Henry Richard, Lord Holland*, ed. his son Henry Edward, Lord Holland (London, 1852–4), i. 96–8.
73. Hall, *British Radicalism*, p. 246; *Monthly Magazine*, January 1798, pp. 65–7.
74. Brit. Mus. Addit. MSS. 27837, ff. 78–9: newscuttings.
75. Holland, *Memoirs of the Whig Party*, i. 130–1; *The Journal of Elizabeth, Lady Holland 1791–1811*, ed. Earl of Ilchester (London, 1909), i. 177; *Monthly Magazine*, February 1798, p. 142.
76. Brit. Mus. Addit. MSS. 27808, ff. 110–11.
77. *Later Correspondence of George III*, iii. 15: Pitt to the King, 31 January 1798; Holland, *Memoirs*, i. 129; Reid, *Fox*, p. 356; Veitch, *Genesis of Parliamentary Reform*, p. 337.
78. Thompson, *The Making . . . Class*, p. 187.
79. *Memoir by A. O'Connor, T. A. Emmet, and W. J. McNevin. With the Substance of their Examination before the Secret Committee of the House of Lords, August 1798* [1798].
80. For the low regard in which the Foxites were held , see *Journal of Lady Holland*, i. 203; *The Farington Diary*, ed. J. Greig (London, 1922), i. 233, 235, 242.
81. *The Whole Proceedings . . . against the Rt. Hon. Sackville, Earl of Thanet, Robert Fergusson, esq. and others for a Riot* (London, 1799).
82. *Journal of Lady Holland*, i. 251.
83. *Parl. Accounts and Papers: Sessional Papers, House of Lords, 1801: A List of Persons apprehended or detained charged with or suspected of Treason between 1 Feb. 1793 and 13 April 1801*.
84. E.g. W. H. Reid, *Rise and Dissolution of the Infidel Societies in this Metropolis* (London, 1800), pp. 93–5, 109. See Maccoby, *English Radicalism*, pp. 113–14, 123–4, 126–7, for the crisis of 1796–8.
85. Tooke, *The Diversions of Purley part ii*, p. 15; F. D. Cartwright, *Life and Correspondence of Major Cartwright* (London, 1826), i. 262: Tooke to Cartwright, 12 December 1800.
86. See Dinwiddy, 'Robert Waithman and the Revival of Radicalism in the City of London', *op. cit.*, pp. 74–5.
87. Corporation of London Records Office, Common Hall Book 9, ff. 108–11, 116–17, 126.
88. Brit. Mus. Addit. MSS. 27818, ff. 16–18, 20, 22, 29, 30, 35, 123; Brit. Mus. Addit. MSS. 27817, f. 101: anniversary dinner, 21 May 1802.
89. For the Middlesex Freeholders' Club, see *Declaration and Regulations of the Middlesex Freeholders' Club, instituted in the year 1804* (London, 1804); *Cobbett's Political Register* 25 October 1806: extracts from Major Cartwright's address to the 1st meeting of the Middlesex Freeholders' Club; Brit. Mus. Addit. MSS. 27818, f. 685; Addit. MSS. 27838, f. 91: printed open letter and newscuttings.
90. See *The Whole Proceedings and Resolutions of the Freeholders of the County of Middlesex at a Meeting . . . 29 Oct. 1800, where it was unanimously resolved that War is the Cause of the alarming high price of provisions* (London, 1800).
91. E.g. Common Hall Book 9, ff. 144–7, 151–2, 163; Brit. Mus. Addit. MSS. 27818, ff. 16–18: Hardy to Cartwright, 24 January 1801, draft; *Life and Correspondence of Cartwright*, i. 290–3: Cartwright to Hardy, 5 February 1801.
92. E.g. Robert Waithman, *War Proved to be the Real Cause of the Present Scarcity* (London,

1800), published by J. S. Jordan; *The Whole Proceedings and Resolutions of the Freeholders ... 29 Oct. 1800*; Brit. Mus. Addit. MSS. 27818, ff. 16–18.

93. *Times*, 29 June, 6, 7, 10, 16, July 1802.

94. Wyvill, *Political Papers*, vi. 39–40, 54–5, 69: Fox to Wyvill [5 November 1799], 26 January, 28 October 1800.

95. *Ibid.*, p. 55: Fox to Wyvill, 26 January 1800.

96. *Report of the Proceedings During the Late Contested Election for the County of Middlesex* (London, 1802), p. 9.

97. Middlesex CRO, WR/PEP: Poll Book Westminster 1802, incomplete.

98. *Journal of Lady Holland*, ii. 146.

99. Reid, *Horne Tooke*, pp. 151–8.

100. *Autobiography of Place*, pp. 181–6.

101. Brit. Mus. Addit. MSS. 27817, f. 212; Bodleian Library, Oxford, MS. Eng. Hist. C296 (Burdett Papers), f. 17.

102. PRO P.C. 1/3526: [Place] to [Richard Hodgson?] n.d. [April 1798].

103. See George Dyer, *A Dissertation on the Theory and Practice of Benevolence* (London, 1795), p. 84.

104. Bodleian Library, Oxford, MS. Eng. Hist. C295 (Burdett Papers), ff. 12–15, 119–27, 162–5.

105. *Parl. Accounts and Papers*, xlvi. no. 943, *Papers relating to HM's Prison in Coldbath Fields*, 5 March 1799, pp. 9–35; *Monthly Magazine*, April 1799, p. 243, May 1799, p. 333, June 1799, p. 411.

106. L. Radzinowicz, *History of the English Criminal Law and its Administration from 1750* (London, 1948), p. 318.

107. *Parl. Accounts and Papers*, lii. no. 1026, *Report from the Commissioners appointed ... to enquire into the State and Management of H.M.'s prison in Coldbath Fields, Clerkenwell, 1 Nov. 1800*, p. 45.

108. Sheridan, like George Tierney, did not participate in the Foxite secession from parliament.

109. *An Impartial Statement of the Inhuman Cruelties Discovered in Coldbath-Fields Prison, by the Grand and Traverse Juries ... and reported in the House of Commons on ... 11 July 1800 by Sir Francis Burdett* (7th edn., London, [1800]); *A Further Account of the Cruelties ... as reported ... 22 July 1800 in the Speeches of Sir Francis Burdett and R. B. Sheridan* (4th edn., London, [1800]).

110. See *Rules, Orders and Regulations for the Management of the New House of Correction* (London, 1795); H. Mayhew and J. Binney, *The Criminal Prisons of London and Scenes of Prison Life* [1862] (new impression, London, 1968), pp. 274 ff.

111. For the *Monthly Magazine*, see Ian Sellers, 'Social and Political Ideas of Representative English Unitarians 1795–1850' (Oxford Univ. B. Litt. thesis [1956]). See Patterson, *Radical Leicester*, pp. 67–78, for Phillips and the *Herald*.

112. See n. 109.

113. PRO T.S. 11. 819/2702: King against John Smith.

114. PRO T.S. 11. 456/1511: King against Joseph Johnson and J. S. Jordan; and see F. K. Prochaska, 'English State Trials in the 1790s: A Case Study', *Journal of British Studies*, xiii (1973), pp. 63–82.

115. Bodleian Library, MS. Eng. Hist. C295, f. 16, MS. Eng. Hist. C296, ff. 41–2, 88, 90, 98.

116. *Ibid.*, f. 88: Duffin to Horne Tooke, 8 August 1800; PRO T.S. 11. 1066/4908, ff. 14–17: Trial between Aris and William Dickie for slander, 2 June 1803.

117. See G. Rudé, *The Crowd in History: A Study of Popular Disturbances in France and England, 1730–1848* (New York, 1964), esp. pp. 59–60, 211–12, 229–30, 240, 242–5, for his analysis of the organization and meaning imposed on even the most spontaneous riots by ideas, a few leaders and commonly-held beliefs in liberties etc.

118. See PRO Home Office Papers, series 42, vol. 50: R. Baker to Duke of Portland, 15

August 1800; series 43, vol. 12, f. 73: Portland to Baker, 17 August 1800, for the riot.

119. *The Celebrated Speech of C. J. Fox at the Shakespeare Tavern, 10 October 1800*, pp. 14–15.

120. *Report from the Commissioners 1 Nov. 1800*, pp. 18–21, 33, 47, 52.

121. See *Report of the Proceedings during the Election for Middlesex*, pp. 13, 14, 23, 24, 26, 29, 36, 56, 62, 75; M. D. George, *Catalogue of Political and Personal Satires* (London, 1947), viii. nos. 9878, 9880–2).

122. *Monthly Magazine*, May 1802, p. 387. The motion was made on 12 April 1802.

123. *Report of the Proceedings during the Election for Middlesex*, p. 36: Burdett's speech, 6th day of poll.

124. See P. Ziegler, *Addington* (London, 1965), chs. 4–6.

125. Final figures, Byng 3848, Burdett 3207, Mainwaring 2936.

126. See Patterson, *Burdett*, ii. 482–4, bye-election for Westminster, 1819.

127. *Copy of the Poll for the Election . . . for the County of Middlesex* (London, 1803); *Report of the Proceedings during the Election for Middlesex*.

128. Black, *The Association*, p. 188; Brown, *The French Revolution in English History*, pp. 86, 91–4; *Trial of Horne Tooke*, i. *passim*.

129. See *ibid.*; Jeremiah Joyce, *An Account of Mr Joyce's Arrest for Treasonable Practices* (2nd edn., London, 1795).

130. See *The Whole Proceedings against Thanet, Fergusson and others for a Riot.*

131. For Frost, see Bodleian Library, Oxford, MS. Eng. Hist. b. 200 (Burdett Papers), notes for the case, Burdett against Frost; Brit. Mus. Addit. MSS. 27817, f. 154: newscutting, obituary 25 July 1842. For Bonney, see Brit. Mus. Addit. MSS. 27838 (Place Papers), ff. 25, 207.

132. For the election and radical personnel, see *Considerations on the Late Elections for Westminster and Middlesex, together with some facts relating to the House of Correction in Coldbath Fields* (London, 1802); [G. Huddersford], *The Scum Uppermost when the Middlesex Porridge-Pot Boils over: an heroic election ballad with explanatory notes etc.* (London, 1802); *Parl. Papers 1804*, iv (3), *Report from the Select Committee appointed to enquire into the Election and Return for the County of Middlesex, 9 July 1804.*

133. *Later Correspondence of George III*, iv. 286: Pitt to the King, 1 February [1805].

134. E.g. J. Bowles, *Thoughts on the late General Election, as demonstrative of the progress of Jacobinism* (3rd edn., 1802), esp. pp. 9, 16–19, 27–9, 43–5, 68–9.

135. *Report of the Proceedings during the election for Middlesex*, p. 38: H. H. Townsend's speech. He was the son of the popular Wilkite Alderman Townsend.

136. *Ibid.*; and see Anon, *The Middlesex Election Candidly Considered in its Causes and Consequences* (London, 1802), pp. 20–1, 30–4.

137. See J. G. Alger, 'British Visitors to Paris 1802–1803', *English Historical Review*, xiv (1899), pp. 739–41.

138. Patterson, *Burdett*, i. 144: Government memo to Thomas Coutts, n.d. [Aug. 1802]. For Despard's arrest, 19 November 1802 and trial 7 February 1803, see Thompson, *The Making . . . Class*, pp. 522–8.

139. See *Report from the Select Committee appointed to enquire into the Election and Return for the County of Middlesex, 9 July 1804.*

140. See Bodleian Library, MS. Eng. Hist. b. 200; Holland, *Memoirs of the Whig Party*, ii. *passim*; Patterson, *Burdett*, i. 147–51.

141. See G. R. Taylor, *The Angel-Makers: a study in psychological origins of historical change 1750–1850* (London, 1958); R. Bendix, 'The Lower classes and the "Democratic Revolution"', *Industrial Relations*, i (1961), pp. 91–116; G. Whale, 'The Influence of the Industrial Revolution on the Demand for Parliamentary Reform 1700–90', *Transactions of the Royal Historical Society*, v (1922), pp. 101–31.

142. Brit. Mus. Addit. MSS. 27817, f. 65: Hardy, Introductory Letter to a Friend, written 1799.

ALICE PROCHASKA

The Practice of Radicalism:
Educational Reform in Westminster

On 23 May 1807 a group of about thirty shopkeepers and lesser
professional men achieved a triumph of no small significance in the
politics of reform. With an expenditure of just over £1,000 and no
bribery they engineered the election of Sir Francis Burdett, the radical
reformer, as Member of Parliament for the City and Liberty of
Westminster.[1] They took their stand on a general platform of rights and
liberties, calling for 'purity of election', the abolition of government
sinecures, the disfranchisement of rotten boroughs, and for a return to
'that independent spirit which Englishmen have so justly boasted; that
spirit which produced the revolution of 1688'.[2] Beneath these slogans
lay a rich seam of reformism potentially far more radical than its surface
manifestation. For the Westminster election committee of 1807 was
composed largely of men who had belonged to the London Corresponding Society in the 1790s. Some of them, like John Richter and Paul
Lemaitre, had suffered imprisonment for their beliefs.[3] They were
influenced by the political and religious theories of Thomas Holcroft
and Thomas Paine and by the far-reaching attack on government
contained in William Godwin's *Enquiry Concerning Political Justice*.[4] Two
of the most influential leaders of radical opinion, Major John Cartwright and John Horne Tooke, were actively involved in the resurgence
of radicalism in Westminster; and their respective theories and styles of
political organization helped to shape the reform movement in the city.[5]
Here was a potent blend of faith in the goodness of man with the
pragmatism and experience that could build a political organization
upon a base of optimism. It is the purpose of this essay to examine a little
known episode in the development of the Westminster radicals'
programme: their attempt to educate the poor children of London. In
seeing how this plan flowed from their political work we may appreciate

more fully how comprehensive were their ideals and how wide the scope of their ambition.

Politics in Westminster after 1807 rapidly became an influential force among reformers. Frequent public meetings and dinners, especially those that celebrated the anniversary of Burdett's election, attracted large crowds of metropolitan reformers with a good sprinkling of MPs and less well known radical politicians from other parts of the country.[6] Although the committee was only formally constituted at election times, its members formed a nucleus both for discussing reform and for the practical organization of meetings and demonstrations.[7]

There were certainly enough political events to engage their attention. In 1808 the committee shared the delight of other reformers in the liberation of Spain, and John Richter framed an address to the king on their behalf, expressing the hope that Spain might enjoy democracy at last.[8] The year 1809 witnessed that great radical triumph, the exposure of the Duke of York's mistress and by implication the Duke himself for selling commissions in the army. The greatest scandal of the decade, it excited the imaginations of the country and called forth tributes from innumerable public meetings to the reformers who had uncovered it. Sir Francis Burdett was among the Duke of York's foremost scourges and received the fervent endorsement of his electors.[9] The next year he was in prison, jailed for contempt by order of the House of Commons because he had defended the right of the journalist John Gale Jones to comment on proceedings in Parliament. When Burdett was freed after an imprisonment of three months, his election committee seized the opportunity for public display. They organized an elaborate procession from the Tower of London to Burdett's town house in Piccadilly, in which they employed all the most full-blown symbols of constitutional purity and righteous defiance. 'Westminster's Pride' brought ridicule on the celebration by slipping away across the river to his house in Wimbledon, eluding his fans completely. But the organization had been superb.[10]

By now the Westminster committee had an unrivalled grasp of organization and electoral management. In a city so excitable and so prone to popular disturbance as Westminster, it was no small achievement to organize popular politics as peaceably as they did. While the elections of 1807 and 1812 were uproarious affairs by twentieth-century standards, and the Crown and Anchor dinner meetings scarcely models of decorum, they were a vast improvement on earlier scenes which had made the leading committee member Francis Place ashamed of his fellow citizens and indignant against the aristocratic politicians who encouraged their animal behaviour. It was of cardinal importance to the Westminster election committee that popular demonstrations should be reasonably seemly. There was a constant threat of over-reaction by the government, for the line was fine between engaging the sympathies and imaginations of a Westminster crowd and provoking the authorities into dispersing it with violence. But it was not only that. The Westminster election committee, nurtured on the most optimistic ideals of the French Revolution and dedicated to giving people a voice in their own destiny, really believed in the dignity of working men. Respectability was not the fetish of a group of middle-aged tradesmen who had themselves become respectable; it was part of the creed of reform.

Nor was it all a one-way process. By the time the committee began preparing for the general election of 1812, the will of their electorate had impressed itself on them. Sir Francis Burdett maintained his Olympian distance from the business of electioneering by virtue of his established popularity. But the candidate for Westminster's second seat was expected to give solid undertakings as a condition of receiving the committee's support. Before they threw their weight behind Lord Cochrane in 1812, the leaders of the committee made him account to a public meeting for his conduct since he became an MP and pledge in writing that he would always vote for reform and for any measure against sinecures. With the exception of Burdett himself, it was essential for any radical candidate to appear on the hustings regularly during the poll and to declare his principles clearly. Another essential ingredient in any radical victory was the lavish flattery meted out to the electorate, 'the free and independent electors of Westminster' whose example was inspiring reformers throughout the country.[11] Their vanity thus was flattered at every turn, but it was their vanity as the independent voice of the people that was important.

Between 1807 and 1812 the activities of the Westminster election committee had become part of the definition of that emergent phrase, 'radical reform'.[12] But after five years of politicking its members were beginning to seek additional outlets for their energy. Their hopes of achieving any kind of parliamentary reform were not high, for overtures to the Whigs in 1810–12 had underlined the differences between radicalism and reformist whiggery. The Union for Parliamentary Reform, which Major John Cartwright hoped would become a national union to promote tax-payer suffrage and annual parliaments, started life with a broadly based membership ranging from members of the Westminster election committee to the moderately reformist Whigs John Christian Curwen and Christopher Wyvill. Cartwright prepared an *Appeal to the Nation* on the Union's behalf and a subscription was opened, but the union as originally constituted made no further progress.[13] A similar apathy overcame the first Hampden Club, founded in 1811 by Thomas Northmore to bring together Whig and radical gentlemen in the cause of reform.[14] The Whigs were not prepared to endorse any scheme more radical than Curwen's Act of 1809 to prevent trafficking in parliamentary seats and Thomas Brand's unsuccessful bill of 1810 which had proposed triennial parliaments, a reform of the polling system and the extension of the franchise to borough householders and copyholders. This was not so far-reaching as the bill that Sir Francis Burdett had introduced in 1809; and his proposals had been themselves a watered-down version of what many of his committee members would have preferred.[15]

They expressly linked constitutional reform with the whole spectrum of social ills; and as the reform movement developed in Westminster its leaders increasingly insisted on the non-political benefits that democracy would bring. Following on the disappointments of 1810–12 they extended their attention both geographically and socially, to the industrial provinces and to the very poor in their own city.[16] Major Cartwright's provincial Hampden Clubs, unlike their original, catered to working men in the industrial regions and looked to leaders in Westminster for inspiration. Francis Place and other members of the election committee replied to requests from other constituencies for practical advice on the conduct of elections, and began to establish links with working men in the areas that were disturbed by Luddism.[17] Meanwhile, their own constituency provided abundant opportunity for experimenting with reform among the 'respectable' poor.

When members of the Westminster election committee embarked on schemes for educating the London poor, some of the wider implications of nineteenth-century radicalism began to develop alongside the campaign for parliamentary reform. Though the movement began with a fairly limited programme of constitutional reform it drew its inspiration from a background of political thought that emphasized the need for reform in all parts of the nation's life. A utilitarian philosophy rooted in the ideas of William Godwin and Horne Tooke and drawing vigour from the teachings of Thomas Paine and Thomas Holcroft, compelled a concern for the whole community. Horne Tooke had written, 'The end [of government] is happiness to all beings capable of happiness . . . as universally extended as possible . . . Even freedom itself is valuable only as a means indispensably necessary to that end.'[18] Godwin also considered that happiness and moral improvement were the proper aims of political activity, although unlike Tooke he held individual freedom to be an integral part of human happiness.[19] Paine and following on from him, Thomas Holcroft, advocated drastic social changes for the same fundamental purpose, and high among the necessary reforms they placed universal education.[20] In the course of their work to educate the Westminster poor, the members of the election committee were to make contact with another influence of great importance, the utilitarianism of Jeremy Bentham and James Mill.[21] It was Bentham's and Mill's teaching more than any other that gave philosophical substance to the links between parliamentary and educational reform.

James Mill placed the education of the people at the core of his article 'On Government', written for the *Encyclopædia Britannica*. By a chain of utilitarian reasoning he arrived at the conclusion that the only good form of government was by popular representation; and if the people were unable to perceive and act in their own interests they must be taught to do so. He did not specifically address the question whether popular education or parliamentary reform should come first, but some time before his article appeared the necessary connection between the two had become a commonplace among radical reformers.[22] Francis Place, always convinced that education of the people must both precede and accompany other reforms, wrote in 1815, 'as brutality is destroyed by intelligence a desire to excel is generated, and this love of distinction directed in the right way is the prime mover towards good in all mankind.'[23] At the inaugural public meeting of the West London Lancasterian Association in 1813 the farmer and political economist Edward Wakefield expressed the same idea in terms of national happiness, taking for granted the utilitarian premise that 'the happiness of the great majority is ... the first of national objects'.[24]

The first three decades of the nineteenth century were critically important in the development of popular education; and the most fruitful educational debate of those years was over the rival claims of Andrew Bell and Joseph Lancaster to have founded the 'monitorial' system of teaching large numbers of children together in one classroom. It was with the camp of Joseph Lancaster that the Westminster radicals threw in their lot. The notion of setting older children to teach the younger ones cannot have been entirely new in the late eighteenth century, but by 1810 it was being adopted with unprecedented enthusiasm and on a large scale. To benefactors of any political or religious colour, the economy with which a great number of poor children could be taught by this method was a strong recommendation.[25] The heated partisanship involved in the debate over its origins brought in religious considerations, since Bell commanded the support of the Church of England and Lancaster that of dissenters. This factor ensured that the method would be taken up on both sides with ardent rivalry; and indeed there soon developed something of a race to build schools and claim small souls.[26] Apart from the two rivals, the National Schools Society and the Royal Lancasterian (after 1813 the British and Foreign School) Association, there were non-sectarian educationists who saw merits in the system. At New Lanark, Robert Owen incorporated it in his model factory school.[27] At the Edinburgh Academy the schoolmaster James Gray claimed that he found monitorial teaching very successful.[28] And a little later the Hill family used a modified monitorial method in their boarding school for middle-class children at Tottenham.[29]

Joseph Lancaster's supporters were an incongruous collection of Quakers and other dissenters, royal dukes and free-thinking radicals. Lancaster himself was a Quaker; and it was the leading London dissenters William Allen and Joseph Fox who founded the Royal Lancasterian Association and obtained the patronage of that strange prince the Duke of Kent.[30] By about 1811 the committee of the Association included Henry Brougham, Francis Place, James Mill, and Edward Wakefield.[31] The Royal Lancasterian Association was founded to support Lancaster's existing school in Borough Road Southwark and with a view to propagating his system of teaching throughout the country. Lancaster himself travelled around England giving lectures, and schools were founded in London and in provincial towns under the active patronage of the parent association.[32] Relations between Lancaster and his sponsors began to turn sour, however. His financial profligacy and ungovernable temper created serious problems and in 1813 he became bankrupt and was pensioned off as 'superintendent' of the Association's schools. The Royal Lancasterian Association changed its name to the British and Foreign School Society.[33] Soon after this, reports came from Lancaster's boarding school in Tooting that he had been more than zealous in administering corporal punishment to his apprentices; and following an inquiry his connection with the British and Foreign School Society virtually came to an end.[34]

In the same year when they broke with Lancaster and changed the name of their organization, several members of the Society embarked on an ambitious programme of providing 'schools for all' on a systematic basis in London. They embodied their plan in a new offshoot of the parent society, the West London Lancasterian Association, whose original members included Francis Place, James Mill, Edward Wakefield, Sir James Mackintosh, and Joseph Fox.[35] According to Wakefield, the idea of forming such an association arose from a conversation between himself and the Earl of Darnley, secretary to the St. Patrick's

Society which had a large fund at its disposal for educating Irish children. Darnley and Wakefield met with some other gentlemen at the house of Joseph Fox, and there it was decided to extend their aims to include children of all religious and national backgrounds.[36]

The West London Lancasterian Association attracted strong support. Both Sir Francis Burdett and Lord Cochrane promised donations, and other philanthropists who were actively interested included Lord Stanhope, the Duke of Bedford, Sir Samuel Romilly, Josiah Wedgwood junior, and Fowell Buxton. James Mill kept Bentham informed of progress. The Duke of Kent extended his patronage to the new association and also involved his brother the Duke of Sussex.[37] Committed political radicals formed the largest single group among the members of the WLLA. William Adams, Henry and Samuel Brooks, Thomas Cleary, Thomas Evans, Francis Place, John Richter, and Messrs. Long and Sturch were all members of the Westminster election committee whose names appeared on the WLLA committee list. In addition to them James Mill, Edward Wakefield, and Joseph Hume, whose formal association with the Westminster radicals began with the Lancasterian projects, all later began to play a part on the Westminster election committee.[38] Wakefield explicitly intended to use the committee as a whole in the work of the organization.[39] Wakefield, indeed, was the organizing genius behind the West London Lancasterian Association. To him unquestionably belongs the credit for the pioneering inquiries into the extent of educational need in part of the City of Westminster, which were made on the Association's behalf and later incorporated into the evidence before Brougham's Education Committee.[40]

At a meeting held in the British Coffee House in Cockspur Street on 2 August 1813, the West London Lancasterian Association for teaching Reading, Writing, Arithmetic, and Good Morals passed a remarkable set of resolutions.[41] It was to offer instruction to children of both sexes and all religious denominations in an area approximately corresponding to the City of Westminster, with a population of 356,000.[42] The avowed purpose of the Association was 'to take the children off the streets and train them up in goodness'.[43] To this end, printed copies of the resolutions were to be distributed to all 84,529 families in the area, and gentlemen volunteers were sought to make a house-to-house survey of the numbers of uneducated children.[44] In soliciting subscriptions the Association made it clear that the parents of uneducated children were particularly welcome to subscribe, and that a modest annual payment of five shillings would secure membership of the Association.[45] It was Wakefield's personal hope that permanent visitors could be secured to gather information on the condition of the working people throughout London.[46] His ambitions far outran the possibilities of such an organization, for the radicals' attitude to popular education did not altogether accord with that of their nonconformist colleagues. Projects of more modest scope were to prove beyond the competence of the West London Lancasterian Association.

At the end of 1813, however, the WLLA embarked on its schemes with great optimism. Edward Wakefield bore the brunt of the early administrative chores, despite the fact that he spent most of his time on his farm near Bury St. Edmunds.[47] He was the first speaker at the public meeting to launch the Association, and was responsible for the novel plan of making a house-to-house survey of children in need of schooling.[48] Francis Place felt that Wakefield would have provided the leadership that the Association needed had he been more often in London.[49] Throughout their correspondence Wakefield demonstrated his talent for publicity and administration: Sir James Mackintosh was very useful because he would appeal to the ladies; a public meeting in Westminster ought to be limited to ticket holders so that those who came would feel important; Place must use not only the Westminster committee but also twenty active district visitors to help him with 'the complete organisation of the whole metropolis'.[50] In his report to the committee on his survey of a small part of the Covent Garden division of the WLLA's area of concern he also displayed a gift for cogent philosophical argument:

> An ancient philosopher has said that a people are formed by laws, manners and philosophy; and narrow would be your pursuit were you only endeavouring to form a herd of reading and writing machines. It is through that instrument, by the study of useful books, that you will form moral habits, and a moral and instructed population will take care to be governed by laws that will suit their habits; and such a people will no doubt learn to exercise the reasoning faculties by which they will be enabled to judge of cause and effect, which is the philosophy of which Aristotle has spoken.[51]

To Wakefield as much as to any of his colleagues, the education of the people was but a means to the greatest of ends. But even when he permitted himself this brief glimpse of the grand design he did not lose sight of the practical problems. District visitors, he remarked in the paragraph following his philosophical exposition, must be instructed to find enough local collectors of subscriptions to enable them to keep an eye on every single family in their district. Parents must be taught their duty to their children, above all the duty of keeping them clean. In Edward Wakefield there was to be found that close alliance of high philosophical aims with attention to practical detail which character- ized the utilitarians at their best.

In his absence, the burden of work fell upon Francis Place, who found himself busier than he had ever been before;[52] and Wakefield became anxious about his friend's lack of tact in a delicate situation. 'You will, I am sure, be cautious how you alarm [the Quakers] by any religious or political declaration,' he wrote; and in the same letter he commended James Mill's 'fine principle and magnificent talent. When you want to carry a point with Allen and Fox, he must be set to work.'[53] But at first all went well. In the wider context of the parent British and Foreign school Society, plans were going ahead for the Borough Road School to become a training school for young teachers who would be sent out to Lancasterian schools 'in every part of the British dominions'.[54] By February 1814, Place could report that it was prospering. Meanwhile, Joseph Fox was doing good work in the south of Scotland, and had persuaded people in Edinburgh and Glasgow to pay £200 a year and travelling expenses to an inspector and superintendent of Lancasterian schools.[55]

'I am by no means out of heart with our association, although I am dissatisfied it moves so slowly,' commented Place.[56] But the WLLA, unlike the parent body, did not thrive on its increasing number of distinguished supporters.[57] The committee members were inactive or occupied with other matters;[58] meetings were cancelled (one of them, to Wakefield's surprise, because Brougham and Romilly were on cir- cuit).[59] The committee's apathy disguised two crucial differences of opinion. The first, which had already caused some dispute in the Association, concerned fees. Wakefield, Place, and Mill maintained that the new schools must levy some small charge; Fox, Allen, and others were equally insistent that it must not. The second issue was religion. Both questions fundamentally divided the radicals from the other philanthropists, and had implications that reached beyond the educational arena.

Francis Place insisted that the Lancasterian schools should charge fees; Edward Wakefield considered it vitally important and found support from Joseph Hume. Others were sympathetic to the idea, and Place felt that he had succeeded in convincing a sub-committee of the Association, which had been set up to consider the matter.[60] There were two main arguments in favour of charging fees. In the first place, charitable donations were an unreliable source of funds, likely to decline after the first wave of enthusiasm had passed. It was therefore desirable that the Lancasterian schools should establish themselves on a firm business footing, issuing shares to subscribers who would expect some kind of return on their investment. This would have the excellent result, in addition, of encouraging other people to set up similar schools. But over and above these considerations, 'the committee must abandon every attempt of degrading the people by drawing them into charity schools'.[61] Wakefield reinforced moral considerations by pointing out that decent shop keepers, the chief potential source of subscriptions to the WLLA, would not be interested in sending their children to free schools which would degrade them to the status of charity-children; and if they did not want to send their own children they would not subscribe at all.[62] Francis Place later recorded his opinion of charity: unthinking people, oppressed by the difficulty of accomplishing any permanent good,

> ... relieve themselves by the performance of what is vulgarly called charity. They give money, victuals, clothes etc. and thus by encouraging idleness and extinguishing enterprise, increase the evil they would remove, make pauperism more general and take from it the shame which is the best guarantee for industry and independence, without which there can be neither honesty, comfort nor virtue among the common people, who become too dependent and too degraded to be useful either to themselves or to the community.[63]

There spoke the laissez-faire liberal, preaching a gospel of self-help that cruelly ignored the realities of poverty. But the more genial side of this gospel was that concern for the dignity of working men which was the keystone of Francis Place's career, as it was of the political careers of several of his colleagues on the Westminster election committee. Years later, in his polemic against J. Silk Buckingham and the 'Drunken Committee', Place wrote bitterly of the moral condescension that the upper classes showed towards the lower:

> The working man must have no relaxation; he who drudges constantly against his will must have no such propensities as are allowed and cherished in his superior ...[64]

A favourable review of this pamphlet commented that 'the worst of the moral sensibility of the English public is that it is so irregularly and partially excited, that it penetrates so little below the surface'.[65] This remote and superficial sensibility was in radical eyes the enemy of self-improvement. It was against this that Place and Wakefield and their fellow radicals fought in the West London Lancasterian Association. Their efforts to attack the problem in a businesslike and unsentimental way showed up the division between the philanthropist's desire to ameliorate the situation and the radical's aim to change it.

Charity was an obstacle to the success of the WLLA, but the real stumbling block was religion. The original intention had been to teach 'reading, writing, arithmetic, and good morals' to children of both sexes and every denomination.[66] Religious instruction was to be based on the Bible alone.[67] But in March 1814 the Quaker Joseph Fox wrote to Francis Place insisting that the Bible ought to be the sole text used not only for religious instruction but for every other subject as well. He admitted that his only purpose in promoting the Association was 'to enable every child to read [the] Scriptures and in Scripture language *only* to enable them to come to a knowledge of the truth'.[68] Place's reply, uncharacteristically moderate in tone, expressed very well the common ground between all the radicals who were involved in the WLLA:

> What appears to you to be truth appears to me to be the reverse of truth, and knowing how widely men differ on matters purely speculative as all religion is and ever must remain, it appears to me that it is my duty as it is the duty of every man to treat one another's notions of truth with the greatest tenderness...
>
> I view [education] as an immense instrument for moral training, you would add – for religious. We all agree in the utility of good morals. We disagree most widely and particularly on religious subjects, and we say let us pull together for the general good as far as we can agree, and let us leave that on which we disagree alone.[69]

His reasonableness did not succeed in deflecting the blow, however, and Fox began to undermine his colleague's position in the Association by accusing him of being an unbeliever.[70] Not long afterwards Joseph Lancaster himself raised the question of Place's religious views within the British and Foreign Society, and despite the good offices of Samuel Whitbread and the Duke of Kent Place was eventually expelled from the committee.[71]

Francis Place continued to give help and advice to both the WLLA and the British and Foreign Society, but after a further eighteen months of wrangles over the religious problem, the WLLA finally expired.[72] It had had a stormy existence, and the atmosphere of suspicion and personal feud that pervaded its committee did not help to smooth over the great problem of the place of religion in the schools' curricula. The radical wing of the Association included at least four free-thinkers (Place, Wakefield, Hume, Mill, and probably several others). In view of the fierce sectarian battle then raging between the Anglican National Society and the nonconformist British and Foreign Society, it was too much to expect of the nonconformists that they would cede an important branch of the society they had founded to wholly non-denominational or to secular teaching.

The members of the West London Lancasterian Association had expended their talents and energies in a thankless cause; and not for several years would any of them be rewarded with greater success in their efforts to provide education for the poor. But this was the first step that Westminster radicals as an identifiable group took towards social reform. As such it clarified some of the features of their movement and helped to distinguish their approach to social problems from that of more conservative or apolitical reformers.

It was of the utmost importance to the radical members of the WLLA that the poor and uneducated should not be patronized. Members of the Westminster election committee, many of them self-educated themselves, showed a consistent concern for the dignity of their fellow citizens. The pride they took in organizing an election without bribery or riots was analogous to their insistence that the Association's schools must be independent of mere charity. In this and in later enterprises such as the London Mechanics' Institute, proud words concealed what was in reality a tenuous distinction; for benefactors like Sir Francis Burdett or Lord Stanhope must have realized that their 'subscriptions' were likely to be outright donations disguised. Nevertheless, the participation of the small tradesman and artisan in his own political destiny or his children's education was at the core of the Westminster radicals' approach to reform. A second distinctive feature carried over from their political habits was the great thoroughness with which the radicals tackled educational reform. The meticulous accumulation of social details later became a hallmark of what has been called 'Benthamism'. In 1813–14 it was simply businesslike. The radicals' developing techniques of thorough canvassing, dividing the city up into manageable sections, found a parallel in their work for education.[73] The form of teaching that they chose may have been narrow and misguided, though its cheapness provided a partial justification. But there was inspiration in the way that Francis Place, Edward Wakefield, and their colleagues set about providing their schools, piling a pyramid of aspirations upon a solid base of fact. Thus, although the West London Lancasterian Association turned out to be a brief and unhappy episode in the history of Westminster radicalism, we can see in it the outlines of a pioneering approach to reform that was comprehensive and professional in both its outlook and its methods.

Notes

1. The history of the 1807 election has been considered in several works, notably: Graham Wallas, *The Life of Francis Place, 1771–1854* (1898); M. W. Patterson, *Sir Francis Burdett and his Times, 1770–1844* 2 vols. (1931); E. P. Thompson, *The Making of the English Working Class* (2nd edn. 1968), chap. 13; and J. M. Main, 'Radical Westminster, 1807–20' in *Historical Studies (Australia and New Zealand)*, (1966). The present essay is based on part of my unpublished Oxford D. Phil. thesis, 'Westminster Radicalism 1807–1832', (1975), in which the election is also treated. I would like to take this opportunity of thanking Miss Betty Kemp, Dr. J. R. Dinwiddy, and my husband Dr. F. K. Prochaska for their help with many of the questions raised in this essay.

2. British Library Add. mss. 27838 f. 158 and *passim*; [Francis Place and John Richter] *An exposition of the circumstances which gave rise to the Election of Sir Francis Burdett for the City of Westminster, and of the principles which governed the Committee who conducted that Election* (1807), p. 6.

3. Thompson, *Making of the English Working Class, op. cit.*, p. 506.

4. Alexander Stephens, *Memoirs of John Horne Tooke* 2 vols. (1813) ii. p. 476; Wallas, *Life of Francis Place*, pp. 29, 57–60; Mary Thale (ed.) *The Autobiography of Francis Place* (1972), pp. 136–7, 143, 217–18; Add. mss. 35153, f. 1.

5. Stephens, *Memoirs of Tooke* ii. pp. 306–8 and *passim*; F. D. Cartwright (ed.) *The Life and Correspondence of Major Cartwright* 2 vols. (1826) i. p. 355 and *passim*. Although Francis Place usually wrote slightingly of Cartwright, he saw a lot of him and cast no doubt on his importance in Westminster in the early years after 1807. Wallas, *Life of Francis Place*, pp. 62–3; Naomi C. Miller, 'John Cartwright and radical parliamentary reform, 1809–19, *English Historical Review* (1968), pp. 711–15; Prochaska, 'Westminster radicalism', pp. 8–13, 45, 52–3.

6. Frequent mention of the proceedings can be found in William Cobbett, *Political Register*, e.g. vols. xiii, 863, xv, 686–92, 820–3, xvii, 243–55, 587–8; *Life and Correspondence of Major Cartwright*, ii, pp. 371–80 and *passim*; Add. mss. 27838–40 *passim*.

7. Add. mss. 27838–40 *passim*.

8. Add. mss. 27838 ff. 325, 328–9, 330.

9. Cobbett, *Political Register* vol. xv (January–June 1809), table of contents; Wallas, *Life of Francis Place*, p. 48.

10. The episode is described in detail in Patterson, *Sir Francis Burdett*, i. pp. 240–94 and in Wallas, *Life of Francis Place*, pp. 48–56.

11. Add. mss. 27840 ff. 3–8, 55, 57, 74.

12. For a discussion of the phrase and its history see Elie Halévy, *The Growth of Philosophic Radicalism* (trans. Mary Morris, 1928), p. 261.

13. *Life and Correspondence of Major Cartwright*, ii. pp. 10–11, 24, 375–80; Sir Samuel Romilly, *Memoirs of the Life of Sir Samuel Romilly* (edited by his sons, 1840), iii. pp. 45–6, 55. Miller, 'John Cartwright and parliamentary reform', pp. 715–19, rightly points to the far greater success of the Union in the provinces as a result of Cartwright's later efforts.

14. Naomi C. Miller, 'Major John Cartwright and the Founding of the Hampden Club', *Historical Journal* (1974).

15. *Parliamentary Debates*, xiv, 15 June 1809, 1041–56; Add. mss. 27840 ff. 7, 10, 74 contain some discussion of the committee's requirements of an mp, in which it was implied that Burdett was exempt largely because he had a popular following and the committee therefore could not afford to alienate him.

16. *Life and Correspondence of Major Cartwright*, ii. pp. 30–45; Samuel Bamford, *Passages in the Life of a Radical* with a preface by Tim Hilton, (1967), pp. 13–14; Add. mss. 27828,

ff. 226–7. Miller, 'John Cartwright and parliamentary reform', pp. 718–24 and 'Major Cartwright and the founding of the Hampden Club', seriously undervalues the attention paid by other radicals to the provinces after 1811.

17. Add. MSS. 27840 ff. 14, 23, 55, 63, 109–10, 113; Add. MSS. 27828 ff. 226–7; Thompson, *The Making of the English Working Class*, *op. cit.*, pp. 541–2; Roy A. Church and S. D. Chapman, 'Gravener Henson and the Making of the English Working Class' in *Land, Labour and Population in the Industrial Revolution* edited by E. L. Jones and G. E. Mingay (1967).

18. *A letter on Parliamentary Reform* (1793), pp. 6–7.

19. E.g. in *An Enquiry concerning Political Justice and its influence on Morals and happiness* (3rd edn., 1798), i. p. xxvi, summary of principles.

20. Thomas Paine, *The Rights of Man*, part 2 (2nd edn., 1792), pp. 126–7; Thomas Holcroft, *Memoirs* (edited by William Hazlitt, 1816), *passim*.

21. Francis Place must have met James Mill by about 1811, when they were both on the committee of the Royal Lancasterian Association, Add. MSS. 27823 f. 14; Chester W. New, *The Life of Henry Brougham to 1830* (1961), pp. 203–4. For the development of their friendship and the extent to which Mill became involved in the West London Lancasterian Association, see Add. MSS. 35152, *passim*.

22. James Mill, *An Essay on Government* with an introduction by Ernest Barker (1937), pp. 63–73.

23. Add. MSS. 27823 f. 67, Francis Place to William Allen, 19 September 1815.

24. *Ibid.*, f. 88.

25. E.g. Sir James Mackintosh's emphasis on cheapness in his address to the West London Lancasterian Association in August 1813, reported in the *Philanthropist*, iii. (1813), pp. 369–74.

26. W. H. G. Armytage, *Four Hundred Years of English Education* (2nd edn., 1970), pp. 89–91. Francis Place remarked on the importance of religious partisanship in making a cause attractive, Add. MSS. 27823 f. 125.

27. Robert Owen, *New View of Society* (1813), pp. 41–52; *The Life of Robert Owen. Written by himself* (1857–8), pp. 289 *seq*.

28. Add. MSS. 35152 f. 16.

29. University College London, Bentham Papers box 18 f. 180, prospectus of Bruce Castle school.

30. The Duke of Kent was a genuine philanthropist with a particular interest in education. Far from being an orthodox Anglican, he favoured religious eccentrics and was a friend of Robert Owen who claimed to receive messages from the Duke's spirit after his death. *Life of Robert Owen*, pp. 192, 225, 229. There is some disagreement about whether Joseph Fox was a Baptist or a Quaker, but Francis Place was certainly under the impression that he was a Quaker and refers to him as such throughout his papers on the WLLA.

31. Add. MSS. 27823 f. 14; New, *Life of Brougham*, pp. 203–4.

32. Wallas, *Life of Francis Place*, p. 94.

33. *Ibid.*, pp. 93–5; Add. MSS. 27823 ff. 16–21. Wallas's account omits the charges of sadism against Lancaster.

34. Add. MSS. 27823 ff. 25–8.

35. *Ibid.*, ff. 80–8.

36. House of Commons Reports from Committees (1816), ii. 1 February–2 July, p. 43.

37. Add. MSS. 27823 ff. 99 *seq*.; Add. MSS. 35152 ff. 8–9, 24–6, 33–4, 56 *seq*.

38. Add. MSS. 27840 f. 35, cash-book for the 1814 Westminster election, shows Mill as a subscriber; f. 109, letter from Edward Wakefield to John Richter, (?) October 1814, shows Wakefield's active involvement in radical politics and with the Westminster committee in particular. Add. MSS. 27845 f. 10, committee list for 1818, is one of many including the names of both Hume and Mill.

39. Add. mss. 35152 ff. 14–15, 56 *seq.*; Add. mss. 27823 ff. 99 *seq.*
40. House of Commons Report from Committees (1816), ii. 1 February–2 July, pp. 36–7, 40–4.
41. *The Philanthropist*, iii. (1813), pp. 361–3.
42. *Ibid.*, pp. 361–2.
43. *Ibid.*
44. *Ibid.*
45. *Ibid.*
46. Add. mss. 35152 f. 27.
47. Add. mss. 35152 f. 26; Add. mss. 27823 f. 88. Wakefield's correspondence with Place is the best single source of information on the wlla.
48. Add. mss. 27823 f. 88.
49. Add. mss. 35152 f. 26.
50. *Ibid.*, ff. 14, 35.
51. Report dated 6 September 1813, inserted in House of Commons Reports from Committees (1816), ii. pp. 40–2.
52. Add. mss. 35152 ff. 14–15, 24.
53. *Ibid.*, ff. 14–15, 35.
54. This was Wakefield's hope. *Ibid.*, f. 6.
55. *Ibid.*, f. 37.
56. *Ibid.*
57. These included Lord Holland, Sir Samuel Romilly and Francis Horner. *Ibid.*, f. 25.
58. John Richter and Francis Place were occupied with the campaign to repeal the Statute of Apprentices, although Place still found time to spend on the wlla. *Ibid.*, f. 38.
59. *Ibid.*
60. *Ibid.* Wakefield urged Place to dwell on the matter with each member of the committee individually. *Ibid.*, ff. 12–13, 35.
61. *Ibid.*, ff. 14–15.
62. House of Commons Reports from Committees (1816), ii. p. 41.
63. Add. mss. 27823 f. 150 (Francis Place to William Allen, 7 March 1814).
64. Francis Place, *Improvement of the Working People – Drunkenness – Education* (1834), p. 13. See also Brian Harrison, 'Two roads to social reform: Francis Place and the "Drunken Committee" of 1834', *Historical Journal*, xi (1968), pp. 272–300.
65. Review by the Unitarian journalist and politician W. J. Fox, inserted in Add. mss. 27825 f. 227.
66. Add. mss. 27823 ff. 88, 118; Add. mss. 35152 f. 45.
67. Add. mss. 35152 f. 45; Add. mss. 27823 f. 88.
68. Add. mss. 35152 f. 43.
69. Add. mss. 35152 f. 45.
70. *Ibid.*, f. 45; Add. mss. 27823 ff. 96–9. At one point the amazing charge was made that Thomas Cleary, a Roman Catholic, planned to introduce deistical instruction into the Lancasterian schools, Add. mss. 35152 f. 120–1.
71. Add. mss. 27823 ff. 25–7, 28–31. Lancaster's attack came just after Place had been on a sub-committee to investigate charges of sadism against him.
72. Add. mss. 27823 ff. 52–3, 66–78, 115–18; Add. mss. 35152 ff. 99–109; Place collection of newspaper cuttings no. LX, *passim* (unfoliated) and Chrestomathic day school minute book, p. 23.
73. Add. mss. 27838–43 *passim*; Wallas, *Life of Francis Place*, pp. 133–4, quotes Place's letter to George Ensor – 1819, in which he describes the high degree of organization that he achieved for the first time at the election of 1819; but many of the tactics then used had already been tried out at earlier elections.

JOHN STEVENSON

The Queen Caroline Affair

On 8 January 1820, a government informer reported to the Home
Office his view of the state of metropolitan radicalism: 'Disaffection and
seditious clamour,' he wrote, 'is at present stopped and silenced in the
Metropolis and its suburbs.' Apart from the millenarian prophecies of
the followers of Joanna Southcott, the country and the capital seemed
quiet.[1] Within six months, however, the calm which had descended
after Peterloo and the Six Acts was rudely shattered. On 29 January
George III died and the Prince Regent came to the throne. In February
the Cato Street conspiracy was uncovered and its leaders brought to the
scaffold. In June occurred the most startling event of all, Caroline of
Brunswick returned from self-imposed exile to claim her rights as the
wife of the new King. The struggle which ensued has often been treated
as a rather farcical epitaph upon the years of agitation and distress
which followed the Napoleonic Wars. For some historians, the affair has
seemed an aberration from the mainstream of reform activity which
stretched from the latter part of the eighteenth century to the Great
Reform Act. But the Queen Caroline affair offers some fascinating
insights into the development of radicalism in general, and London
radicalism in particular. In terms of coverage in the newspapers, radical
agitation, and popular involvement it was the most impressive display
of public opinion in the capital since the days of Wilkes. It brought the
Ministry near to resignation or dismissal more than once during its
course and even seemed at times to threaten revolution. Not only did it
form the high-water mark of the post-war agitation, before the
relatively calm years of the eighteen twenties, but it was also the last of
the old-style metropolitan agitations in which London gave a lead to the
rest of the country.[2]

The Prince Regent and Caroline had been married in 1795. Almost from the beginning the marriage was unhappy – George had been married already, secretly and illegally to a Roman Catholic widow, Mrs. Fitzherbert. George did little to alter his profligate ways and Caroline was sufficiently indiscreet to be accused in 1805 of having an illegitimate child. Although exonerated from the graver charges by 'the delicate investigation', her reputation was destroyed and George began to contemplate divorce. But in a way which forshadowed later events, she was able to attract to herself the support of a number of Whigs and radicals who turned her home at Kensington Palace into a 'rival court'. Brougham cynically admitted that she was useful as 'a Constitutional means of making head against a revenue of 105 millions, an army of half a million, and 800 millions of debt'. In addition, Caroline kept a small house at Bayswater where she entertained a wide range of friends and acquaintances, including Canning, Byron, and Sir Francis Burdett. In 1813 when the Prince Regent tried to prevent Caroline from seeing her daughter, she had considerable backing from Whig and radical sources. Cobbett supported her in the *Political Register*, while the City of London presented her with an address. Deputations were sent to Caroline from Westminster and Middlesex, linking her grievances with the need to reform the House of Commons. Other towns and cities were also called upon to demonstrate their support for Caroline against the 'tyranny' of her husband. But in spite of these professions of support, she wearied of the battle and took ship for the Continent in August 1814.[3] Already, however, she had shown the ease with which conflicts within the royal family could be turned to advantage by the opposition and by reformers. No divorce had been obtained and she remained the legal wife of the Prince Regent.

His ascent to the throne in 1820 turned what was a half-forgotten episode of the regency into an awkward dilemma. If the Regent was now King, was Caroline also Queen? As preparations were made for a lavish Coronation, the matter became increasingly urgent. The King had a new mistress and determined to divorce his existing consort. The day after his father's death, George IV insisted that Caroline's name should be excluded from the prayers for the health and safety of the Royal Family. On 12 February the changes were acknowledged in the *Gazette*. This precipitate action by the King immediately created a live political issue out of the Queen's affair. It alerted opponents of the Ministry that the Queen might become a rallying point for them if she chose to defend her position. Equally, it threw the Ministry into confusion. They had no desire to instigate divorce proceedings against Caroline, fearing that the King's reputation would be as liable to damage as his consort's. They hoped to achieve a compromise with

Caroline by offering her an annuity in return for staying abroad. When, however, they put this plan for separation rather than divorce to the King, he reacted angrily with talk of dismissal. Eventually, after much persuasion, the King was brought round to the idea that separation would be the best solution for the 'peace of the country' and his own 'dignity and peace of mind'. The question now was whether Caroline would accept. The Ministry's intermediary was Brougham whom Liverpool trusted as an envoy because of his past friendship with Caroline. Brougham on his part hoped to use his position of influence to obtain a suitable sinecure or position from the Government.[4]

It was scarcely an auspicious moment in which to imperil further the prestige of the monarchy. While the immediate threat of sedition had been thwarted with the discovery of the Cato Street conspiracy, it did little to calm the country at large. Lord Sidmouth at the Home Office was convinced that the plotters had intended the total overthrow of the Government in conjunction with a widespread conspiracy among the manufacturing districts. He wrote to Wellington that 'a simultaneous explosion appears to be meditated at an early period'.[5] The trial and execution of Thistlewood and his fellow conspirators gave little cause for satisfaction with embarrassing revelations about the use of *agents provocateurs*. The continent was also in a state of upheaval, with revolutions in Spain and Portugal and liberal stirrings in Italy and Germany. It was in March that Peel wrote to Croker, expressing his feeling that 'the tone of England' had changed in a more 'liberal' direction and that some form of accommodation would have to be found for it. Peel felt that the situation might become such that Whigs and Tories would have to come together to pass reform in order to beat off the forces of radicalism.[6]

Only three years earlier, Peel had warned of the potentially dangerous consequences of any division within the royal family at a time when ill-feeling amongst the populace was running so high: 'I expect to see the clouds burst furiously. If there should arise any division in the Royal Family, it will be the match to fire the gunpowder.' Such a moment seemed to have arrived, but Caroline's attitude would prove crucial. Since her departure from England in 1814, her progress through the Continent had been a source of gossip. At one point she was touring Italy in a blue-lined gilt and mother-of-pearl phaeton, shaped like a sea-shell and driven by a child dressed as an operatic angel in spangles and flesh-coloured tights. Lady Bury encountered her at a party in Geneva in 1814, 'dressed *en Venus*, or rather not dressed further than the waist'. At Milan she took a lover, Count Bartolomeo Bergami and travelled about the Mediterranean with him. So blatant was her conduct that the Ministry had already begun to collect evidence about her behaviour in 1819, with the so-called 'Milan Commission'. With the King's death, however, Caroline determined to return to England, intending either to establish her rights as Queen or bargain for them as stoutly as possible.[7]

Almost as soon as the Queen's name was excluded from the Liturgy, London radical circles began to stir at the prospect of a new cause with which to attack the Ministry. On 15 February Anne Cobbett wrote that 'a Queen's Party is forming'. She went on: 'It is expected there will be sad work about the new Queen. She is abroad, and there is a strong party here for her, who want her to come home and be crowned with her husband and she has quite spirit enough to do anything. But Prinny will not let her be crowned ... If she comes to England there will certainly be a row, many will espouse her cause out of mere *obstinacy* to the new King.'[8] Although the Queen remained in Italy until the end of April, she wrote to Liverpool on 16 March, declaring her intention to fight for her title. A longer letter to the London newspapers explained her motives and appointed Brougham and Denman her Attorney and Solicitor Generals. In May the Home Office was informed that there had been a revival among the 'disaffected' as a result of the encouragement given to them by Alderman Wood, Sir Robert Wilson, and other MPs sympathetic to the Queen's cause. By the end of the month it was claimed that the radicals had set up a 'Liberal alliance' and appointed a 'Directory Committee' in London to seek out the 'most efficient means of carrying on sedition'.[9] On 17 May Cartwright, the veteran radical, took the chair at a meeting in London to celebrate the Queen's birthday. Anticipating a grave turn in events, Thomas Fowell Buxton feared that 'we are going into an inquiry which will lay bare the most disgraceful scenes in the royal family on both sides; the probable consequence will be the impeachment of the Queen. The nation will be divided, and all the lower orders will be on her side; and the certain consequences, disturbances, riots, and bloodshed.' Sir Robert Wilson, Whig MP for Southwark, told Grey that 'The present arrival of the Queen will, however, produce some decisive results. If she comes it is my firm belief ministers will resign.'[10]

The most important contact the Queen made with the English radicals was with Alderman Wood. Wood was a Whig, MP for the City of London, and one of the leaders of City radicalism. Place held a fairly low opinion of him, but described him as a 'useful City man' and 'a friend to improvement and a parliamentary reformer'. As an active City radical he had played a prominent part in earlier agitations, especially in the campaign in support of Sir Francis Burdett in 1810 when Wood has used his position as Sheriff of London and Middlesex to embarrass the Government in their attempts to arrest Burdett for a libel upon the House of Commons. A firm upholder of the City's rights and liberties, he had also played an active role in the campaign on behalf of the Queen in 1813. His support provided Caroline with the backing of the City radicals and the possibilities of wider support in the capital. Wood in turn, seems to have reciprocated the favour of the Queen, and became one of her strongest supporters in the struggle which was to ensue.[11] The Queen wrote to Wood on 15 April asking him to meet her at Calais. Wood left for the Continent in May with Lady Anne Hamilton; Wilson informed Grey that 'Wood is certainly gone to get her.'[12] He met the Queen at Montbeliard, near Basancon in Burgundy. Together they journeyed to St. Omer where the Government's emissary, Brougham, was carrying the offer of a pension if the Queen would stay out of the country. Brougham was both the Queen's adviser and the Ministry's representative. He was trusted by Liverpool and was genuinely convinced that the offer he bore was a reasonable compromise. Unfortunately he aroused the Queen's suspicions and she refused the compromise offered to her. When Lord. Hutchinson intervened, she presented him with an ultimatum which it was impossible for him to accept. On 5 June Caroline and Wood took a packet-boat from Calais and arrived in Dover the same afternoon. She was greeted with a propitious sign: the garrison fired a Royal Salute and she journeyed to London amid enthusiastic crowds and the ringing of church bells.

Wood had written in advance to his friends in London to warn them of the Queen's embarkation. According to the Government's informant: 'The disaffected are all in a motion to raise the population of the metropolis to receive her in triumphant manner from a spirit of hostility to His Majesty and not from any goodwill to Her Majesty.' He mentioned a number of radicals who were becoming involved in the Queen's cause, including Thomas Wooler, editor of *The Black Dwarf* and John Thelwall, the ex-LCS member.[13] In London interest was suspended in all other subjects. Croker had warned that the Queen's arrival would make 'a great sensation among the lower and middling orders'. Grey feared 'a Jacobin Revolution more bloody than that of France'. Another saw it as the last possibility of 'a convulsion' when 'the violence of political agitation appeared to be fast subsiding'.[14] Wilson recorded: 'The inhabitants of London seem alarmed as the day approaches ... the mob is pressing in more and more open expressions in favour of the Queen – so that there are many of the officers who are unwilling to stick out with confidence as to the conduct of their men in the time of peril.' The first of many suggestions, not all unfounded, that the soldiers garrisoning the capital might support the Queen.[15]

Caroline's progress from Dover was a triumphal procession. On 6 June she entered the capital with Wood at her side to the acclaim of a large crowd. The mob dragged her coach through the streets and as it passed Carlton House, Wood rose to give three cheers. The sentries at the gates presented arms and the procession was followed by a large crowd to Wood's house in South Audley Street where the Queen was to lodge. One witness wrote: 'I never saw more and such agitation in the public mind and amongst all classes – even White's cheered the arrival of the Queen when it was known . . .'[16] Already there was abundant evidence that the populace had found a new champion. Croker reported that the mob was enforcing a general illumination. Sidmouth was unable to get into his own house for a hostile mob and Wellington's coach had its windows broken. The Duke, held up by a gang of workmen with pickaxes who demanded that he show support for the Queen, unburdened himself of the memorable reply: 'Well, gentlemen, since you will have it so, God save the Queen – and may all your wives be like her.'[17]

The Queen's arrival in the capital created a great stir. Greville wrote: 'It is impossible to conceive the sensation created by her arrival. Nobody either blames or approves of her sudden return but all ask, what will be done next? How is it to end?' Brougham recorded: 'It is impossible to describe the universal, and strong, even violent, feelings of the people, not only in London but all over the country . . . The crowd collected wherever they knew her to be, and called her to appear at the windows of whatever house she was in.'[18] It took a little time for various shades of opinion to assess the situation. The Government had two courses of action open to it: it could attempt to continue negotiations or instigate proceedings to obtain a divorce. Wilberforce suggested that negotiations be recommenced and received encouragement from the Queen. The King, however, remained unhappy with the idea of compromise and even began to sound out the Whigs to see if they would instigate the divorce proceedings which he regarded as the most preferable course of action. Thus the first weekend of the Queen's arrival saw the Ministry in crisis. Just when the administration seemed to have weathered the worst of the post-war difficulties, it was faced with the situation so feared by Peel in 1817. By 11 June the King had recovered his calm and negotiations were opened with the Queen. It soon became obvious that there remained a wide gulf between the two sides. The Queen would only accept a settlement if it implied no misconduct on her part: she required some recognition of her status as

Queen, either by the insertion of her name in the Liturgy or by the appropriate formalities when living abroad. After a last attempt at compromise by Wilberforce, negotiations broke down. The Ministry had now to turn to legal attempts to deprive the Queen of her title. They proceeded with a Bill of Pains and Penalties based upon the evidence they had collected of her misconduct while out of the country.[19] The trial of the Queen was also to be a trial of strength between the Ministers and the supporters which Caroline had gathered about her.

An important factor in the Queen's refusal of compromise was the support she was getting from radical circles in the capital. One of the earliest and most prominent followers of the Queen was Cobbett. He was one of the people contacted by Alderman Wood the night before the Queen's arrival in the country. Cobbett and Wood had met only once before, but Wood must have known that Cobbett had supported the Queen before she left England in 1814 and that the brilliant publicist would make a formidable recruit to her cause. Although Cobbett somewhat resented the way in which Wood controlled correspondence and access to the Queen, he put his talents and influence at her disposal. As early as 8 June he was advising the Queen against compromise, arguing that her 'powerful, active, vigilant, and implacable' enemies would use any suggestion of negotiation to 'convince the people there is some truth in the allegations'. Two days later he urged the Queen not to accept 'any compromise', informing her that the print shops already depicted her in royal robes with a crown and sceptre. A week later he was advising the Queen to make a direct appeal to the House of Commons over the heads of Ministers. On 20 June he registered a 'violent shock' at the publication of details of the negotiation between the Queen and the Ministers. By the end of June, however, when negotiations had virtually broken down, Cobbett was urging her to rely upon the strength of public opinion. Parliament, he argued, would do nothing for her except in so far as it was influenced by public opinion.[20]

Indeed, opinion did seem to be with her. Not only was Cobbett ready to throw his skills into the struggle, but there appeared to be almost inexhaustible support for the Queen from the London populace. The Government was informed that the Queen was convinced that the people were on her side and that every effort was being made to create 'tumult and insurrection'.[21] And, for a few days in June, it did appear that the worst fears of disturbances and disorder might be realized. On 15 June there was a tremor of mutiny in the 3rd Regiment of Guards in the Mews Barracks. The First Battalion refused to stand to duty through one night and on the following morning a group refused to give up their arms and ammunition when requested. This followed persistent rumours that the soldiers were openly drinking the Queen's health. Eventually the mutinous solders were talked round and marched out of the capital to Portsmouth. Mobs which collected around the barracks after they had gone were dispersed by loyal troops from the Horse Guards. Lord Sidmouth later recorded that the mutiny was the most serious crisis in the whole of the post-war period. In fact, the grievances of the troops were almost entirely concerned with pay and conditions. The alarm of the government had given them an onerous round of duties for which they claimed they ought to receive extra-pay. Nonetheless, the Queen had proved a focus for complaints. The troops were reported by Greville to have marched through Brentford crying 'God Save the Queen'.[22]

It was as a focus for a miscellany of discontents that the Queen now appeared dangerous. In the debate in the House of Commons on the restoration of the Queen's name to the Liturgy, Denman used a significant phrase when he said that 'If her Majesty was included in any general prayer, it was in the prayer of all who are desolate and oppressed.' She was beginning to act as the representative of all manner of groups and interests, in the traditional role of the 'reversionary interest'. Not least she brought some sort of unity to the divided forces of London radicalism. The City, under Wood's guidance, was throwing its weight behind her; Freemantle informed the Duke of Buckingham: 'The City is completely with her, not the Common Council, but the shopkeepers and merchants.' Common Council did, however, pass a series of anti-ministerial motions, one of them protesting against the stationing of military forces in the City while they were debating the Queen's affair. A City address to the Lords signed by 61 members of Common Council condemned the Bill of Pains and Penalties as militating 'against the established rules of justice and equity' and 'calculated to weaken the stability of the throne'. It continued: 'It appears to this Court that by persisting in these measures the peace, the security, and the welfare of the realm may be endangered, and the succession to the crown weakened and impaired.' This was the most strongly worded address from the City of London to the Crown since the height of anti-war activity in the mid-1790s.[23]

Other reformers were active too. Cartwright was engaged in attending public meetings in support of the Queen and presenting addresses to her. In July he was trying to organize a public dinner in support of the revolutions in Spain and Italy. He linked the revolutions abroad, demands for reform of Parliament, and the Queen's affair. 'If it ever (the authority of Parliament) before could have been doubted,' he wrote, 'it must now, I conceive, in consequence of the present outrageous proceedings against majesty itself, in the person of the Queen, impress itself on the public mind, with irresistable force.' Thus Dr. Samuel Parr expressed his view in a letter to Cartwright: 'I hold with you that the honour of the Queen is closely connected with the constitutional rights of the people; and at all events we are gaining ground against a venal and oppressive crew in the palace, in the council chamber, and in both houses of Parliament.'[24] At first J. C. Hobhouse, the Whig MP for Westminster, dismissed the affair as of little importance, writing four days after the Queen's arrival that: 'I own I do not think the matter of much importance except so much as it may aid the programme of reform.' By 18 June, however, he recorded meetings with Burdett and Wood in which the Queen's affair was discussed.[25] A meeting of the Westminster Electors early in July brought the forces of Westminster radicalism behind the Queen, even though Burdett remained aloof from the cause.

Most impressive of all, however, was the support of the London population. Not only did the mob attack any failure to show proper respect for the Queen, but support also took the form of organized processions. One witness recorded that:

> When the Queen took up her residence at Brandenburg House on 3rd August, there began a series of processions, from the extreme East to the extreme West, that manifested at once the energy and the folly of democracy in its wildest hour of excitement. Often riding to Windsor have I been detained by an army of working men, with bands, and banners, and placards, headed by deputations of their several committees with wands of office – all terribly in earnest – all perfectly convinced of the Queen's immaculate purity – all resolved that oppression should not triumph – a peaceful multitude, but one that in any other country would have seemed the herald, if not the manifestation of, Revolution.[26]

Addresses and deputations continued to arrive in the Queen's support. Creevey saw the sailors present their address:

> I heard a noise of hurrahing and shouting in the street; so I ran out to see. I may say, the navy of England marching to Brandenburg House with an address to the Queen. I have seen nothing like this before – nothing approaching to it.[27]

The radicals were convinced that the Queen's cause depended upon her ability to mobilize public opinion. Cobbett's daughter wrote to the Queen at the end of June to say how disturbed she was that Caroline was not going to the theatre and urged her to maintain her public appearances. The Queen, she claimed, 'has no real and efficient reliance, except on the people'. Six weeks later, Anne Cobbett was clearly better pleased with Caroline's performance. Having seen the Queen drive by she reported that 'She is in fact just what one could fancy a *Queen* ought to be.'[28]

Support for the Queen was certainly both impressive and extensive in the capital. Creevey wrote that:

> Every Wednesday the scene which caused such alarm at Manchester is reported under the very nose of Parliament and all the constituted authorities and in a tenfold degree more alarming. A certain number of regiments of the efficient population of the town march on each of these days in a regular lock-step, four or five abreast, banners flying, music playing. I should like anyone to tell me what is to come next if this organised army loses its temper.[29]

The second reading of the Bill of Pains and Penalties on 17 August led to renewed addresses and deputations. So alarmed was the Government, that the artillery were moved up from Woolwich. Two regiments of Life Guards were posted in Palace Yard and another in Westminster Hall, where a train of field-pieces was also stationed. Although no serious disturbances broke out, a large crowd assembled at 8.00 a.m. and stayed throughout the day, only dispersing about 10.0 p.m.[30]

Although the bill passed its second reading there was a growing conviction that the affair was getting out of hand. Peel wrote to Croker:

> I do think the Queen's affair very formidable. It is a famous ingredient in the cauldron which has been bubbling a long time, and upon which, as it seemed to me, the Government could never discern the least simmering. They added a blow-pipe, however, when they omitted the queen's name in the Liturgy: when they established a precedent of dethronement for imputed personal misconduct. Surely this was not the time for robbing Royalty of the exterior marks of respect and, for preaching up the anti-divine right doctrines . . . What is to be the end of it?[31]

The Black Dwarf had few doubts, 'Depend upon it, the house is tottering . . . and all the exertions of all the ministerial mob can not prevent it from falling.'[32] Popular hand-bills were openly hinting at the threat of the succession and appeals were being made to the example of revolutions on the continent. Under the title of 'Revolution in Naples, effected by the Soldiers', a hand-bill printed by William Benbow praised the conduct of the army of Naples for imposing 'a representative free Constitution'. It concluded: 'Feeble indeed is the tenure of the throne that depends on the arm of power, and is not fixed in the love of the subject.' Another ferociously lampooned the King as an 'infirm elderly gentleman' who 'fancies himself the politest man in Europe'. Its last lines ran: 'It is of the utmost consequence to himself that he should be at his post, or he may lose his place; one of his predecessors having been cashiered for his misconduct.'[33]

It was impossible for the Whigs to remain unaffected by a popular cause which offered an excellent opportunity for embarrassing or even toppling the Government. Some, however, were restrained by their belief in the Queen's guilt and the distaste she had engendered by her conduct abroad. Erskine, Donoughmore, Hutchinson, and Lauderdale were all hesitant about supporting her. Brougham and Denman had pledged to act for Caroline, though the former's involvement owed more to self-interest than any great affection for the Queen. Grey, Russell, Mackintosh, and Tierney remained undecided and relatively uncommitted. Several made a distinction between opposing ministerial actions and approving of the Queen's character and conduct.[34] Even Burdett, one of the most potent forces in metropolitan radicalism was lukewarm about the Queen's cause. He took a somewhat cold-blooded attitude to the proceedings against her, arguing that it would probably be more useful if the Bill of Pains and Penalties passed, 'then for the tug of war'.[35] His attitude was more typical of the Whigs than of the Queen's enthusiastic supporters, such as Cobbett and Wood, seeing her cause as a useful one which might be the source of restoring the party's fortunes.

Caroline also tapped a strong strain of dislike for the Prince Regent. The distress of the post-war years and his reputation for profligacy had led to him being mobbed in the streets of the capital twice since 1816. Croker argued that no revelations about the Queen's conduct could dampen popular support. He told Peel:

> I can only tell you that all the disgusting details proved against her seem to make no change in the minds or numbers of her partisans. This is natural – they adopted her because she was in opposition to the King and the Government, and her personal conduct, if it only continues impudent and violent enough, is of no kind of importance to the mob.[36]

Benjamin Haydon also reflected that the 'fury of the people for the

Queen is not from any love of her, but from that innate propensity to seize any opportunity of thwarting, annoying, and mortifying those who by their talents or station enforce obedience'. Crabb Robinson, when asked by Coleridge whether he was a 'Queenite', replied, 'No ... only an anti-Kingite.'[37] It was this aspect which the anti-radical *John Bull* harped upon when it described the Queen 'as the pole to hoist the revolutionary Cap of Liberty on'.[38]

But the Queen's cause was popular for its own sake among a wide section of the population both within and outside the capital. The themes of the 'injured Queen' channelled an element of chivalrous and romantic feeling. A hand-bill, printed by William Benbow and entitled the 'Glorious Deeds of Women', recounted the names of famous women of ancient Rome and of the Old Testament, ending 'And a Queen will now bring down the corrupt Conspirators against the Peace, Honour, and Life of the Innocent.'[39] Haydon wrote of an encounter with 'a little Whig-hater, loyal but a Queen's man – a picture of healthy independence ... loved the King, thought the Queen a whore – but he would be damned if any woman should be ill-used, whore or no whore'.[40] Similarly, the journalist Charles Knight had few illusions about Caroline, recording that he had met her on board ship while she was travelling around Italy: 'She dined at the Admiral's table, and left an impression that will never be forgotten. Her talk was of such a nature that Lord Exmouth ordered the midshipman to leave the cabin.' But he continued, 'not the less did I feel that Caroline of Brunswick was an injured wife, although I could not doubt that she was a depraved woman.'[41] Some hand-bills seriously set out to show that the Queen's trial would lead to her execution. One entitled 'Proposal to Murder the Queen' described her trial as 'a direct instigation to murder the Queen'. It concluded: 'Englishmen, look well at these things ... Will you stand by, while such monsters dip their hands in the blood of a woman; an INNOCENT WOMAN; an INNOCENT AND INJURED QUEEN?'[42]

Undoubtedly the agitation was remarkable for the torrent of radical caricatures, lampoons, and literature of all kinds which it evoked. A foreign visitor remarked upon the 'boundless range of the press and liberty of speech'. 'Every day,' he wrote, 'produced its thousand fiery libels against the King and his adherents, and as many caricatures, that were hawked about all the streets.'[43] This literature drew upon the tradition of caricature and pamphleteering which had developed in spite of the attentions of Liverpool's Government. The Queen had the most able journalists and satirists of the day working on her behalf. As early as July a government informant told the Home Office that 'Men and boys have been employed by Benbow and Fairburn to circulate in the Metropolis and for 50 miles around it, vast quantities of Bills, Placards, and publications of a seditious and inflammatory nature with a view to inflame the passions of the lower orders into acts of violence against the constituted authorities.'[44] Hone and Cruikshank's *The Political House that Jack Built* was published even before Caroline arrived and was followed by such successes as *The Queen's Matrimonial Ladder* and *The Divine Right of Kings to Govern Wrong*. Song-sheets for street sale had titles such as *God Save Queen Caroline* and *Caroline Triumphant*. The caricaturists had a field-day with cheap prints which lampooned the King's past conduct in blunt and obscene terms. Never had a reigning monarch been so savagely and coarsely attacked in print and in cartoon. For a time, wrote a contemporary, 'the whole people was obscene'. Virtually none of these products could be prosecuted in spite of the Six Acts, for fear that they might only inflame and publicize the Queen's cause.

London tradesmen demonstrated openly on the streets against the Bill. On 30 October the Brass Founders bore a crown in procession to the Queen, Creevey reported that there may have been 100,000 people in Piccadilly to watch. Earlier in the month it was reported that 25,000 people were expected to assemble at Brandenburg House, when the London carpenters, bakers, and glass-blowers were to present an address. The parishioners of St. George, Hanover Square and St. John's Wapping were also expected. The parishes of Cripplegate, Bishopgate, St. Mary, Lambeth, St. Giles and St. George Bloomsbury also presented addresses.[45] By the end of the month of October the Queen was receiving up to thirty deputations per day from London parishes or groups of tradesmen. Moreover, the Queen's cause had spread to the country at large and addresses were coming in from several towns.[46] On 26 October, when Cobbett attended upon the Queen for the first time since her return to England, he carried with him two addresses, one from Warwick and another from Bury St. Edmunds.[47] In mid-October, Greville wrote that 'The town is still in an uproar about the trial, and nobody has any doubt that it will finish by the Bill being thrown out and the Ministers turned out.'[48] Opinion, he claimed, was still polarized between those who thought the Queen completely innocent and others who were convinced of her guilt. Several members of the Government appeared demoralized by the trial. Wellington declared that it had degraded the King 'as low as he could be'. Sidmouth was especially grieved, but put on a brave face:

> ... all that just and honest pride which once gave conformity and dignity to a state of existence in this country is nearly annulled and

obliterated – But even in despair, as was said by Burke, we must perform the offices of hope. I am, however, much more under the influence of indignation, of disgust than of any feeling which approaches to despondency.[49]

Among the radicals there was some disquiet as to management of the agitation. J. C. Hobhouse met Caroline on 2 October and talked of her relationship with 'the people'. 'I told her the people were unanimous, almost,' he wrote, 'but I never counted on them as they had been so often opposed to government and always failed.' When Caroline asked him about the loyalty of the troops, Hobhouse replied that he did not believe the stories about them and that he knew of only two regiments that had expressed any discontent. With the admission that 'this was delicate ground' they left the subject, Hobhouse having indicated that the Queen could place no reliance upon the troops. By the end of the month Hobhouse, for one, believed that great care would have to be taken not to exhaust public feeling, and claimed to have told Wood so, but the latter 'was a vain man' and insisted on keeping up the spectacle of public deputations and addresses.[50] Hobhouse's desire for the addresses to end, however, brought a tirade from Cobbett. While committing himself to a defence of the Queen, he complained of the 'enormous damage' done to her cause by the non-receipt of addresses. He thought it likely to cool the ardour of the people 'at the very moment when she stands in need of all the warmth of their friendship . . . It has excited *great suspicions* as to her ultimate views!' Two days later, he reiterated this theme, complaining that 'The notice about the *non-receipt of addresses* will be found to be a most fatal step for the Queen!' He alleged that there were complaints against it from 'all over the country' and blamed Brougham and Denman for driving away the Queen's 'real friends, just at the moment when she will stand in heed of them'.[51] In the last days of October there was also evidence that Burdett was holding back his support; Hobhouse recorded, 'I find that Burdett feels very diffident at identifying himself in any way with the Queen.'[52]

Meanwhile, the Queen's trial was coming to its climax. But though Ministers persevered, their majorities for the readings of the Bill of Pains and Penalties were falling, Castlereagh complaining that the Whigs were playing the issue purely as a 'party' matter. The second reading of the Bill was passed by only twenty-eight votes and the third reading by only nine. At this point the Ministry gave up the struggle. The prospect of fighting the Bill through the Commons raised not only the spectre of defeat, but also of widespread civil commotion in which it was feared that Caroline would be backed by the forces of London radicalism and by the mob. Ministers sought a prorogation of Parliament to allow public feeling to die down and after a sullen period of non-communication with his ministers George IV agreed. His immediate reaction, however, was to test out the Whigs once again. A letter of dismissal was prepared, but eventually the King thought better of it. On 13 November Croker recounted that the Speaker thought that 'Lord Liverpool would go out conditioning with the King to take Lords Grey and Lansdowne.' Croker himself felt that a spell of government by the opposition would relieve the King from a great deal of pressure, but expected Lord Liverpool to carry on. He reflected, however, that if the Queen also stood her ground and refused to go away 'the trouble is only beginning'.[53] Indeed, the Queen's Chamberlain, Keppel-Craven, had on the same day requested a palace and establishment 'suited to the rank which she holds in the country'. Likewise the Queen had pledged to her friends that she would not leave the country nor agree to come to terms. Croker remarked ominously that if 'she has strength and courage to push her advantage, she must turn out the Ministers, and may overturn the country . . .'.[54]

The abandonment of the Bill was greeted by tremendous rejoicing in the capital. Anne Cobbett wrote that within half an hour of the decision being known 'guns were firing in all directions, bells ringing, and illuminations in every street and suburb', celebrations which continued for several nights. Carriages which did not display white bows or laurel leaves were stopped in the streets, while the house of Benbow the printer was 'a mass of blaze'. She described the spectacle as 'fine beyond anything you can imagine. All the ships in the river lighted to the mastheads, processions marching with bands of music carrying busts of the Queen with the crown on her head covered with laurel, playing God Save the Queen and bearing torches.'[55] Creevey described the river as 'the most beautiful sight in the world; every vessel is covered with colours, and at the head of the tallest mast in the river is the effigy of a Bishop, 20 or 30 feet in length, with his heels uppermost, hanging from the masthead'. Not only the main streets, but also 'the most obscure and most quiet streets' were illuminated.[56] The Common Council of the City of London proposed an address to Caroline, offering: '. . . our sincere and joyful congratulations upon the triumphant refutation of the foul charges brought against your Majesty's character and honour and the exposure of a conspiracy still more powerful and detestable than any of those, of which your Majesty has formerly been the object'. The Queen's reply emphasized that her stand had saved the nation as a whole from oppression: 'If my enemies had prevailed the people who are now feared would have been despised, their oppression would have been indefinitely increased.'[57] She claimed that the Press and the people had saved her and vowed that in future she would 'live for the people'. In the country there were many demonstrations of support. Several Cornish boroughs witnessed illuminations and in Oxford the Riot Act had to be read when the celebrations led to fighting between town and gown.[58]

The radicals were jubilant. The Cobbett household was especially so: 'The greatest triumph has been gained by the People of England,' wrote Anne Cobbett. She continued: 'There will be a change of Ministers, but though the Whigs *want* to get in, still they seem shy, for they know they cannot get in unless the people help them, and in that case they know they must give *some* reform; and the Governor (Cobbett) says unless they do that they *shall not* come in, and if they give *a little* the rest will soon follow.' A few days later, the euphoria had still not subsided. 'All is *triumph* here for the people. The change must come now.' By the end of the month, it was being said that the Ministry was only staying in because of the fear of letting in the Whigs at a time when they 'would have to attend to the voice of the people'. The Whigs were also felt to be dubious about accepting office from a King who might insist that they take up proceedings against Caroline: 'The ministers stay in to save their heads, and the Whigs stay out, because they cannot perform what they *must* promise before they will be let in.'[59]

On 29 November the Queen attended a thanksgiving ceremony at St. Paul's. Although she was given no formal marks of respect by the Government, she was accompanied by the Common Council of the City of London and a guard of honour composed of 1,000 gentlemen on horseback, organized by Wood. Sir Robert Wilson described it as 'a most imposing exhibition and the enthusiasm as high and general as can be imagined'. He estimated there were almost half a million people on the streets. Anne Cobbett described it as an 'immense mob' and *The Times* as the largest crowd in the history of the capital.[60] Hobhouse, Cobbett, and Wilson acted as her courtiers. Although the government had placed the police and soldiers on the alert, there were no disturbances during the procession. At St. Paul's the Psalm chosen was 'Deliver me, O Jehovah from the evil man: Preserve me from the violent man'. Encouraged by the great show of support – even the King's Guard saluted the Queen – Wilson hoped that the country at large would sustain the patriotism of the capital.[61]

The triumph, however, soon began to appear hollow. Once the Ministry decided to stand firm and not resign, Caroline was placed in a difficult position. Although she retained the option of holding out for her full rights as Queen, there was the difficulty of maintaining public feeling and the problem of defining what she stood for. In addition, there was the growing volume of anti-Caroline satire, led by Theodore Hook's *John Bull*, established in December 1820. It achieved a substantial circulation and turned the radicals' own weapons of obscene caricature and witty lampoon against the Queen's cause. Loyalist opinion too, was beginning to make itself felt. In December the Government received loyal addresses from the Universities of Oxford and Cambridge and by the early months of 1821 the number had risen to several hundred.[62]

The radicals were also showing signs of division now that the immediate object of defeating the Bill of Pains and Penalties had been achieved. Personal and political antagonisms between Cobbett, Wood, and the Westminster politicians once again began to bedevil radical agitation as it had many times before. Wood and Brougham were also reported to be at odds, a dangerous division between two of Caroline's closest advisers, but symptomatic of the frequent conflicts of interest between Whigs and radicals which had also been so frequent in the post-war period. Grey painted a depressing picture in a letter to Sir Robert Wilson:

> I cannot doubt that the proceedings of Wednesday last may be taken as a genuine and avowed expression of the feeling which at this moment animates a very great majority of the people of England, but I am afraid that this is still too much confined to the middle and lower ranks of society and I cannot help feeling a good deal of apprehension of the ultimate success of any measures which are not supported by that class which ought to lead in any expression of whiggish opinion. Such a state of things if pushed to extremity can only produce one of two results, either a democratic revolution or the destruction of our constitution.[63]

The position for the Queen's supporters began to look even bleaker in the first months of the new year. The Whigs attempted to restore the Queen's name to the Liturgy by parliamentary pressure and build up a momentum in the Commons which might lead to a favourable climate for reform. Attempts to mobilize county meetings on the Queen's behalf, however, met with difficulties. Not all the leaders of Whig opinion were prepared to campaign on Caroline's behalf and others found that feeling for reform was much stronger than for the Queen. Although some meetings were held in the country, the petitions which resulted differed in their demands. The Whigs were undoubtedly tapping a degree of popular support, but this support was diverse in its aims and intermittent in its intensity. On 26 January the Whigs tested their strength in the Commons; proposing a motion that the removal of the Queen's name from the Liturgy was ill-advised. They mustered 209 votes against the Government's 310. Although a good showing, it was not enough. A further vote on 5 February also led to a Whig defeat. The mass of country gentlemen would not vote with the Whigs and the Ministry was safe from a 'revolt of the independents'. Although a group of wilder spirits wanted to carry on opposition 'out of doors', the Whig leaders quietly dropped Caroline's cause. Her use to them was over.[64]

But the desertion of the Whigs did not end support for the Queen, it merely removed the parliamentary wing of it. Caroline still had the support of the City radicals, especially Wood and Wilson, and also of Hobhouse, Hume, and Cobbett. Nor was popular support lacking in the capital. On 30 January a public meeting of the inhabitants of St. Pancras voted a 'loyal and affectionate' address to the Queen and passed resolutions in favour of parliamentary reform.[65] In January 'Working Mechanics and the Industrious Classes' were called to present an address to the Queen at Brandenburg House. The meeting was advertised by John Gast, a veteran organizer of the London shipwrights since the 1790s. Those wishing to attend were asked to be of respectable appearance and bring with them 'any model or ornament of their trade or professions, respectable banners or flags, with appropriate mottoes, as shall be approved by the committee'.[66] The mention of a committee suggested that even if the Whigs were dropping out of the affair, a group remained who were determined to bring the Queen's supporters out on to the streets. That lower and middle class support for Caroline was still strong can also be seen from the address presented by Kensington at the end of the year. Of 900 signatures, the majority appear to have been respectable householders, artisans, and servants. The upper classes, however, generally remained aloof from it.[67] In the Cobbett household, support for the Queen remained firm. Cobbett was reported to have become 'mighty fond of dress' when called upon to attend Caroline and spent two or three evenings a week playing blind man's buff with her.[68]

However, feeling for Caroline was gradually being replaced by interest in the King's Coronation plans. Even Anne Cobbett was forced to admit that his speech to Parliament 'has astounded and at the same time conciliated his loving subjects; it is mild and gentle in the extreme, not a word about sedition and blasphemy or anything of the sort, in short, it is all graciousness'.[69] The combination of popular excitement at the prospect of a Coronation, and the dropping of the Queen's cause by the Whigs marked a serious turn in the Queen's fortunes. Moreover, the Ministry were still offering her a settlement. Ministers had gambled upon a decline in popular support for the Queen's cause and even stilled some of the most scurrilous abuse in the loyalist prints in order to bring her towards a settlement. In January, against the advice of Brougham and Cobbett, she accepted a pension of £50,000 per year. With this, as another historian has remarked, 'She was no longer a symbol of resistance to oppression; she had passed over to the side of the pensioners.'[70]

Caroline still had a desire to establish her position, however, and to clear her name. Her support was not entirely exhausted and she had a last chance to bring her followers on to the streets with the King's Coronation. As early as April, Caroline was informed that she would not be allowed a place in the Abbey, still less accorded any official marks of honour. She determined to attend the Abbey. In this she was mainly encouraged by Alderman Wood. Cobbett was excluded from the arrangements by Wood and Sir Robert Wilson declined to come to London to assist the Queen in spite of a personal appeal from her.[71] The Queen set out for Westminster Abbey accompanied by what Croker described as a 'thin and shabby mob'. At the entrance to the Abbey she was refused admittance and was forced to make her retreat in an embarrassing anti-climax. Although her partisans claimed that the venture had been a success – that the crowds supporting her had been large and the soldiers had once again shown favour towards her – her opponents noted the surprising warmth shown towards the King and the ludicrous spectacle of Caroline going from door to door in Westminster Abbey and being refused admittance. Croker summed up his feelings:

> We had rumours all day of mobs and riots. I went myself to see what had happened; it turned out that half a dozen windows were broken in half a dozen places, and that was all. There was no more crowd opposite the Queen's door than served to fill the pavements.[72]

Even the precautions taken by the authorities were designed more to preserve the peace against an excess of enthusiasm in the general illumination which followed the Coronation than to resist disorder by the Queen's followers. Croker went so far as to report that Caroline and Wood were hooted by the spectators and that far from demonstrating her strength 'it only proved her weakness'. Brougham too was insistent that the Queen had 'lost incalculably', for 'getting out of her carriage, and tramping about; going and being refused, and damaging the Coronation was all very bad, but the way of doing it was very, very bad'.[73]

The Queen's health proved incapable of withstanding the physical and emotional shock of the episode. She was taken unwell on the evening of the Coronation and in spite of a brief recovery died on 6 August. Lord Londonderry wrote to Eldon that 'it was the greatest of all possible deliverences both to his majesty and the country'.[74] Nor was relief confined to her opponents, Burdett wrote: 'So the poor Queen is gone and made an honourable exit: poor thing it is well over: no one wishing her well could wish it otherwise. She could not have remained with dignity, nor have departed in better time or manner.'[75] Lord Sidmouth, however, was aware that even Caroline's death would not bring an end to the agitation and wrote that 'the voice of faction will cry; and the lifeless remains will be made, if possible, the instrument of irritation'. As a result the Government wanted to dispose of the Queen's remains as quickly and discreetly as possible. They seized upon her deathbed wish to be buried in Brunswick as providing an opportunity to avoid further embarrassment. It was planned to move the Queen's body from Hammersmith to Harwich by the route least likely to lead to demonstrations. At first it was thought that a route by water down the Thames could be used, but a nervous Lord Liverpool decided it would facilitate obstruction by the City of London. It was finally decided to send the Queen's cortege by road on a circuitous route north of the City of London. An escort of Horse Guards was provided and other soldiers, police, and magistrates were put on the alert for the funeral procession.[76]

Early on 14 August the Queen's funeral procession set off. Almost immediately, the Government's plans were thrown out by the very large numbers of people on the streets. Carts were found to be blocking the intended route with masses of people behind them. After consultation with Lord Liverpool, the procession was rerouted through Hyde Park by the magistrate in charge, Sir Robert Baker. The Life Guards were called out and the crowd began to pelt the troops with dirt and stones, crying, 'Through the City, through the City.' Baker became alarmed as the crowd increased and all routes except that through the City seemed blocked by carts or wagons. In the meantime a detachment of Life Guards became involved in a fracas with the crowd who were at Cumberland Gate. The troops attempted to keep the gate clear and were forced to draw their swords. The mob, however, twice succeeded in shutting the gates and the troops were pelted heavily with stones and mud, injuring many and unhorsing two. The troops charged the crowd and when this proved of no avail they opened fire. Two men were shot, Richard Honey, a cabinet maker of Compton Street, Soho, and George Francis, a bricklayer. Sir Robert Wilson, who was riding in the funeral procession, remonstrated with the troops, saying that 'the people will have her go through the city'. Sir Robert Baker still hoped to find a route avoiding the City, but as the embattled procession made its way forward, 'an immense concourse of people' and new barricades 'of coaches and carts which seemed chained together and loaded with people' blocked alternative routes and inexorably turned the procession towards Temple Bar. At Fleet Street the procession was met by the City Marshal who informed Baker that the Lord Mayor was on his way to escort the procession through the City. The troops were dismissed and Sir Robert Baker retired defeated to the Home Office in Whitehall. The Lord Mayor then escorted the procession through the streets of the City on to the Romford Road for Harwich.[77]

The Government's attempts to bring the affair to a speedy and quiet conclusion had been thwarted. The Government's agent, Sir Robert Baker, had been hounded by the mob into disobeying his orders and allowing the procession to go through the City. Lord Stowell wrote to Sidmouth:

> I don't wonder that every well-affected man everywhere ... should contemplate such events with the deepest affliction ... we all feel that in the present times the safety of the country depends upon the superiority of the army, governed by the civil authority, over the force of the heated and disaffected multitude in the capital; and if that is suffered to be over-ruled it shakes every man's idea of his own personal safety ... I met the mob that day in Holborn; and they halloed out to me, 'Ay, you gemmen thought you could carry everything your own way; but we'll show you the difference': and they will show it if this victory of the mob is suffered to pass over unnoticed.[78]

John Bull fulminated against a 'head of police, who evidently had no head of his own' and warned that 'a magistrate incompetent in times of difficulty, either from moral or physical imbecility to enforce laws and ordinances of the government is the most dangerous character in the country'.[79] But although Baker paid for his conduct of the procession by losing his post as Chief Magistrate at Bow Street, the Government blamed the metropolitan radicals for orchestrating the popular demonstrations. Hobhouse, Under Secretary at the Home Office, reported to Lord Sidmouth that 'immense assiduity has been used by the radicals with Sir Robert Wilson, Joseph Hume, and J. C. Hobhouse at their head'. He went on: 'I dread the moral effect of this day. The mob glory in having carried their object by force, in having beaten the military ... It strikes me that it is highly important to postpone all military reductions until the effect of this day is seen.'[80]

The *Courier* claimed that a number of men with white truncheons had been seen in public houses near the New Road recruiting men to drag carts across the road.[81] Suspicion especially focused upon Sir Robert Wilson, who had returned from Paris the day before the funeral. Several witnesses said they had seen him organizing the crowd at different parts of the route. Above all he had openly remonstrated with the Life Guards about their conduct.[82] The Government was prepared to proceed against him on the two grounds of encouraging the people and insulting the troops, but it was decided that the evidence of the former was too unreliable and the King was prevailed upon to dismiss him from his commission. Wilson's own evidence suggested that he had been mainly motivated by fury at the behaviour of the troops. He wrote to Grey: 'Never did any government behave so sillily as ours did yesterday and never did people behave better. The Life Guards quite lost their temper – fired without orders from magistrates or commanding officers and when I got up amongst them they were so wild, so very wild.' He explained that he had urged going through the City 'or else the mischief would have been very great indeed.' His only reference to the obstruction of the procession was the ambiguous comment that 'the barricades as a first experiment of the system were admirably constructed and I admire the resolute attitude of the defenders'.[83]

These remarks could be taken simply as the interested comments of an ex-military attaché, but Wilson had clearly been implicated in some way; so too had others among the metropolitan radicals. J. C. Hobhouse revealed in his diary that the Queen's funeral had been organized by the same committee as had organized the procession to St. Pauls in the previous year. Place was little involved, but Wood was prominent. At a meeting at the Freemasons' Tavern, with Joseph Hume in the chair, it had been decided to try to obtain permission for the procession to go through the City. When, however, this was refused, J. C. Hobhouse recorded that there was 'great confusion' and that feeling was 'very intense'.[84] It is very likely that a group attempted to ensure that their intentions were carried out. The references to 'men with white truncheons' suggests that the City constables may have taken a part, acting under the aegis of Wood or Waithman, the latter being Sheriff of London and Middlesex. While the procession was taking place, Waithman sent a letter to the Lord Mayor, asking him to attend at Temple Bar and await its arrival, suggesting that he expected the procession to be diverted. Undoubtedly, a degree of collusion occurred between Wilson and other London radicals in wrecking the Government's plans of bringing the Queen Caroline affair to a speedy close.

The events of the funeral procession played further into radical hands. Wilson's dismissal led to the formation of the 'Friends of Sir Robert Wilson'. Brougham claimed Wilson had been at his side all day and a meeting at the City of London Tavern condemned his dismissal as 'a wanton act of arbitrary power under a plea of prerogative'. A public subscription for him was opened by the electors of Southwark. But even more useful to the radicals were the two deaths arising from the actions of the soldiers, giving an opportunity to recreate, in a minor key, the furore caused by Peterloo. On 19 August Sidmouth was warned that, 'Watson and Co who had fallen into a state of torpor have been resuscitated by the events of Tuesday and are now busied in getting up a public funeral for the two unfortunate men who fell at Cumberland Gate, with a view to cause further mischief if possible.'[85] The radical press made as much out of the incident as they could, *The Black Dwarf* headlining the deaths for three weeks. A formidable organization of London tradesmen and radicals prepared the funeral. It was held at the expense of the bricklayers, carpenters, and joiners of the metropolis who formed a joint committee for the purpose. The designing hand appears to have been a group of radicals led by John Gast, Dr. Watson, Gale Jones, and Waddington. With the aid of Robert Waithman, who as Sheriff was Chairman of the inquests on the dead men, ample scope was given to embarrass the Government.[86]

The inquests made it clear that the Riot Act had not been read and no order to fire received by the troops. Some of the Life Guards on duty at the funeral were forced to parade before the Coroner's jury, but no specific charges could be made. A verdict of manslaughter 'against a Life Guardsman unknown' was brought in.[87] The public funeral of Honey and Francis on 26 August provided the last 'spin-off' from the Queen's affair. It was estimated that seventy or eighty thousand people were involved. A rendezvous was made at Smithfield at noon and the route of the procession took it past the Knightsbridge Barracks used by the Life Guards. On the return from the graveyard, fighting broke out between some of the procession and off-duty soldiers outside the barracks. The Riot Act had to be read, and although Waithman intervened to break up the fighting, he was blamed for behaving in peremptory manner. This reopened old quarrels between the City and the Home Office about the respective jurisdiction of the civil and military powers. After an acrimonious correspondence with Lord Bathurst, the affair gradually subsided, but not before the Common Council of the City had set up an inquiry and the anti-ministerial press had vented their displeasure at 'praetorian licentiousness', 'military dominion', and the descent of the army into a 'lawless mob'.[88]

The Queen Caroline affair marked a watershed between the post-war agitation and the calmer years of the eighteen twenties. One of its most striking characteristics was that it was essentially a metropolitan agitation, for though there was support for Caroline in the country, it was primarily the expression of opinion in the capital which made her cause so dangerous for the administration. Of all the post-war agitations, it was the affair of Queen Caroline which came nearest to bringing down the Ministry and bringing the Whigs back to power. As Peel had recognized in 1817, dissension within the royal family was extremely serious, providing focus and legitimacy for a wide range of discontents. The Caroline affair dominated popular politics in a way which completely overshadowed the years of the Luddite outbreaks, the introduction of the Corn Laws, and the Peterloo 'Massacre'. For both radicals and ministers, the Queen's affair appeared one of the most important of the years between the revival of radicalism at the end of the Napoleonic Wars and the First Reform Act. That the affair should have developed around the dubious conduct of the King's wife, did not detract from its power to mobilize radical and popular opinion in the capital.

The involvement of Cobbett, for example, can not be regarded as mere opportunism. Cobbett was quite genuine in his regard for Caroline as was shown in his comments about her death. A letter of 17 August bears unmistakable signs of real grief: 'I have never before known what depression of spirits was; but I really feel it now.'[89] The role of the City radicals, Wood, Waithman, and Wilson, was also testimony to the power of the Queen's cause to focus opposition.

Some sections of radical opinion, like some later historians, were irritated about the involvement of radicals in a cause which they regarded as a diversion from more important issues. Thus *The Black Dwarf* complained:

> It is too much the custom of this country to be amused with trifles ... All national interest in public business is suspended because a man and his wife cannot agree! Tell a true political *quid nunc*, that a military despotism is rapidly rivetting the fetters which an interested legislature has imposed – he will interrupt you with astonishment, that you should mention such trifling matters, while it remains unknown, whether the Queen will be permitted to live at home, or abroad![90]

The radical reformers, it alleged, would learn nothing from the affair, while 'The "lower orders" have grown out of their baby clothes, and are not to be interested in nursery or bedroom disputes.'[91]

But one of the most remarkable features of the affair was the involvement of the London populace. Demonstrations in support of the Queen seem to have tapped more general enthusiasm than any agitation since the days of Wilkes. The addresses, petitions, resolutions, and deputations from the London trades were far too numerous to be just the result of manipulation by the radicals. The participation of the London trades, for example, illustrated the extent to which a form of loyalism could still mobilize some of the most advanced and well-organized workers in the country. The involvement of a man like John Gast, one of the pioneer trade union leaders of the early nineteenth century, showed the ability of Caroline to play upon ideas of the 'injured Queen' and act as a form of legitimation for protest movements. Her cause was clearly popular among a wide section of the working population of London, where her appeal may have been that of the 'good Prince' – a popular and legitimate alternative monarch to George IV. Popular loyalism was far from dead among London artisans and the populace at large. Whatever the reservations of some sections of radical opinion, the power of this sentiment to bring people on to the streets was one of the most impressive features of the whole affair. Popular demonstrations against the Government were often not 'radical' and the appeal of Queen Caroline was evidence that popular loyalism could survive alongside new forms of organization among the working population. Indeed, its survival even after the death of Caroline was to be a significant feature of the ideology of the working classes in the nineteenth century as a whole.[92]

The Queen Caroline affair was seen by many contemporaries as a victory for the Whigs. Lord John Russell believed that 'the Queen business had done a great deal of good in renewing the old and natural alliance between the Whigs and the people and of weakening the influence of the radicals with the latter'. Similarly, Spencer Walpole saw the Queen's trial as a watershed in the emergence of the Whigs as a popular party.[93] There was little doubt that the Queen's affair affected a wider cross-section of opinion in the country than had been seen for many years. The Ministry was in serious danger of being ground between the desires of the King and the increasingly powerful demands of 'public opinion'. The mobilization of opinion, however, was largely metropolitan. The caricatures and prints put out in the agitation served an informed clientele mainly based on the print shops, taverns, and coffee houses of the capital.[94] Nonetheless, for all their reservations, the Whigs and City radicals developed an agitation which stretched from the streets of the capital to the Houses of Parliament. Anne Cobbett registered the unifying effect of the Queen when she wrote in November 1820:

> In the first place, with one accord, the people, the whole of the people Church people, Methodists and sectarians of all sorts, Tradesmen, *Farmers*, labourers and *soldiers* as much as any had all long ago declared for the Queen, leaving for her enemies, the King, Ministers and all courtiers and all Parsons and Priests of every description. This, in the first place, was almost a Revolution; for the Queen is a radical and has consequently joined all together against the Government.[95]

One of the features which most impressed contemporary opinion was the orderly nature of the demonstrations in support of the Queen and the powers of organization which they seemed to indicate among the radicals and trade groups. Creevey recorded his impression of the sailors who marched to present an address to the Queen:

> There were thousands of seamen all well-dressed, all sober – the best looking, the finest men you could imagine. Every man had a new white silk or satin cockade in his hat. They had a hundred colours, at least, or pieces of silk with sentiments on them, such as 'Protection to the innocent'.[96]

Creevey wrote of the enthusiasm for the preparations made to celebrate the dropping of the Bill of Pains and Penalties:

> Waithman ... tells me that the arrangements made in every parish in and about London on this occasion are perfectly miraculous – quite new in their nature – and that they will be of eternal application in all our public affairs ...[97]

By avoiding the violence which had frequently occasioned both repression from the authorities and dissension among reformers, the agitation to force the government to give way had proved remarkably effective. A united effort had been obtained from Whigs, City and Westminster radicals, and the London trades. The radical journalists and printers, Hone, Wooler, Benbow, and Dolby had produced an immense output of caricatures and satires. It has been argued that during the course of the proceedings against Caroline the Liverpool Government 'came to terms with the "rise of public opinion"'.

Coercion proved impossible against a torrent of abuse which used ridicule as its major weapon and was clearly supported by a large section of opinion in the capital. By conceding, the Ministry survived by a very narrow margin the fate it was to suffer in 1830.[98] The Queen Caroline affair marked a new stage in the articulation of opinion in which peaceful demonstrations, processions, and meetings were the popular wing of a broad-based alliance of support. It was Creevey who wrote: 'The people have learnt a great lesson from this wicked proceeding, they have learnt how to marshal and organise themselves, and they have learnt at the same time the success of their strength.'[99]

But Waithman's belief that the popular organization seen in the Caroline agitation would be of 'eternal application' proved ill-founded, at least as far as London radicalism was concerned. Metropolitan radicalism failed to live up to the promise envisaged by Waithman and others, either in the reform agitation of 1831–2 or in the 1840s. The Queen Caroline affair was the last great agitation in which London gave a lead to the rest of the country and outstripped the provincial cities and towns by the size and impressiveness of its demonstrations. There were many reasons for this. Place blamed the size and diversity of the capital which rendered it less effective as a political force.[100] Moreover, Caroline's cause provided the last occasion upon which the City radicals gave a lead to political agitation in the capital. The City contained an ever smaller proportion of London's population and had increasingly specialized political interests. Although there was a revival of City radicalism in the form of men like Waithman and Wood, the City as a whole was often predominantly Tory in the complexion of its MPs and Lord Mayors.[101] Thus one time that a significant stirring of the City of London took place was over the Property Tax, when the commercial interests of the merchants and financiers seemed at risk. The City radicals took up Caroline's cause as a case of 'injured rights', very close to the concept of 'liberties' which had infused City radicalism in the eighteenth century.[102] Neither economic issues nor reform were explicitly espoused by Wood and his co-adjutors during the agitation. The City radicals, especially Wood and Waithman, were representative of what has been called 'shopkeepers' radicalism', having little in common with the more patrician Whiggism of Burdett, the open demagoguery of Hunt and the Spenceans, or the utilitarianism of Place and the Westminster radicals.[103] As a result, the City was less able to act as the representative of metropolitan opinion as a whole. The City was only one of a number of political groupings in the capital, each with a distinct tone and personnel of their own.

Moreover, beneath the temporary co-operation of the London

radicals in the Caroline affair lay the personal and political divisions which were a prominent feature of radicalism during this period. The Queen's cause provided the last occasion upon which the forces of metropolitan radicalism were drawn together under a personality with sufficient appeal to impose some unity upon the various groups. For a few weeks, Caroline could have swayed feeling in the metropolis in whatever direction she chose. Like Wilkes, she was able to give some cohesion to the disparate political groups in the capital; she was also able to channel the less articulate feelings and aspirations among the population of the capital. This cohesion, however, was based upon the very vagueness of her cause – that of the 'injured Queen'. Once, however, the Bill of Pains and Penalties was dropped and Caroline began to be tainted with compromise, the political movement she headed began to disintegrate under the rivalries of the metropolitan radicals. No permanent liaison between the forces of London radicalism resulted from the affair. As a result the capital ceased once again to bring its full weight to bear upon politics. Without co-ordination between its political groups, the inevitable result was diffusion of effort.

This diffusion of effort partly helps to explain why London began to play a proportionately smaller role in the agitations of the nineteenth century. It was not that the capital lacked activists, nor that it lacked interest in issues such as reform – London was, as Thomas Oldfield had pointed out, grossly under-represented in terms of its population – it had at least as much claim to extra representation as the manufacturing cities of the north and midlands. Rather, the capital failed to develop an adequate substitute for the role filled earlier by the City of London as the representative of metropolitan opinion. Divisions among reformers and radicals, the growth in size and diversity of the capital, and the loss of the City as a mouth-piece for opinion in the capital as a whole reduced London's effectiveness in the political life of the nation. Caroline marked the end of a tradition of political figure-heads who had given cohesion and purpose to the activities of politicians and populace. Wilkes, Gordon, Burdett, Hunt, and Caroline all left something to be desired as political leaders, but by this period the major obstacle to personalities providing surrogate organization to London radicalism was the growth and composition of the capital itself. The decay of the Queen Caroline agitation after the dropping of the Bill of Pains and Penalties was testimony to the way in which the political groupings in the capital were pulling in different directions. After 1821, the focus of radical agitation passed to more cohesive and homogeneous communities in the provinces.

Notes

1. HO40/15: report of 'J.S.' to Home Office, 8 January 1820. 'J.S.' was John Shergoe, a regular informant throughout the Queen Caroline affair. I owe his identification to Dr. J. A. Hone.
2. For traditional interpretations see S. Maccoby, *English Radicalism 1786–1832* (London, 1955), pp. 370–4; E. P. Thompson, *The Making of the English Working Class* (2nd edn., London, 1968), pp. 778–9. For a recent view of the ministerial side of the affair, see J. E. Cookson, *Lord Liverpool's Administration* (Edinburgh, 1975), chs. 4, 5.
3. E. Tangye Lean, *The Napoleonists* (Oxford, 1970), pp. 90–6; A. Briggs, *The Age of Improvement, 1783–1867* (3rd edn., London, 1964), p. 191.
4. See J. E. Cookson, *op. cit.*, pp. 206–13.
5. Devonshire CRO, Sidmouth Papers: Sidmouth to Wellington, 21 March 1820.
6. L. J. Jennings, *The Croker Papers* (London, 1884), i. p. 170.
7. *Ibid.*, p. 110; E. Tangye Lean, *op. cit.*, p. 114–17.
8. Nuffield College Library, Cobbett Papers: A. Cobbett to J. P. Cobbett, 15 February 1820.
9. HO 40/15: reports of 'J.S.', 10, 24, 30 May 1820.
10. F. D. Cartwright (ed.), *The Life and Correspondence of Major Cartwright* (London, 1826), pp. 183–4; C. Buxton (ed.), *Memoirs of Thomas Powell Buxton* (London, 1849), p. 105; British Library, Wilson Papers, Add. MSS. 30123, ff. 151–2.
11. For Place's comments, see Add. MSS., Place Papers, 27550, ff. 189–90. Matthew Wood (1768–1843); Alderman 1809; Sheriff of London and Middlesex 1810; Lord Mayor 1815–16 and 1816–17. MP for the City of London from 1812 to his death.
12. Add. MSS. 30123, ff. 163–6, 24 May 1820.
13. HO 40/15: Report of 'J.S.', 6 June 1820.
14. L. J. Jennings (ed.), *op. cit.*, p. 173; E. Tangye Lean, *op. cit.*, p. 118; C. Knight, *Passages of a Working Life* (London, 1864), i. p. 259.
15. Add. MSS. 30123, ff. 189–90.
16. *Ibid.*, ff. 169–70.
17. L. J. Jennings (ed.), *The Croker Papers, op. cit.*, f. p. 174.
18. P. W. Wilson (ed.), *The Greville Diary* (New York, 1927), i. p. 126; H. Brougham, *The Life and Times of Henry, Lord Brougham* (London, 1871), ii. p. 366.
19. See J. E. Cookson, *op. cit.*, pp. 235–48 for the details of the negotiations.
20. Cobbett Papers: letters of W. Cobbett to Queen Caroline, 8, 10, 12, 15, 25, June 1820.
21. HO 40/15: report from 'J.S.', 12 June 1820.
22. L. J. Jennings (ed.), *The Croker Papers, op. cit.*, i. pp. 175–6; G. Pellew, *Life and Correspondence of First Viscount Sidmouth* (London, 1847), iii. pp. 330–1. For a fuller discussion of the incident, see my unpublished D.Phil. thesis 'Disturbances and Public Order in London, 1790–1821' Oxford University, 1973, pp. 143–4.
23. *Memoirs of the Court of George IV* (London, 1859), i. p. 51; Corporation of London Record Office, Common Council Journal 94, ff. 184, 199–203.
24. F. D. Cartwright, *The Life and Correspondence of Major Cartwright, op. cit.*, pp. 197–9.
25. Add. MSS. 56541, Broughton Papers (J. C. Hobhouse), diary entries for 10 and 18 June 1820.
26. C. Knight, *op. cit.*, i. p. 259.
27. H. Maxwell (ed.), *The Creevey Papers* (London, 1905), i. p. 320.
28. Cobbett Papers, Anne Cobbett to Queen Caroline, 29 June 1820; Anne Cobbett to Miss Boxall, 14 August 1820.

29. H. Maxwell (ed.), *The Creevey Papers, op. cit.*, i. p. 332.

30. HO 41/26, ff. 25–6.

31. L. J. Jennings (ed.), *The Croker Papers, op. cit.*, i. pp. 176–7.

32. *The Black Dwarf*, 14 June 1820, p. 808.

33. HO 40/14: hand-bills sent in to Home Office, 1820.

34. A. Mitchell, *The Whigs in Opposition, 1815–1830* (Oxford, 1967), pp. 145–6.

35. Bodleian Library, Burdett Papers, MS. Eng. Hist. d. 217, f. 192, Sir Francis Burdett to Bickersteth, 21 October 1820.

36. L. J. Jennings (ed.), *The Croker Papers, op. cit.*, p. 177.

37. W. Bissell Pope (ed.), *The Diary of Benjamin Robert Haydon* (Cambridge, Mass., 1960), ii. p. 290; D. Hudson (ed.), *The Diary of Henry Crabb Robinson* (Oxford, 1967), p. 66.

38. *John Bull*, 24 December 1820.

39. HO 40/14: hand-bill sent in to Home Office, 1820.

40. W. Bissell Pope (ed.), *The Diary of Benjamin Robert Haydon, op. cit.*, ii. pp. 296–7.

41. C. Knight, *op. cit.*, i. p. 252.

42. HO 40/14: hand-bill sent in to Home Office, July 1820.

43. R. Rush, *A Residence at the Court of London* (London, 1845), i. p. 346.

44. HO 40/15: report from 'J.S.', 10 July 1820.

45. H. Maxwell (ed.), *The Creevey Papers, op. cit.*, i. p. 334; HO 40/15: report from 'J.S.', 21 October 1820 and 24 November 1820.

46. Add. MSS. 56541, Broughton Papers, diary entry for 25 October 1820.

47. Cobbett Papers, A. Cobbett to J. P. Cobbett, 26 October 1820.

48. P. W. Wilson (ed.), *The Greville Diary, op. cit.*, i. p. 131.

49. Sidmouth Papers, Sidmouth to C. Yorke, 24 September 1820.

50. Add. MSS. 56541, Broughton Papers, diary entry for 2 October 1820.

51. Cobbett Papers, W. Cobbett to M. Wood, 29 October and 31 October 1820.

52. Add. MSS. 56541, Broughton papers, diary entry for 31 October 1820.

53. L. J. Jennings (ed.), *The Croker Papers, op. cit.*, i. p. 174.

54. *Ibid.*, p. 175.

55. Cobbett Papers, A. Cobbett to J. P. Cobbett, 15 November 1820.

56. H. Maxwell (ed.), *The Creevey Papers*, i. p. 341.

57. Corporation of London Record Office, Common Council Journal 94, ff. 276–9.

58. W. R. Ward, *Victorian Oxford* (London, 1965), p. 42.

59. Cobbett Papers, A. Cobbett to J. P. Cobbett, 15 November 1820; A. Cobbett to J. P. Cobbett, 24 November 1820; W. Cobbett to J. P. Cobbett, 24 November 1820.

60. Add. MSS. 30123, Wilson Papers, ff. 213–16, 30 November 1820; Cobbett Papers, A. Cobbett to J. P. Cobbett, 6 December 1820; *The Times*, 30 November 1820.

61. See R. E. Zegger, *John Cam Hobhouse: A Political Life, 1819–1852* (Columbia, 1973), p. 87.

62. J. E. Cookson, *op. cit.*, pp. 279–82.

63. Add. MSS. 30109, Wilson Papers, ff. 140–2, Grey to Wilson, 5 December 1820.

64. A. Mitchell, *op. cit.*, pp. 156–7.

65. F. D. Cartwright (ed.), *The Life and Correspondence of Major Cartwright, op. cit.*, p. 207.

66. HO 40/16: notice sent in to Home Office, undated, January 1821. For Gast's career, see S. and B. Webb, *The History of Trade Unionism* (3rd edn., London, 1920), pp. 84–5, 107, 111; also E. P. Thompson, *The Making of the English Working Class, op. cit.*, pp. 851–5.

67. E. Tangye Lean, *op. cit.*, pp. 121–2.

68. Cobbett Papers, A. Cobbett to J. P. Cobbett, 6 December 1820.

69. *Ibid.*, A. Cobbett to J. P. Cobbett, 31 January 1821.

70. L. Woodward, *The Age of Reform, 1815–1870* (2nd edn., Oxford, 1962), p. 68.

71. For Cobbett's exclusion from the arrangements, see Cobbett Papers, A. Cobbett to J. P. Cobbett, 22 July 1821; for Wilson's refusal see Add. MSS. 30103, Wilson Papers,

ff. 19–24, Queen Caroline to Wilson, 19 July 1821 and Add. MSS. 30103, Wilson Papers, ff. 24–8, Wilson to Lushington, 19 July 1821. Wilson gave two reasons for not helping the Queen. He said his wife was ill and that as the King had helped him in the past he did not want to interfere with his Coronation.

72. L. J. Jennings (ed.), *The Croker Papers, op. cit.*, i. p. 196.

73. *Ibid.*, p. 197; H. Maxwell (ed.), *The Creevey Papers, op. cit.*, i. pp. 361–2.

74. H. Twiss, *Life of Lord Chancellor Eldon* (London, 1844), ii. p. 432.

75. Burdett Papers, MS. Eng. Hist. d. 217, f. 693.

76. G. Pellew, *Life of Lord Sidmouth, op. cit.*, iii. p. 356; for the funeral arrangements see HO 44/9: Memorandum on moving the Queen's body by water, 14 August 1821 and Memorandum on military arrangements for the Queen's funeral, August, 1821.

77. For the events at Queen Caroline's funeral, see HO 44/9. See also Sidmouth Papers, H. Hobhouse to Sidmouth, 14 August 1821 and J. Stevenson, 'Disturbances and Public Order in London, 1790–1821', *op. cit.*, pp. 153–60.

78. G. Pellew, *Life of Lord Sidmouth, op. cit.*, iii. pp. 356–6.

79. *John Bull*, 16 August 1821.

80. Sidmouth Papers, H. Hobhouse to Sidmouth, 14 August 1821.

81. *Courier*, 16 August 1821.

82. See HO 44/9: evidence of Lt. Storey, 18 August 1821; evidence of Lt. Col. Hill, 16 August 1821.

83. For attitudes to Wilson's behaviour, see Sidmouth Papers, Bathurst to Sidmouth, 5 September 1821; for Wilson's comments, Add. MSS. 30123, ff. 239–42, 16 August 1821.

84. H. Brougham, *Life and Times of Henry, Lord Brougham, op. cit.*, ii. p. 427; *The Traveller*, 26 October 1821.

85. Sidmouth Papers: H. Hobhouse to Sidmouth, 19 August 1821.

86. *Ibid.*; *The Black Dwarf*, 22 August, 29 August, and 5 September 1821; *The Times*, 27 August 1821; Robert Waithman (1764–1833), Whig MP for the City of London 1818–20, 1826–32; Lord Mayor 1823. For his political career prior to the Caroline affair, see J. R. Dinwiddy, 'The Patriotic Linen-Draper: Robert Waithman and the Revival of Radicalism in the City of London, 1795–1818', *Bulletin of the Institute of Historical Research*, vol. xlvi (1973).

87. *The Times*, 16–25 August 1821; *Annual Register*, (1821), History, p. 128.

88. *Ibid.*, 27 August 1821; Corporation of London Record Office, PAR Book 3, Report of Committee of General Purposes on the Knightsbridge Riots; HO 44/9: Captn. MacNeill to Lt. Col. Lygon, August 1821; report of Lt. Col. Lygon to Home Office, August 1821. For comments on the behaviour of the troops, see *The News*, 2 September 1821.

89. Cobbett Papers, W. Cobbett to S. Clarke, 17 August 1821.

90. *The Black Dwarf*, 28 June 1820, p. 895; see also comments on p. 808.

91. *Ibid.*, p. 808.

92. See R. McKenzie and A. Silver, *Angels in Marble* (London, 1968).

93. R. E. Zegger, *op. cit.*, p. 87; C. W. New, *The Life of Henry Brougham to 1830* (Oxford, 1961), pp. 261–2.

94. See E. P. Thompson, *op. cit.*, pp. 809–10; M. Dorothy George, *English Political Caricature* (Oxford, 1959), i. ch. 10 and ii. ch. 10.

95. Cobbett Papers, A. Cobbett to J. P. Cobbett, 26 November 1820.

96. H. Maxwell (ed.), *The Creevey Papers, op. cit.*, i. p. 320.

97. *Ibid.*

98. J. E. Cookson, *op. cit.*, pp. 270–1; see also R. Rush, *op. cit.*, i. pp. 345–6, who believed the Ministry showed 'great wisdom' in surrendering up their measure. Lord Malmsbury believed the affair siphoned off the discontents of the post-war period, see Lord Malmsbury, *Memoirs of an ex-Minister* (London, 1884), i. p. 16.

99. H. Maxwell (ed.), *The Creevey Papers, op. cit.*, i. p. 341.
100. For Place's views on this question, see the letter to Croker (1840), quoted in G. Wallas, *Life of Francis Place, 1771–1854* (5th edn., London, 1951), p. 393.
101. Although the City returned only one Tory MP in 1818 and three Whigs, in 1820 it reverted to the pattern which had dominated since 1790, returning three Tories to one Whig. After 1826 the City swung Whig once again and remained so until the Reform Act of 1832. In 1801 the City represented 10 per cent of the capital's population as a whole, by 1821 it was 5 per cent.
102. See Dame Lucy Sutherland, 'The City in Eighteenth-Century Politics', in *Essays presented to Sir Lewis Namier*, (ed. R. Pares and A. J. P. Taylor, London, 1956).
103. See J. Dinwiddy, *op. cit.*, pp. 92–4; also G. Rudé, *Hanoverian London, 1714–1808* (London, 1971), chapters 8 and 9.

D. J. ROWE

London Radicalism in the Era of the Great Reform Bill

There has recently been a considerable amount of publication on political radicalism in London at the time of the agitation for the first Reform Act; and the National Union of the Working Classes (NUWC) has received particular attention.[1] It is not intended here to provide another general survey but to look at some aspects of the subject. It is intended to concentrate entirely on the popular agitation for reform – that of the public and parochial meetings and the activities of the political unions. Inevitably in an agitation as major as that for the first Reform Act it might be expected that the capital city, which contained the offending institution, the House of Commons, and which accounted for one in eight of the population of England and Wales, would play a major role. While there was a good deal of action in London and contemporaries believed that there was a wide range of support for reform there, it is likely that the response was relatively less significant than for other towns. That the national press was centred on London, as was the unstamped, largely working-class, press, meant that more publicity was given to radical activity there than strict justice might have allowed. It could certainly be argued that in terms of its impact on reform legislation London was only important in that it housed Parliament. But this paper is not concerned with parliamentary debates, nor with the behind the scenes discussions, intrigues, and dinners which may or may not have influenced the way in which particular Members of Parliament and Lords cast their votes. Such a disclaimer is necessary, when contemplating concentration on the popular agitation, to avoid the criticism of Edmund Burke:

Because half-a-dozen grasshoppers under a fern make the field ring with their importunate chink, whilst thousands of great cattle, reposed beneath the shadow of the British oak, chew the cud and are silent, pray do not imagine that those who make the noise are the only inhabitants of the field; that, of course, they are many in number; or that, after all, they are other than the little shrivelled, meagre, hopping, though loud and troublesome insects of the hour.[2]

I

The reform organizations reflect the interests of and devotion to political reform of a small proportion of the total population of London. This is not intended to denigrate the contemporary interest in reform but is merely an expression of fact. At no point during the period 1831–2 were more than a few thousand of London's population of about 1·8 million enrolled in political unions,[3] and only a small proportion of those played any part in the formal activity of the unions. The maximum number of votes cast for any candidate in the election to the Council of the National Political Union (NPU) in February 1832 was only 600 which implies that it is unlikely that more than one thousand members actually voted. As in more recent examples it is clear that most people who join an organization hold its general beliefs but will not actively foster them, a useful corrective to paying too much attention to the significance of the actual organization in the minds of its members.

It is, of course, true that the impact of an organization may be spread widely beyond its membership and Francis Place, in particular, made grandiose claims for the influence of the NPU. But in the same way that that union managed to enrol both much smaller total numbers and a much smaller proportion of its potential membership than did, for instance, the Birmingham Political Union, it seems likely that Place's claims were unjustified. Even the claims of political union leaders in London, were often not impressive. William Benbow, not the most objective of sources, only claimed 'at least 10,000 *efficient* members' of the NUWC in June 1832.[4] It is, therefore, clear that the political unions in London were relatively insignificant in so far as total membership was concerned and it is likely that unions in other towns were more successful in obtaining members. The significance given to London unions by historians appears more to be based on the fact that they existed in the capital and were, therefore, thought to be influential, than on their size. The London unions did, however, have access to the national press, whose reporting of their meetings diffused their opinions much more widely. It is likely that the opinions expressed in the unstamped newspapers had a much wider effect on working men in

London than did the NUWC and that the *Morning Chronicle*, *The Times* and other national dailies were more formative influences on, largely, middle-class opinion than was the NPU. In discussing the unions and their members it must be made clear that we are looking at the minority of activists and not at the broad range of people who favoured reform.

Already the discussion in this paper has tended to divide the interest in reform along class lines and it is undoubtedly true, although perhaps exaggerated by historians, that there was a working-class interest in reform and a middle-class one, epitomized in organizational terms in London by the two main unions to which reference has been made. I have suggested elsewhere[5] and do not wish to repeat the argument in detail, that the working-class reformers in London divided between support for the NUWC and support for moderate reform (with some overlapping); a division which appears more to be related to psychological and other factors than to economic and social structure. In addition, within the largely working-class organization of the NUWC there was more tolerance of middle-class reformers and the Whig Reform Bills than has often been suggested. These modifications must continually be borne in mind during the following discussion.

II

One area to which particular attention has been paid is that of the formative influences on the radicals. Working-class radicalism clearly had some base in those reformers who had been active in post-1815 radicalism, including Benbow, Richard Carlile, Allen Davenport, Charles Neesom, and Thomas Preston (several of them associates of Thistlewood's). It is less easy to show the influence which co-operative and, more difficult still, economic thought had. Owenism has often been cited as the be-all-and-end-all influence on the thought of the extreme London radicals but this has recently come under attack.[6] It has been pointed out that earlier writers had put forward the argument that all output depended upon labour and was, therefore, labour's due. Nevertheless this became a more common radical viewpoint under the influence of co-operation, although not necessarily of Owen, and the anti-Ricardian economists.[7] It is important that the significance of Owenite teaching is not overlooked in the revulsion. In the address of the British Association for the Promotion of Co-operative Knowledge (BAPCK) in December 1830, many of the leading members of the soon to be formed NUWC expressed the opinion that Owen had impressed on them that they 'sowed and reaped all the corn – built all the houses – made all the clothes; and yet that we were the worst fed, the worst housed, and worst clothed part of the community'.[8] Owen did have an influence and one which was probably greater than that of the anti-Ricardian economists.

The overall impact of the new economic ideology on the working-class political reform organizations of the period appears to have been limited. The new thesis that profits, and therefore all employers, were the reason for the poor state of the working classes, failed to oust the old favourites of high taxation and aristocratic power. The new analysis hardly touched the Radical Reform Association (RRA), in spite of the links of many of its members with co-operation. Its October 1829 'Address to the People of the UK' was entirely concerned with Cobbett's 'Old Corruption':

> The nation is divided into two castes, whose views, interests, habits, and sympathies, war with each other. One caste, constituting the great bulk, are unrepresented, pay the taxes, and are dropping into pauperism; the other caste, forming an inconsiderable minority, are almost exclusively represented, receive the taxes, revel in luxury and hourly augment their income ... the source of all our evils ... the direction of the civil and political state is engrossed by a few wealthy families ... the immense sum of eighty millions is annually raised by taxes, charges, or impositions from the people.[9]

For political unions subsequent to the RRA it was even more difficult in one sense for the economic analysis to make headway, since the introduction of the Reform Bill reinforced the significance of 'Old Corruption' by drawing attention to the small group which opposed reform. But historians have been influenced by Francis Place's exaggerated comments on the NUWC leaders; 'their notions that every thing which was produced belonged to them and them only ... prevailed to a very considerable extent'. Such ideas prevailed to only a very inconsiderable extent among working-class radicals and, as Dr. Hollis has shown from an extensive reading of the unstamped press, 'At best working-class speeches and letters were a somewhat undigested mixture of both attacks.'[10] This is even true of Bronterre O'Brien and Henry Hetherington, whom Hollis cites as users of the language of economic radicalism. O'Brien, for instance, once described aristocracy as that system which 'would maintain an unnatural division of society into classes *viz.*, those who labour and produce as well as consume, and those who consume only ...' and his computation, that the aristocracy robbed the working classes of £150m. annually through taxation, harks back to the old analysis.[11] The relationship of Hetherington to the new analysis depends heavily on his ownership of the *Poor Man's Guardian*, which, in its editorials, certainly used the language of economic radicalism but could also devote much space to exclusive attacks on 'Old Corruption'. It may well be that the variation in the *Guardian*'s approach owed a lot to the editor and leader writers and that Hetherington, whose subsequent activities show no deep commitment to the new ideology, should not be considered a major proponent of it. Hetherington's other papers were certainly more traditionally oriented. *The Radical* considered that 'a Radical is one who, impatient of enormous taxation imposed by a set of tax-imposers, over whose rapacity he has no control, is determined to procure a remedy for such a foul disease'; and *The Republican* advertised its character solely in terms of the elimination of 'Old Corruption', beginning with 'Extirpation of the Fiend Aristocracy'. The difference may be that Hetherington did not interfere with editorial policy and in *The Radical* and *The Republican* James Lorymer went his own way in 'the language of natural rights and taxes, not the language of economic analysis'.[12]

Whoever wrote it, the economic analysis was included in the *Guardian*. Early in its life the paper reprinted an article of Carlile's attacking 'Kings, Priests and Lords' but argued that it did not go far enough and that it was property which gave power. A fortnight later an editorial on the Reform Bill clearly showed the two analyses:

Remember, friends and brethren, that you and you alone produce *all* the real wealth of the country; remember also that you enjoy not [*sic*] but a very scanty portion of what you in fact produce: then *who* do enjoy it? – why, you will say, our 'kings,' and our 'priests,' and our 'lords,' ... but are they the only ones who fatten in idleness and uselessness upon your labour? ... do not your 'masters,' your traders – from the banker and merchant down to the £10-a-year-coal-shed-keeper, – in fact from lord mayor down to '*middle man*,' – do not they also enrich themselves at your expense?[13]

There is little evidence, however, to show that it had much effect on the attitudes of members of the NUWC. There are occasions when one thinks that the analysis has sunk in. Part of a resolution at a meeting in January 1832 ran 'that until arrangements are made for uniting both the capitalist and the labourer in the same person, no permanent benefit will be obtained for the working classes'. James Watson, who proposed the resolution, went on to say:

Capital, whether it meant food or gold, or clothes could not come into existence without industry (hear.). Then those who possess all these things, one would think, were the most industrious persons in the world, for they were the richest (hear.). But how was it that the reverse was the case? How was it that they were the most profuse and extravagant, and yet produced nothing? ... The reason was manifest; because capital monopolised that to which it had no claim, and labour was deprived of its proper right (hear.).

Although he defined capital as the 'produce of labour' it is apparent that Watson regarded this as relating to capital owned by the rich, rather than as a universal system pertaining to all who employed labour and he showed the confusion which existed among the radicals by referring to Owen's plan for labour exchanges as what the people needed. That Watson had little knowledge of or was only a recent convert to the ideas of economic radicalism is suggested by one speech in which he said, 'He had discovered that a book containing lectures on popular political economy by Mr Hodgkins [sic] had been condemned by that society [for the Diffusion of Useful Knowledge] ... and that was a sufficient proof that it contained something worth their attention.' Much the more standard pattern of Watson's thought was to be seen in his comments on an NUWC resolution to abolish primogeniture:

The abolition of this law would tend to raise the labourer to his proper standard in society, and to produce an equalization of wealth ... He was one who thought he could live without kings, lords, or bishops, and he believed that they never would prosper until the aristocracy was abolished (Cheers).[14]

If this was the level of understanding of the new analysis of a major leader, Watson's weekly meeting of the NUWC at the Philadelphian Chapel, Finsbury Square being second only to the main meeting in the Rotunda or the Institution, Theobald's Road, it is hardly surprising that the minor leaders were confused in their understanding of the new analysis, or kept entirely to an 'Old Corruption' approach. In one debate Woodhouse argued that capital provided machinery which undercut small masters and asked, 'What was the cause of all this? – The King's evil (laughter) – the aristocracy and the law of primogeniture'; and a fortnight later he commented, in a debate on the National Debt, that he 'had a great objection to the National Debt because it deprived him of the produce of his labour'.[15] But even this confused mixture of the old and new analyses was much less common than the traditional view of the wrongs of society. NUWC debates were most likely to be on tithes and taxes, the Church, the Corn Laws, or 'The Effects of Aristocratical Domination'. The common interpretation of poverty might be that of Goode in a debate on tithes:

> They had many bees in his country; and he had well observed them; there was the working bee, the drone bee, the thieving bee, and the king bee. He must compare them with the community, there was the productive class; the placemen, pensioners, or drones; and the thieving bee he could not but compare with the bishops; as to the king bee he was a good king for he protected the working bees.[16]

The last section on the king was, of course, optional and the king might be included with the drones according to taste.

Basically the NUWC was concerned with obtaining the franchise for working men, as being the way to influence their general environment, and was not concerned with worker control in employment. This meant opposition to aristocratic power and brought the argument full circle that property and theft of land were the prime reason for poverty and wealth divisions. It seems likely that there were also difficulties in putting over the new analysis in London. There was often no grand division between employers and employees in its largely artisan occupations, which made it difficult to show a division between productive and unproductive labour, hence Watson's interpretation of the new analysis as the rich capitalists stealing from the poor. There were many examples among the radicals of artisans who had made small master status, including the many radical printers and publishers, Watson, Hetherington, and John Cleave and, in other trades, Benjamin Warden, Place, and Alexander Galloway. These and many small shopkeepers did not fit the bill as oppressors of the poor. Early in its existence the NUWC showed an interest in the new economic ideology by discussing motions to restrict committee membership to 'wealth producers' but these were strongly opposed, especially by Hetherington, Foskett, and Warden, the three members deputed by the BAPCK to form the NUWC. There were too many self-employed members and, indeed, employers of labour, who would have been excluded by such a regulation. The new union, therefore, added 'and others' to its title, an addition which was soon forgotten or ignored. Although there has been some attempt to claim that the NUWC projected socialist ideas,[17] profit is too rarely the villain of the piece to support such an argument and that union has to be seen in the orthodox line of Paine, Cobbett, and Hunt.

Within this general picture, however, it is difficult to define the main influence on any individual's thought. Hence Hollis has argued that Benbow's thought was based on Painite radicalism and Prothero that he was close in his analysis to Cobbett, while Parsinnen argues that Benbow was influenced by and incorporated the new economic analysis in his pamphlet, 'Grand National Holiday and Congress of the Productive Classes', published in January 1832.[18] It is, however, clear that 'Old Corruption' was the prime source for Benbow. In his pamphlet he divided oppressors and oppressed in the ratio 1/499, which excludes any serious use of the new analysis, which could hardly fail to make the ratio of unproductive/productive persons less than one to four. It appears likely that those radicals who had been active in the period 1816–20, had their analysis of the problems of society formed by 'Old Corruption' and were largely unaffected by new approaches.

For some of the radicals, such as Benjamin Warden, who had come through co-operation in the 1820s, political argument was found wanting and they were drawn back completely into co-operation.[19] This rejection of political radicalism by those whom the *Poor Man's Guardian* called 'philosophical Owenites' caused many angry scenes at NUWC meetings and acrimonious correspondence in the columns of the *Guardian*.[20] Charles Duffey, a co-operator, who, unlike Warden, did not break his links with the NUWC but endeavoured to carry his arguments at its meetings, was frequently in conflict with the general opinion of the political radicals. When the NUWC discussed a motion to challenge the House of Commons to depute some of its members to a discussion on the claims of the non-electors, Duffey was horrified that 'the committee could propose such buffoonery'. He argued that they had to behave wisely in order to 'conquer the prejudices of public opinion' and that they should co-operate with friendly politicians such as Hume and Cobbett. He failed to get the motion withdrawn and his speech 'was followed by a furious altercation which continued for some time when the meeting broke up without any resolution having been passed'.[21] As with all London reform organizations of the time the NUWC was a disparate body of men with many ideas of immediate aims and how to achieve them and with little willingness to compromise with the opinions of others. The effectiveness of the NUWC was accordingly limited by the need to try to please a wide range of reformers and co-operation, which had provided a partial base for the NUWC also detracted from it and distracted attention from political reform. Such squabbles over policy and methods of action were undoubtedly of significance in limiting the union's attraction of members.

III

Although the NUWC was the major working-class reform organization, it was preceded by several short-lived organizations, whose failure was perhaps symptomatic of the problems of establishing viable organizations from reformers with a wide range of opinions. After the success of the Catholic Emancipation movement the RRA was formed in 1829,[22] with a similar organization and some personnel to the Association for Civil and Religious Liberty. Although there were similar bodies in Leeds, Oldham, and other towns, the RRA was an exclusive association.[23] Its meetings were mainly held in the Mechanics' Institute, Theobalds Road, with some at the Rotunda, Blackfriars Road. Although non-members were admitted at the door, the general impression is of a small group assiduously discussing the evils of the existing political structure. In a speech on the need for universal suffrage Warden stated the Association's position, 'The unequal distribution [sic] of wealth arose, in fact, from two causes; excessive taxation, and profligate expenditure ... We had to pay £66,000,000 of taxes ... The only remedy for these things was to give the people a salutary control over their representatives', a position which was only to be expected of an association whose mentors were Cobbett and Hunt.[24] It is unlikely that the RRA had any marked impact, although Hunt had some drawing power and meetings of 3,000 were claimed, while the *Weekly Free Press*, the main newspaper read by working men at the time, reported the meetings. The Association's October 1829 address to the people encouraged the setting up of local societies for universal suffrage in an attempt to extend its influence. Within the London parishes, however, contemporary agitation was aimed at the power of the select vestry and the imposition of church rates and there was little response.[25]

From the RRA onwards one gets a feeling of *déjà vu*. There is a consistent pattern of the attempts of a small number of committed men to find the moment in time and method of organization which would enable them to achieve an end, which, despite their disagreements, was for all of them the benefit of working men. The RRA was the political arm of some of the leaders of the BAPCK – Hetherington, Lovett, Warden, and Watson were members. But it also contained John Grady, Daniel French, F. A. Augero, and Emmanuel Dias Santos, who were to be among the more extreme members of the NUWC. There were subsequent rumours that Grady was involved in revolutionary plotting, although the NUWC worked within the constitution and there were continual rifts between the various cliques.[26]

In response to the setting up of the Birmingham Political Union, the
RRA decided, on a proposal from Hunt, to call 'a great Metropolitan
meeting, to appoint a Metropolitan Political Council'.[27] As the general
climate of opinion became more favourable to political reform the
leaders of the RRA saw the opportunity to develop the mass organization
which would make their ideas influential, and Hunt, no doubt, saw the
opportunity to boost his personal following. A public meeting was held
on 8 March 1830 in the grounds of the Eagle Tavern, City Road, with a
large crowd, estimated by Hunt at 20,000, at which the Metropolitan
Political Union (MPU) was formed.[28] It was firmly based on the
Birmingham precedent and although heavily dependent on the RRA for
personnel for its first council its approach was different. The RRA had
been critical of such moderate reformers as Joseph Hume but the MPU
had four Members of Parliament, including Hume, on its council of
thirty-six members. Although the major object remained 'radical
reform' it was becoming realized that a compromise was necessary to
widen support. Despite the presence of some MPs the MPU was not to the
taste of certain reformers. Burdett and Hobhouse, the radical MPs for
Westminster, were invited to attend but refused and one of the latter's
friends wrote, '*If you go there* then I shall feel bound to *go likewise – that you
may not be left alone in such company.*'[29] The union held occasional meetings
during the summer and endeavoured to persuade 'the TRADE
SOCIETIES of the METROPOLIS' to communicate with the secretary in
order to draw them into the agitation. This was unsuccessful and the
Union failed to achieve a firm base. Place claimed that its failure was a
result of the appointment of Hunt as treasurer, since 'nobody would
subscribe money to be under the controul [*sic*] or care of Mr Hunt'.
Since Hunt was the chief proponent of the MPU it is unlikely that it
would have been supported initially unless the members accepted that
he was to have a considerable influence. The failure of the MPU seems
more likely to result from the lack of response from the London
population and the inability of the small group of active leaders to be
able to run both groups. At an RRA meeting on 12 July Waylen perhaps
recognized the latter problem when he proposed that the association be
disbanded in order to strengthen the MPU but his motion was ruled out
of order by the chairman.[30] It was possibly too late since dissension was
breeding among the leaders over aims, methods and, no doubt, power.
The occasion for a major break-up was a MPU meeting on 9 August to
discuss the revolution in France. George Rogers, the Bloomsbury
tobacconist, and subsequent member of the NPU, was in the chair.[31]
There was disagreement between the chairman and some speakers who
implied that a revolution was needed in Britain and finally confusion

when Gale Jones moved extra resolutions including, 'That taxation, without representation is tyranny, and ought to be resisted'. Rogers subsequently declined to take further part in public meetings and the council revoked the membership of Jones and the Rev. Robert Taylor for uttering sentiments at variance with their duties as members.[32] Neither action was particularly significant since the union did not recover from its dissensions and disappeared. The autumn of 1830 also saw the disappearance of the RRA, although it has been stated that it lasted until the spring of 1831.[33] There is no evidence of activity by the Association at the time of the proposed Mansion House visit in November 1830 nor that there was continuity to the formation of the NUWC in March–May 1831.

The collapse of the two associations did not mean a break-up of the group of radical working men who had been involved in their leadership. Meetings continued to be held in the Rotunda, at which familiar leaders spoke on universal suffrage, taxation, church pluralities, etc.[34] In January 1831, for instance, a meeting held at the London Tavern was addressed by Cleave, Grady, and John Savage, to congratulate the electors of Preston for electing Hunt as their MP. Parochial agitation also expanded at this time. Injustices which offended radicals in local affairs began to be seen as a reflexion of corruption and oligarchic power on the national stage. Parochial reform activity was, therefore, an important feeder for parliamentary radicalism since people's interest could more easily be aroused about matters concerning their local community. The leaders of the RRA, and no doubt their followers if we could identify them, played their part. Fall, Grady, and Augero were the leading lights in the reform movement in Lambeth, gaining control over the select vestry, reducing the rate and the vestry clerk's salary, and appointing a 'committee to review the pension list of the parish'. Other parishes also had their share of radical activists and there was considerable communication between reformers – at one annual dinner of the Lambeth Parochial Reformers, Thomas Potter, John Savage, and Thomas Murphy were the guests from the St. Marylebone and St. Pancras Associations.[35] At this level there was some fraternization between middle- and working-class reformers, although the RRA should not be regarded as an entirely working-class body – Augero was a teacher, Grady a lawyer's clerk, and Daniel French a barrister. The divisions among reformers were fluctuating ones, not always determined along class lines. Potter, Savage, and Murphy were consistently on the fringes between the working- and middle-class reform associations and there were working men such as J. D. Styles who remained in both the NUWC and the NPU.

It is clear that there was continuous activity from the autumn of 1830 to the spring of 1831 and that the turning of a small carpenters' union into the NUWC was not fortuitous but merely the opportunity for the extreme radicals' next step. We have perhaps been misled by Lovett's account of the formation of the NUWC and made too much of the switch from co-operation and the BAPCK, rather than seeing the NUWC as depending upon a continuous line of radical activity.[36]

The NUWC aimed at radical reform and was therefore little impressed with the Whig reform proposals but Hollis has argued that the Union considered the Reform Bill 'inadequate, irrelevant to working men, but acceptable as a first step' and that Hetherington was the only member who 'systematically opposed the Bill'. While it is true that the *Poor Man's Guardian* consistently attacked the Bill, others of Hetherington's papers adopted a different viewpoint. *The Radical* commented, 'The Reform Bill must pass, and incomplete, inconsistent, insufficient as it is, it is tolerable as a stepping-stone,' a view supported by Carlile's *Union* and other unstamped papers.[37]

The *Guardian's* view does seem to have obtained some support in the NUWC and the Bill was denounced 'as of no use to the People and that they will never be satisfied with it or without the Ballot, Equal Laws and Equal Rights and they are quite sure we shall ere long have to fight for it'. Similarly much of the criticism of the NPU was couched in terms of opposition to partial measures, such as the Reform Bill, which might distract interest from radical reform. Benbow, for instance, 'thought the Reform Bill was calculated only as a trick to cheat the people . . .[it] set up an *Idol* of £10 shopkeepers, for the purpose of excluding the working classes'.[38] This was not a consistent attitude, since the loss of the second Bill in October 1831 led to a resolution calling for a refusal to pay taxes (repeated in May 1832). Some weeks later, however, a resolution was passed not to sign any petition which did not demand radical reform and another commented that the Bills were 'mere expedients and mere gulls to deceive the public'.[39]

A general impression is that the NUWC was rather more opposed than indifferent to the Bill but that at times when the Bill was in danger it swung towards grudging support. It remained on the sidelines in the Reform Bill agitation, merely capitalizing on the general interest in reform in order to try to gain support for its more extreme views. Its attitudes, however, were no more representative of London working men than were those of the *Guardian*. That paper might write, 'That a very large portion . . . of the poor and working people do not approve of this measure is sufficiently evidenced by the . . . hundreds of thousands who peruse our penny papers, in which . . . we have . . . expressed the strongest opposition to it' but it felt it necessary to devote three and a half pages to Lord John Russell's speech introducing the third Bill; published a special second edition to give the news that that Bill had passed its second reading and recognized its readers' interest in the rejection in May 1832.[40] Francis Place supports the *Union*'s comment that the NUWC 'contains in reality but a very small fraction of the "working class"; [and] that there are as many of the "working class"' in the NPU: and William Carpenter refuted Hunt's claim 'that the working classes are not satisfied with the Bill', commenting that 'the meeting at the Rotunda [which Hunt had used as his evidence] was *not* a meeting of the working classes of the metropolis, as such, but a meeting of "the Radical Reformers" of the metropolis . . . I take upon me to say, that the working classes ought not to be identified with it'.[41] A modern version of the *Guardian*'s approach is seen in Plummer's claim that working people were denied their desire of universal suffrage by the middle classes, who were, after 1832, 'about to enjoy the fruits of their successful chicanery'.[42] Such a claim is unsubstantiated by evidence that the working class generally felt cheated or that the middles classes enjoyed greater 'fruits' (or, for that matter, the working classes fewer fruits) after than before 1832.

IV

The middle-class reform movement in London was particularly dependent on parochial activity and the NPU had stronger contacts with the London parishes than is usually suggested. Initially the Union resolved to form branches and although this policy was officially rejected, in order to avoid breaching the law, several unions were formed, such as the NPU for the Parish of Bethnal Green. Similarly NPU leaders were influential in the parishes, Major Revell, Thomas Bowyer, and J. H. Powell being leading members of the Clerkenwell Political Union. It is, therefore, probable that the NPU was more influential through its branches and connections with local activity than through the main body and this may also be true of the NUWC.[43] There were certainly many occasions on which Place was concerned about the level of support for the NPU and historians have tended to follow him and claim that it was not influential and pay a great deal of attention to the divisions between London reformers.[44] Before looking at these divisions it is important to say that they were among the minority of activists and that the majority of London's population wanted the Reform Bill to pass.

Divisions make it inaccurate to talk of a reform movement, for although most agitation was thrown behind the Reform Bill, once it was published, there were in reality many movements and the divisions reduced their effectiveness. They were perhaps more marked in the working-class organizations but they certainly existed in middle-class bodies.[45] Between the two groups there were much more obvious differences, epitomized between the NUWC and NPU but even here there was some communication and the division was not complete.[46] Even after the withdrawal of most of the NUWC members after their failure to influence the policy of the NPU, there remained several pluralists, including William Carpenter and W. D. Saull and other members of the NPU, such as John Savage and Thomas Murphy, remained in sympathy and limited communication with the NUWC.

The basic problem for the reform agitation was to bring about a compromise between many different groups and individuals in order to obtain the most powerful force to support reform. 'To support reform', because the Whigs' reform proposals of March 1831 formed a pre-emptive strike, after which there was no possibility of forming a major campaign for more extensive, or, for that matter, less extensive reform. It is likely that the position chosen by the Whigs was largely arbitrary and that a more or less extensive reform, within limits, would equally have called the tune for public support. The extent of the illumination in London on 27 April 1831, however, shows that the actual Bill had wide support, and this ranged from the Common Council and Livery of the City, through some businessmen (George Grote was active in getting bankers to petition for reform, although there was also a counter-petition) to parts of the unstamped press. Thomas Wakley, in an editorial in *The Ballot*, commented that soon after the Reform Bill

came into our hands, we threw it down with feelings of pain, indignation, and disgust, because it did not contain any proposition for SHORT PARLIAMENTS and VOTE BY BALLOT . . . [but] our choler having subsided, we resumed the investigation; and now, after mature research, we feel justified in most sincerely thanking Ministers for the bill which they have introduced into the House, and do not hesitate to express our admiration of their firmness, integrity, liberality, and patriotism, and to declare, further, that they are entitled to the unqualified support of every honest and intelligent Englishman.[47]

The *Morning Chronicle* commented accurately that 'the movement in the Metropolis is universal, and extends to all classes of the population'.

Within this broad range of support, however, the divisions existed. Firstly there was dissatisfaction with existing reform leaders. Many reformers regarded their attempts during the 1820s to obtain the transfer of seats from corrupt boroughs to industrial towns as merely temporizing and a barrier to more effectual reform. Existing leaders were being outpaced by public opinion.[48] At a meeting of the RRA Grady queried, 'Had it served the cause of reform, or of the country, that Burdett and Hobhouse had represented Westminster? Where was their motion for reform? When was the gauntlet thrown down in that house where they sat?'[49] The degrees of enthusiasm for reform were such that Hobhouse could comment after dining with a group of Whig reformers, 'My impression was that these men are utterly ignorant of the state of the country, and will persevere deliberating on the miseries of petty political factions till the storm bursts over them, and all is over with them and the country' and yet be astonished by the extent of the Reform Bill, 'there was hardly one of us [parliamentary radicals] that believed such a scheme could, by any possibility, become the law of the land'. According to Brougham, Burdett, and Hobhouse 'greatly doubted if we did not go too far' in the Reform Bill.[50] Burdett's distance from the main stream of moderate reformers became obvious in his dealings with the NPU. To compare Hobhouse's and Place's accounts of the inaugural meeting of the union is to be in two different worlds.[51] Place wrote that Burdett's conduct was 'absurd and particularly offensive to those who were endeavouring to form the Union. To such a length were disagreements pushed by him that it was every minute expected he would abruptly leave the chair and break up the meeting.' Hobhouse noted that 'Sir F. Burdett unadvisedly took the chair at a meeting of the working-class [sic], constituted under the name of the "National Union". I knew some of the most active of these gentlemen and that this was a scheme for watching and controlling Members of Parliament.' According to Hobhouse, Burdett's reasoning was that if he did not head the NPU then 'some designing man or men would'. At best he supported the Union providing that it made the passing of the Reform Bill its only object and 'To all other Reformers who thought that the Union went too far, or did not go far enough, he would say – "Do not make any declaration that would clash with us, and by producing disunion occasion the triumph of the common enemy".' It is hardly surprising that Benbow's reaction at a meeting of the NUWC was to castigate 'the Whig Union of which Sir Francis Burdett was at the head [as] a jesuistical attempt ... to cajole the working classes' to put forward their support for a Bill which offered them nothing and Julian Hibbert warned them 'to beware of certain aristocrats, calling themselves "the NPU of the *Middle* and Working Classes"'.[52]

Thomas Murphy adopted a similar but more placatory approach than that of Burdett. Having argued that, despite their differences, London reformers would unite having seen 'a prospect of obtaining Reform', he commented that 'he knew that there were many who were not disposed to go so far as he wished to go, but he would say, let them come with me until we get as much as they want, and leave me then to strive for the rest by myself'. The later stages of this meeting of the NPU showed that Murphy's call for tolerance was unavailing. The occasion was an attempt by some of the NUWC to propose four additional names for the provisional Council of the NPU which had been carefully selected by Place and his friends. The *Morning Chronicle* gave the following report

> The first was Mr. Wakley (great uproar, hisses, and cries of 'No, no!' being predominant); the second name was Mr. Warden (cries of 'No, no!'); the third was Mr. Cooper ('No, no!'); and the fourth Mr. Henry Hunt, MP (tremendous cries of 'No, no – off, off! – No Rotunda! – No White Conduit!').

Seen from the other side, *The Radical Reformer* commented, 'We perceived a fat, oily-faced, pursy, indolent-looking, shopkeeper-like person bellowing out *"None of 'em"*, *"No Rotunda People"*, before the names had been read. Such was the animal's prejudice.' But Lorymer was not prepared to use prejudice to erect divisions and in the following week's editorial he told his, largely working-class, readers, 'For the present, let all Radicals call for the Bill, the *whole* Bill, and as soon as possible, as the North Americans would say, a pretty considerable d—d deal MORE than the Bill.'[53]

The NPU meeting of 9 November 1831 has still one more piece of evidence on the gradations of divisions among reformers. Having heard his name rejected by the meeting Thomas Wakley managed to obtain a brief hearing and finished, 'As to being a Member of the Council, he could not spare the time ["We don't want you"]; and, more than that, he would never form a part of any Society to which Henry Hunt belonged – that heartless and cold-blooded traitor [uproar].'[54] Wakley was only a relatively minor influence on the reform scene but he was taking sides in what had been a massive saga of disagreement between Hunt, Cobbett, and Carlile, perhaps the three biggest figures at the end of the 1820s. Although they were less influential in London in 1831–2, as a result of the rise of many working men and small masters to leadership, their disagreements had left their mark and were still likely to cause divisions.

The divisions between the middle- and working-class reformers were not a result of the NPU's attempt to recruit working-class support for the Reform Bill. Large has argued that the MPU failed because it could not adequately merge the RRA with middle-class reformers and there were many earlier occasions where middle-class reformers had rejected the extreme radicals.[55] Inevitably distrust between the two groups hardened and it affected all reformers. Hence personalities rather than beliefs became all important. Dias Santos's resolution to add 'radical reform' to the objects of the NPU was howled down, while Daniel O'Connell's statement to the same body that he was 'a friend to Universal Suffrage' was received with 'immense cheering'.[56]

The divisions between the NPU and NUWC were the most obvious and may have been influential in turning some working men against the Reform Bill but divisions within the various organizations certainly reduced their effectiveness. The Rotunda saw regular disagreements among Carlile, Hunt, Hetherington, Taylor, and others and Large commented that the RRA 'dissolved in a welter of dissension'.[57] While its successor, the NUWC was a much more long-lived and successful body, it too suffered the same problems, largely as a result of inheriting similar personnel. The NUWC attracted a rag-bag of radicals, some of whom, such as the co-operators, were not interested in political reform as an end, but only as a means to an end, and all of whom were faced with the problem that their aims were too advanced to be widely acceptable. Additionally the NUWC had to face the problem of working ineffectually within the system or overcoming it. Although some members toyed with a revolutionary position it was largely rejected and the frustration of not being able to achieve the Union's aims was a major cause of divisions.

The extremity of the views of some members was also a factor and Benbow is a good example. His extreme language at NUWC meetings was opposed by many of the moderates; his plan for a Grand National Holiday was continually delayed by the Committee of the Union, was attacked by Hibbert and others and known as 'Benbow's mad scheme'. He was forced to withdraw his motion critical of the NPU and finally his action over the Fast Day procession and subsequent trial led to the withdrawal of Lovett from the NUWC.[58] The regular spy reports on the NUWC make it clear that there were many internal divisions both within the main union and the committee. In January 1832 one report commented, 'A great number of the Members of the Union have left in disgust or displeasure at their [the leaders'] conduct and not a committee night for the last six weeks passed without a quarrel, confusion or disunion among themselves.' A few days later Julian Hibbert resigned from the Union (although he did not stick to his resignation) because of confusion in the committee and uproar at the Rotunda when he was chairing a meeting. The spy commented, Hibbert 'is certain from the furious and divided manner of them that some of them will go too far and be punished'.[59]

The internal divisions of the NPU were of similar type but less marked in degree. The initial decision to divide the Council equally between working- and middle-class men and the early disagreements with the NUWC members who joined the Union, undoubtedly frightened some middle-class reformers away from the Union. The continual bickering between Sir Francis Burdett as chairman and the leaders of the Union may well have had a similar effect. Basically divisions within the Union were over the question as to whether reform demands should go beyond the content of the Reform Bill.[60] Such divisions, however, paled into insignificance once the Bill itself was under attack and it became necessary to put all resources behind ensuring that it passed. Divisions within the NPU could therefore be patched over because all members wanted to achieve at least the Reform Bill while this was not true for the NUWC.

Divisions are a lot easier to pick on than are similarities but it would not do to leave this section without commenting on the fact that there were common areas of belief among even the most disparate of reformers. Hence many members of NPU who believed in universal suffrage disagreed with their NUWC counterparts only in their attitude towards the possibility of achieving it. And, to take a specific example, Francis Place, who had imbibed a belief in the common ownership of land from Godwin, had that in common with the Spencean members of the NUWC.

V

A final area which merits specific discussion is the possibility of the agitation for reform extending into violence and causing revolution.[61] The evidence enables one to outline three possible sources which give weight to such a possibility. Firstly there were a few extremists, whom it is not unreasonable to regard as mentally disturbed.[62] William Knight, who was arrested during the disturbances in November 1830, provides one example. His will, dated 7 November, stated, 'First, my strength I do give to support the cause of liberty in the ensuing revolution. Secondly, my body, if I fall in the night, I give to form a barricade against the advance of the military . . . Thirdly, my pistols I give to my father . . .' Sometimes evidence within this category was put forward for general consumption. A printed handbill, picked up in the street in November 1830, was headed 'Liberty or Death' and included the words 'The time has at length arrived – all London meets on Tuesday – come armed.' Nearly a year later a similar handbill picked up in Clerkenwell queried

> Why should we work hard to support a set of idle Bishops, Dukes, Lords etc? ... Arm yourselves in the best way you can! Assemble on Kennington Common at 1 o'clock on Wednesday morning, and proceed from thence to those parts where it may generally be approved of. After a very short contest the soldiers will join us, then we shall be free.[63]

It may be argued that the printing of handbills represents a level of organization which puts the author beyond classification as mentally deranged but the substance of the handbills remains visionary in the extreme. There is no organization and no plan of campaign and inevitably no obvious response. Evidence such as this may be dismissed since there is no possibility that it could have led to a revolution.

The second group consists of the, mainly, working-class ultra-radicals which merges at one end indistinguishably into the group outlined above. The existence of a revolutionary tradition in this category is well established from the late eighteenth century through to the Cato Street conspirators. Close compatriots of Thistlewood were involved in the reform agitation of the early 1830s and violent language abounded. Edward Lee is reported as having told one meeting in November 1830 that 'If the King went into the City the —— would never come out alive.' And even Hetherington stated 'that nothing but force would ever gain the people's rights and the sooner they prepared themselves for resistance the better'.[64] Outspoken language does not necessarily betoken revolutionary intent, although it caused much contemporary concern and led to the stopping and reading of correspondence to a number of leaders including Dias Santos, Cleave, Osborne, and Benbow.[65] There is no evidence that the search produced relevant information and, given the spy infiltration of the NUWC, both at general and committee meetings and in several of the local classes, it is only to be expected that it was a transparent body unconnected with revolutionary plotting.[66] A spy report of 4 November 1831, while noting that the radicals might resist attempts to prevent the NUWC's White Conduit House meeting, commented, 'I now find that so far from any secret Society or Committee having any controul [*sic*] over the proceedings each Union and each individual is to act as they think proper as to their preparations.'[67] There is no doubt that arming, mainly with pikes, was taking place on some scale among the more extreme radicals but there was no organization aimed at turning the armed members into an offensive group and the arming remained largely for personal protection against the possibility of a meeting of radicals being attacked by the military. At the time of the NUWC's procession on the Fast Day, 21 March 1832, a spy report noted, 'There is no organisation in us as a body but many do calculate that on that day we shall have "a good opportunity to do something".'[68] It is, however, particularly noticeable that the NUWC was very quiet during 'the days of May' 1832, a time at which the middle-class reformers were talking in revolutionary language, when there would surely have been evidence if there had been revolutionary plotting.[69] The occasions when spies reported the possibility of trouble but nothing materialized, as on the Fast Day when police interference with the procession actually encouraged violence, are illustrations of the old proverb that it is better to travel hopefully than to arrive. It is probable that the only occasions on which the NUWC considered an even potentially revolutionary activity were its discussions on Benbow's Grand National Holiday and Congress of the Productive Classes, which Prothero argues was intended to provoke a revolutionary situation. It is, however, noticeable that the Committee of the NUWC delayed the publication of Benbow's plan for several months from the time when it was first raised in August 1831, perhaps because it was reluctant to cause such a confrontation. Similarly, when Benbow, in May 1832, proposed the calling of a national congress, this was rejected.[70] The NUWC recognized the weakness of its position and was not prepared to do anything foolish – a position which only changed in the winter of 1832–3 as the more extreme members gained control, with the results of Cold Bath Fields.

The third group which might be regarded as potentially revolutionary was the middle-class radicals at times when the passage of the Reform Bill was in jeopardy. Although this possibility has been convincingly rejected by Hamburger a few points may be made.[71] Middle-class support for reform was marked only at peaks of excitement – thus the NPU was very weak in the early months of 1832 – which meant difficulties for any planned revolution.[72] There was, however, considerable evidence of violent language in NPU publications. A petition to the House of Lords in May 1832 commenced 'That your petitioners believing, that there is yet time to save the country from a frightful convulsion ...' and an earlier resolution warned

his Majesty's Ministers in particular, and the Aristocracy in general, that a mutilation [of the Reform Bill] will produce consequences fatal as would a rejection; for the storm which has been allayed by the Political Unions, will 'rage with violence', and prevent the voluntary payment of taxes to the dismemberment of society and the extinction of the privileged orders.[73]

The language used at meetings could be similarly forceful. In May 1832 Wakley asked, 'will not this meeting [of the NPU] declare that it will not dissolve itself till the Reform Bill be passed (cheers)? ... will not members from every district meeting be called? What is to prevent us from having a National Convention (loud cheers)?' And at a subsequent meeting, Rowland Detrosier, the NPU secretary, said, 'We have found out the way "To Stop the Duke" (cheers and we have) without spilling one drop of blood. We have put a few paper bullets through the body of the "old lady of Threadneedle Street" (cheers).' Those who heard him contrasting the reformers' measures with the Duke of Wellington's threat to use force clearly understood his allusions. Parochial meetings also heard similar language. Commenting on the possible use of troops by the Duke, Col. L. G. Jones told a Marylebone meeting, 'He had been at the head of some of the most desperate attacks during the late war, and he now declared that if a necessity arose he would again lead on his countrymen to glory ... They all now knew that the men of the North were ready to march upon London (cheers).'[74] It is clear that statements such as these were made and cheered under the psychological pressures of the excitement of early May 1832. It is inconceivable that the NPU would cheer a proposal from Benbow for a National Congress and it is at the least unlikely that they would have taken active measures to support Wakley's proposal. The second point is that all the threats were made in response to an assumption of a flat rejection of reform. A climb-down was eminently more probable, as in fact happened, since the continued political upheavals of the reform agitation were seen by Conservative peers as less attractive than actually accepting the Reform Bill. It is, however, eminently unlikely, as Hamburger suggested, that the middle-class reformers were sufficiently well organized or agreed in their ideas that they could have met a flat rejection with sufficient power to overthrow a united King and House of Lords.

The last words may be left with the almost contemporaneous comments of two newspapers which reflected the major wings of reform opinion. The *Poor Man's Guardian* wrote

When 'the Bill' is safe, which we are not yet quite confident it is, we cannot think so ill of human nature as to think that those who will then have gained their own freedom, will not aid us to gain ours. We must, as they have done, endeavour to show by our own conduct, that we deserve to enjoy our Rights.

And the *Morning Chronicle* commented

There is a great deal of truth in the complaints of the labouring classes in England, that their grievances never will be attended to in a Parliament chosen by the Upper Classes and Middle Classes exclusively. The Reform Bill will be productive of immense benefit, but it leaves this evil where it was. The caste to which the working man belongs is below the Legislature and the Legislature takes no concern in him. In our manufacturing towns, where the Working Classes are becoming intelligent, the heart burnings between the Middle Classes and them are very great; and some day or other we may feel the effects of them.[75]

And so the unhappy compromise was to go on through the 1830s into Chartism and eventually to 1867 and beyond. But it was a compromise.

Notes

1. These works include, J. Hamburger, *James Mill and the Art of Revolution* (New Haven, Connecticut, 1963), P. Hollis, *The Pauper Press* (1970), P. Hollis (ed.), *The Poor Man's Guardian* (1969), D. Large, 'William Lovett' in P. Hollis (ed.), *Pressure from Without* (1974), D. J. Rowe, 'Class and Political Radicalism in London, 1831–2', *Hist. J.* xiii, 1 (1970), pp. 31–47, and D. J. Rowe (ed.), *London Radicalism, 1830–43: A Selection from the Papers of Francis Place* (London Record Society, vol. 5, 1970).
2. E. Burke, *Reflections on the Revolution in France* (Scott Library edn., 1900), pp. 105–6. I owe this reference to Prof. N. McCord.
3. No precise figures exist. The NUWC had a maximum membership of 3,000 if one multiplies the number of classes which existed by 25 (the number at which it was suggested that classes should divide). The NPU is more difficult but may have achieved more than 5,000 members at the peak of the crisis in the 'days of May' 1832. The peak quarters for subscriptions were November–January 1831–2 and May–July 1832 (the accounts are given in British Museum, Add(itional) MSS. 27,796, ff. 290–1, reprinted in Rowe, *London Radicalism*, p. 118). Assuming that there were no donations and that no-one gave more than the minimum quarterly subscription of one shilling, unlikely assumptions, these would give a paying membership of 9,253 at peak. See also Hamburger, *op. cit.*, pp. 129–30. Even with those enrolled in parochial unions it is unlikely that more than 20,000 people were members of political unions in London.
4. Quoted in B. M. Add. MSS. 27,796, f. 313. On Benbow see I. J. Prothero, 'William Benbow and the Concept of the "General Strike"', *Past and Present*, 63 (1974), pp. 132–71.

5. See Rowe, 'Class and Political Radicalism', especially pp. 41–2.

6. Prothero, *op. cit.*, pp. 155–8. See also Hollis, *Pauper Press* pp. 214–17. A reasonable summary of the radicals' position might be that provided by Julian Hibbert at an NUWC meeting, 'They agreed with Mr. Hunt in Universal Suffrage and Vote by Ballot (hear.) and the plan of Mr. Owen could not be followed out until a proper foundation was cleared away. (Hear.).' *Poor Man's Guardian*, 3 December 1831.

7. It is impossible to define the respective influences on the NUWC radicals of Owenism and anti-capitalist economics, since Owen was clearly influenced by the anti-capitalists in the late 1820s and was to denounce private property in *Lectures on an Entire New State of Society* (1830), as did the *Poor Man's Guardian* which rejected Owenism.

8. Quoted in W. H. Oliver, *Organisations and Ideas behind the Efforts to Achieve a General Union of the Working Classes in the Early 1830s* (Oxford University D. Phil. thesis, 1954), p. 41. The Owenite version of the new economic analysis did include the manufacturers in the productive class whereas the anti-Ricardians included capitalist employers in the non-productive group which was parasitic on the workers.

9. *Working Man's Friend*, 24 October 1829.

10. B. M. Add. MSS. 27,791, f. 19; Hollis, *Pauper Press*, p. 286; see generally *ibid.*, pp. 203–11, 220–58 and 285–90.

11. Quoted in A. Plummer, *Bronterre* (1971), p. 35; Carpenter's *Political Letters*, 18 February 1831. O'Brien was subsequently to draw more heavily on the new ideology and compare the 'molehill' of taxation with the 'Mont Blanc' of profits.

12. *The Radical*, 20 August 1831; quoted in S. Maccoby, *English Radicalism, 1832–1852*, p. 32; Hollis, *Pauper Press*, p. 214. Lorymer edited both *The Radical* and *The Republican*.

13. *Poor Man's Guardian*, 16 and 30 July 1831. The most complete exposition of the new ideology published in the paper came not from a London source but from a Manchester correspondent who signed himself variously 'ONE OF THE KNOW-NOTHINGS' and 'ONE OF THE OPPRESSED', *ibid.*, 26 November 1831 and 7 January and 14 April 1832.

14. *Ibid.*, 4 February 1832; 24 December 1831, a reference which throws further doubt on Place's claim that Hodgskin was a major influence on NUWC leaders; and 7 January 1832.

15. *Ibid.*, 4 and 18 February 1832.

16. *Ibid.*, 24 December 1831 and 5 May 1832.

17. Oliver, *op. cit.*, pp. 64–7.

18. Hollis, *Pauper Press*, pp. 204–5; Prothero, *op. cit.*, pp. 141–6; and T. M. Parsinnen, 'Association, Convention and anti-Parliament in British Radical Politics, 1771–1848', *E.H.R.* 88 (1973), pp. 519–20. I am grateful to Mr. F. C. Mather for drawing my attention to this conflict with regard to Benbow's thought. In discussing the calling of the Calthorpe St. meeting in 1833 to consider a National Convention, Parsinnen (p. 520) states that 'the NUWC agitation was so successful that "the people all over the country, were able and nearly willing to take their own affairs into their own hands"', a quotation which he attributes to Place and which he obtained from Oliver's thesis. This implies that Place believed that a working class rising was possible. What Place wrote referred to 1831 and not 1833 and he actually wrote, 'The leaders of all these unions [of working men] had but few exceptions had succeeded [*sic*] in persuading themselves that the time was coming when the whole of the working men would be ready to rise en masse and take the management of their own affairs, i.e. the management of the affairs of the nation into their own hands', B. M. Add. MSS. 27,791, ff. 333–5 (*London Radicalism*, pp. 51–2).

19. Oliver, *op. cit.*, pp. 47–50. It is of interest that two of these, Foskett and Warden, were, with Hetherington, the members of the BAPCK who formed the NUWC. The co-operators perhaps saw co-operation as a way to change society and universal suffrage

as only an improvement to existing society, cf. Lovett's speech to the BAPCK quoted in *Weekly Free Press*, 17 October 1829.

20. In commenting on the inaugural meeting of Owen's Association, Hetherington wrote, 'When the people have EQUAL RIGHTS, and their consequent EQUAL LAWS, the superiority of Mr. Owen's principles will admit of demonstration, but not till then.' This was followed by a reply from Warden in which he stated that he left the NUWC because of its lack of union and there followed an attack on him by Hetherington. *Poor Man's Guardian*, 24 December 1831 and 21 January and 10 March 1832. There was considerable controversy in active working-class circles, the Western Co-operative Institute holding a discussion as to whether Owen's or Hetherington's proposals would best benefit the working classes; *ibid.*, 28 January 1832. Prothero (*op. cit.*, p. 156) divides the NUWC 'between Owenites like Watson, Hetherington and Lovett, and the opponents of Owenism led by Benbow'. This may be misleading and it is important to stress that in the Reform Bill period Hetherington, at least, moved to a position of opposition to Owen as a distraction to what he regarded as the main immediate aim of working men, universal suffrage. A number of well-known NUWC radicals managed, however, to combine that activity with co-operation without any obvious conflict. Lovett, for instance, remained in the First London Co-operative Society; J. D. Styles was secretary to the general meeting of the London co-operatives in March 1832 and William MacDiarmid was delegate from the Metropolitan Co-operative Society. Individual personality caused variations in the pattern – Charles Rosser, for instance, a member of the BAPCK, joined the NPU and not the NUWC.

21. Quoted in B. M. Add. MSS. 27,796, ff. 336–8, (*London Radicalism*, p. 116).

22. There is some confusion as to when the Association was formed. Hollis, *Poor Man's Guardian*, p. xi, gives the 'spring of 1829', although it seems more likely that it was July 1829 since a meeting of the Friends of Civil and Religious Liberty on 13 July decided to change that body's name to the Friends of Radical Reform in the Commons House of Parliament. *Weekly Free Press*, 18 July 1829.

23. Members were to be nominated and seconded at a monthly meeting and then balloted by the committee, *ibid.*, 8 August 1829 and 17 July 1830.

24. *Ibid.*, 8 August 1829. At this time Cobbett was a popular figure in the Association. Hunt's ascendancy of 1830 was still to come and the two were on speaking terms until a disagreement in September led to Cobbett's resignation, *ibid.*, 12 and 26 September 1829.

25. It seems likely that activity in parochial affairs in the late 1820s nurtured radicalism at a time when a wider campaign for parliamentary reform offered limited returns. In the Reform Bill period they ran concurrently and probably reinforced each other. On one occasion Dias Santos was reported as having come to a meeting of NUWC from a meeting in the parish of St. Martin-in-the-Fields to celebrate triumph over the select vestry. *Poor Man's Guardian*, 4 February 1832. The *Morning Chronicle* published accounts of numerous parochial reform associations November 1830–January 1831 and one specific account is in F. H. W. Sheppard, *Local Government in St. Marylebone, 1688–1835* (1958).

26. On Grady see Public Record Office (PRO), Home Office Papers (HO) 40/25, J. W. Brick to S. M. Phillipps, 5 November 1830 and for divisions in NUWC see, for instance, the report of a meeting in *Poor Man's Guardian*, 8 October 1831.

27. *Weekly Free Press*, 6 and 20 February 1830.

28. The inaugural meeting of the MPU took place on a Monday afternoon at 1 p.m., like so many other contemporary radical meetings – reflecting the continuing influence of 'St. Monday'. It was reported in *Weekly Free Press*, 13 March 1830. A printed copy of the resolutions of the meeting and objects, rules, etc. of the MPU is in B. M. Add. MSS. 27,822, ff. 11–14 (*London Radicalism*, pp. 1–7).

29. Col. L. G. Jones to J. C. Hobhouse, *ibid.*, 37,949, f. 78.

30. *Weekly Free Press*, 17 July 1830.
31. There was also a G. Rogers, who chaired a meeting of the NUWC on 30 April 1832, when his language, as reported in the *Poor Man's Guardian* (5 May), was so unlike that of George Rogers that one is inclined to believe that there were two reformers with the same name and initial. It is certainly true that there were two reformers called J. Savage, who are sometimes confused. James Savage was a member of and regular speaker at the NUWC, while John Savage, the St. Marylebone radical whose goods were distrained for refusal to pay rates, was a member of the NPU.
32. *Weekly Free Press*, 14 August 1830.
33. I. J. Prothero in *Dictionary of Labour Biography*, 1, p. 167 and Hollis, *Pauper Press*, p. 102. Large, 'William Lovett', suggests that the RRA met until October 1830 but had dissolved by December.
34. The Secret Service reports reinforce this. See, for instance, PRO HO 40/25, 15 November 1830.
35. *The Ballot*, 17 April, 3 July and 25 December 1831 and 22 January 1832.
36. B. M. Add. MSS. 27,822, ff. 15–27. That the NUWC owed a large debt to the MPU for its organization may be seen from a comparison of the rules, etc. of the two bodies, which are identically worded in some parts (cf. *London Radicalism*, pp. 4–7 and 29–33).
37. Hollis, *Pauper Press*, p. 282; *The Radical*, 27 August 1831; for the view of the *Poor Man's Guardian* see 19 November 1831 and 19 March and 16 June 1832.
38. PRO HO 64/12: Secret Service report, 22 May 1832; *Poor Man's Guardian*, 3 September 1831.
39. *Ibid.*, 22 and 29 October and 10 December 1831 and 7 January 1832. See also Watson's view that the Bill 'was grounded on property and not on rights, and therefore iniquitous and unjust', *ibid.*, 21 April 1832.
40. *Ibid.*, 1 October and 17 December 1831, 14 April and 12 May 1832.
41. B. M. Add. MSS. 27,790, ff. 22–5 and 27,791, ff. 333–5 (*London Radicalism*, pp. 38–40 and 51 and 53); *Union*, 3 December 1831; *The Ballot*, 16 October 1831. There is not scope here for detailed discussion of Carpenter's position but it is an interesting one which would repay attention. An early working-class hero in the unstamped press campaign, he had imbibed a good part of the new economic ideology but was still able to argue during the Reform Bill campaign that there was an identity of interest between the middle and working classes and he remained the strongest link between the NUWC and the NPU. He experienced a good deal of criticism from working-class radicals for his pains. See W. Carpenter, *Address on the Reform Bill* (1831); *Poor Man's Guardian* 19 and 26 November and 3 and 24 December 1831.
42. Plummer, *op. cit.*, pp. 31–2.
43. *The Ballot*, 6 November 1831; B. M. Add. MSS. 27,791, ff. 79, 91 and 98; B. M. Place Collection, Set 63, vol. 1, ff. 25–8, 32 and 40; *ibid.*, Set 63, vol. 2, ff. 76 and 81. Although the NUWC moved officially from a branch to a class system during the winter of 1831/2 the branches remained in effect by means of weekly meetings in various parts of the town. It is not true to say, as Hollis has done (*Pauper Press*, p. 264 and *The Poor Man's Guardian*, p. xviii) that 'The N.U.W.C. was forced to reorganise itself' because of the government ban on political unions with branches. The union was already developing its class structure before the ban, presumably because it saw this as a more effective way of obtaining and retaining members. *Poor Man's Guardian*, 29 October and 26 November 1831.
44. M. Brock, *The Great Reform Act* (1973), p. 296. Brock's implication that Place could not get up a large reform demonstration appears to exaggerate the divisions between reformers and ignores the evidence of the large demonstration of October 1831. See B. M. Add. MSS. 27,790, ff. 39–47 (*London Radicalism*, pp. 40–5) and *Morning Chronicle*, 13 October 1831.
45. Although the NPU had many working-class members, it was dominated by a small

middle-class group on its council, in which working-class members spoke rarely and then half-apologetically.

46. On this point see Rowe, 'Class and Political Radicalism'.

47. For the illumination see *The Times* and *Morning Chronicle*, 28 April 1831; for the support of the Livery see *Morning Chronicle*, 20 September 1831 and Brock, *op. cit.*, p. 214, which gives an account of the censuring of Alderman Thompson for voting against one clause in the Bill and his promise to vote for the whole Bill in future; for the support of businessmen, *Morning Chronicle*, 28 April and 15 October 1831, although there was a petition against the Bill from '800 merchants, bankers and traders of the City of London', Brock, *op. cit.*, p. 242; *The Ballot*, 6 March 1831.

48. One example, albeit of a man who was no longer in the forefront of the reform campaign, was Thomas Hardy, who, on the publication of the Reform Bill wrote to J. C. Hobhouse, 'You will perhaps smile when I say that I am now for the *first time*, a ministerial man.' B. M. Add. MSS. 36,466, f. 309.

49. *Weekly Free Press*, 10 October 1829. The extreme radicals were, however, pragmatists and could bury the hatchet if they believed it to be in their best interests. Dias Santos, as secretary to the MPU, wrote to Hobhouse requesting his support for Hunt at the Preston election and ended by 'wishing you and Sir Francis Burdett every success tomorrow [in the Westminster election] in which every genuine reformer must join us', B. M. Add. MSS. 36,466, f. 223. Hobhouse and Burdett were also being passed in reform fervour by most of their traditional Westminster supporters, *ibid.*, 27,789, ff. 276-8 (*London Radicalism*, pp. 13-15).

50. Lord Broughton (J. C. Hobhouse), *Reflections of a Long Life* (1910), iv, pp. 61 and 87-8; quoted in Brock, *op. cit.*, p. 160.

51. Broughton, *op. cit.*, p. 146 and B. M. Add. MSS. 27,791, ff. 47-57 and 66-79 (*London Radicalism*, pp. 53-9).

52. *Morning Chronicle*, 11 November 1831, report of NPU meeting. One might reflect that since the forces being grouped in favour of reform were far from homogeneous, it is not surprising that the 'common enemy' was in fact an unclear concept, which to some reformers included Burdett himself. B. M. Add. MSS. 27,791, f. 94 and *Poor Man's Guardian*, 5 November 1831. French told a meeting in Clerkenwell that he should not become a member of the NPU if Burdett were chairman, since that would be 'stamping it an Aristocratical Union'. B. M. Place Collection, Set 17, vol. 2, f. 255.

53. *Morning Chronicle*, 11 November 1831 and *The Radical Reformer*, 12 and 19 November 1831.

54. *Morning Chronicle*, 11 November 1831.

55. Large, *op. cit.*, p. 106 and *Poor Man's Guardian* 23 July and 27 August 1831.

56. *Morning Chronicle*, 2 December 1831 and 26 January 1832.

57. Large, *op. cit.*, p. 106. While it suffers from the same dangers as dividing Chartists as to moral and physical force opinions, there is some evidence that the internal divisions of the RRA and subsequent bodies were along similar lines with Augero, Grady, Dias Santos, Benbow, and subsequently Petrie, Mee, and Lee on one side and Hetherington, Lovett, Watson, and Cleave on the other, among the main leaders. See reports of RRA meetings in *Weekly Free Press*, 7 November 1829, 13 March and 12 June 1830; *Poor Man's Guardian*, 28 January and 4 and 18 February 1832; PRO HO 64/11; Secret Service report 16 November 1830; and Hollis, *Pauper Press*, pp. 148-9.

58. Plummer, *op. cit.*, pp. 124-8; Prothero, 'William Benbow'; B. M. Add. MSS. 27,822, ff. 15-27 and 27,791, ff. 94-5 (*London Radicalism*, pp. 138-46 and 64-6). In a letter accompanying his account of the NUWC Lovett wrote to Place, 'I am no ways desirous than any save yourself should know of what I have written, it might beget bad feelings especialy [*sic*] amongst the prejudiced in my own class.' B. M. Add. MS. 27,822, f. 15.

59. PRO HO 64/12: Secret Service reports 12 and 30 January 1832.

60. See reports of NPU meetings in *Union*, 3 and 17 December 1831.

61. This possibility is put forward in E. J. Hobsbawm, *Industry and Empire: an Economic History of Britain since 1750* (1968), p. 55 and E. P. Thompson, *The Making of the English Working Class* (2nd edn., 1968), pp. 889 and 898–9; it is analysed and convincingly rejected in Hamburger, *op. cit.* See also D. J. Rowe, 'Francis Place and the Historian', *Hist. J.* 16, 1 (1973), pp. 59–62.

62. This is written advisedly. Despite the work of several distinguished historians in recent years in attempts to understand the psychology of working men involved in mass activity, there will always remain an element which cannot be explained by logical analysis. The people evidenced below were not rational in their ideas and provide no evidence of any organised revolutionary activity.

63. PRO HO 40/25: papers relating to William Knight; *ibid.*, *ibid.*, 52/14, police report 11 October 1831.

64. *Ibid.*, 40/25: report from F police division of meeting at Clare Market, and secret service report (n.d. but mid-December 1830). See also 52/14, secret service reports for early November 1831.

65. *Ibid.*, 79/4, Lord Melbourne to the Post Master General, 29 December 1830 and 5 November 1831. For the level of concern in November 1830 see *ibid.*, 40/25 and for October/November 1831 see *ibid.*, 52/14. It is significant that the volume of disturbances correspondence rises dramatically a couple of days before an incident like the proposed NUWC meeting of 7 November 1831 and as soon as the affair is over declines dramatically.

66. See Hollis, *Pauper Press*, pp. 40–1.

67. PRO HO 52/14: Secret Service report, 4 November 1831. A report the following day mentioned a belief held by some of the NUWC leaders that 'the Bethnal Green people would insist' on the White Conduit meeting taking place irrespective of Government action, but two of the spies, themselves silk-weavers, considered that 'the respectable part of the weavers' would be pleased if it were cancelled because they felt that they were being pushed on by the unions. The East End was the strongest area of NUWC support – see the list of class leaders with their addresses in *Poor Man's Guardian*, 4 February 1832.

68. *Ibid.*, 64/12: Secret Service report, 12 March 1831. A plan proposed by Petrie to the NUWC Committee for drilling the members of the union was opposed by several leaders and dropped, which reflects their basically constitutional behaviour. B. M. Add. MSS. 27,791, f. 94. Nevertheless some drilling was taking place; Watson's class was practicing sword exercises under an ex-cavalryman. It is perhaps significant that the authorities, having banned the November meeting, allowed the Fast Day procession to take place, albeit with some precautions. It may be that by then they had decided that the NUWC did not pose a serious threat.

69. A report of 1 May 1832 stated that an NUWC meeting at Finsbury 'was to take place at eight but it was nine o'clock ere 40 persons met and then no speakers ... I have found as I have stated that our Meetings fall off and on this occasion no more than 61 was [*sic*] admitted'. PRO HO 64/12.

70. Prothero, 'William Benbow', pp. 147–9; *Poor Man's Guardian*, 27 August and 3 December 1831; PRO HO 64/12: Secret Service report, 17 May 1832.

71. His argument is basically that the middle-class campaign was aimed at persuading the Government of the fearful results of failure to stick to their reform proposals, without actually intending or planning those results. Although many reformers may have been convinced by the propaganda there was no chance that this would backfire on Place and company because there was no organization.

72. Attendance at NPU Council meetings reflects this. B. M. Place Collection, Set 63, vol. 1. See also Place's comments, B. M. Add. MSS. 27,791, f. 126.

73. Copy in *ibid.*, 27,793, f. 24; B. M. Place Collection, Set 17, vol. 3, f. 147. This volume contains some of Place's collection of documents and newspaper cuttings relating to

the NPU. A number of the NPU documents, some of them rejected by the Council, contain extreme language, see ff. 12b, 12e and 12f. See also NPU handbill 'Crisis', 14 March 1832, copy in B. M. Add. MSS. 27,791, f. 153 (*London Radicalism*, p. 79).

74. B. M. Place Collection, Set 17, vol. 3, f. 174, newspaper cutting; B. M. Add. MSS. 27,794, f. 171; *ibid.*, 27,793, f. 203.

75. *Poor Man's Guardian*, 26 May 1832 and *Morning Chronicle*, 16 June 1832.

DAVID LARGE

London in the
Year of Revolutions,
1848

There can be no mistaking the gloom that prevailed in polite circles in London as the year 1847 drew to its close. Henry Reeve provides a representative view when he ended his diary for the old year with the entry, 'remarkable depression ... in society; general illness; great mortality; innumerable failures; funds down to 76; want of money; no society at all'.[1] A few weeks later on 18 February 1848 the Prime Minister, Lord John Russell, making his financial statement for the coming year to the House of Commons, in which he proposed an unprecedented virtual doubling of income tax, echoed such sentiments maintaining that the past eighteen months had been the most distressing ever known in peace-time in Britain.[2] And there was warrant for such dejection. 1847 had truly been a bad year, combining Irish famine and in late spring and again in early autumn two occasions of acute commercial crisis, when hunger and unemployment on the massive scale of 1842 seemed poised to return.[3]

Two main effects of this intense gloom may be discerned. In certain circles it became only too easy for all kinds of prophecies and rumours of further disasters to gain credence, while outside such circles, among those who aspired to provide political leadership for the unenfranchised an air of optimism prevailed. In January 1848 some sections of the London daily press were full of the notion that Britain was in imminent danger of a sudden invasion by France without even a declaration of war[4] and this was *before* anyone had dreamed of such dramatic developments as the continental revolutions of February and March in Paris, Berlin, and Vienna. As might be expected from the existing panicky state of opinion in the capital, when news of these remarkable events reached London, the invasion bogy, as we shall see, was replaced by an even more frightening apparition. In the same month of January the Chartist Metropolitan Delegate Council, addressing its London supporters, spoke of this time as being 'the most favourable opportunity since 1839 for agitation for the Charter', adducing as evidence the existence of severe distress and the incompetence of Lord John Russell's government. The *Northern Star* in its first editorial of the new year reinforced this optimism, referring to the past year as memorable for the election of 'the Chartist chief', Feargus O'Connor, to parliament and claiming that 'throughout England, lectures, public meetings and assemblages of local delegates attest that the dry bones were quickening into life and action'. With pride, it maintained that membership of the Land Company had reached 50,000.[5]

What evidence is there that London Chartism was 'quickening into life and action' by early 1848? First it should be recalled that, by this time, Chartism in London already had a substantial history behind it. In the 1830s, down to the Birmingham Political Union's conversion in November 1837 to the cause of universal suffrage rather than household suffrage and the rise of Feargus O'Connor's Great Northern Union and *Northern Star*, founded in the same month and year, it may justly be claimed that it was the leaders of London working class radicalism who made the front running in launching Chartism.[6] Lovett, Hetherington, Watson, and Cleave had won their spurs in the ultra-radical cause by their major role in creating and sustaining the unstamped press.[7] They had gone on to found the London Working Men's Association in 1836, which not only fathered the Charter itself,[8] but through its missionaries to the provinces in 1836–7 did much to stimulate the revival or formation of similar bodies up and down the country.[9] Nonetheless, important though the services of individual leaders of London Chartism were during the first phase of the movement – Lovett was the indispensable secretary of the National Convention of 1839 and Hetherington's *London Dispatch* was the outstanding ultra-radical newspaper prior to the *Northern Star* – Londoners themselves had shown only a limited interest. Delegates to the National Convention had been dismayed by the capital's apathy. In January 1839 there were only five Chartist organizations in the whole of the metropolis; in March there were only 19,000 London signatures of the National Petition and only £50 had been collected for the National Rent. London's Palace Yard meeting to choose delegates for the Convention could not compare in numbers with the vast gatherings at Lancashire's Kersal Moor or Yorkshire's Peep Green.[10] Quarrels between rival groups, of which that between the LWMA and Harney's London Democratic Association[11] is well known, further weakened London Chartism, as did the absence of any central delegate organization to bring together local groups of ultra-radicals that existed in many parishes but who had no connection with formal Chartist bodies such as the LWMA or the London Democratic Association. Yet it was among such groups that the real strength of metropolitan Chartism lay as was to be demonstrated in the early 1840s.

Thanks to the encouragement of the National Convention itself in 1839, to the initiative of many local leaders such as Edmund Stallwood of Hammersmith, Charles Westerton of Knightsbridge, Henry Ross and John Simpson of Camberwell, to mention but a few, and to the emergence of the National Charter Association in 1840 to provide a vital organizational framework, many of the weaknesses of London Chartism as it was early in 1839 had been overcome. The second National Petition was borne through London in 1842 by a huge procession of Chartists, now joined by many of the trades who had formerly provided little support; the number of Chartist societies had shot up from five in January 1839 to thirty-seven in October 1842; and from July of that year onwards a fully functioning central delegate organization was established after several abortive attempts. The London signatories to the National Petition of 1842 reached the impressive figure of 200,000.[12] As Dr. Prothero has convincingly argued, 1842 represented the high water mark of support for the Charter in London. By this time the movement had been transformed: working-class leaders dominated it, class antagonism was expressed more freely and sharply than ever before, and recruits had been won on a considerable scale from the less 'aristocratic' trades, such as those of the building workers, in contrast to the narrow base of support from a small number of more 'aristocratic' trades, such as compositors, on which the LWMA had rested. Indeed, the evidence points to the trade unions and trade societies displaying considerable enthusiasm for the Charter in the London of 1842: some NCA localities appear to have been composed almost exclusively of members of particular trade societies in their district.

Following the peak of activity in 1842 there was certainly a considerable decline in support between 1843 and 1847. The number of Chartist societies in the capital fell from thirty-five in December 1842 to twenty-three in December 1843 and to ten by June 1847. This, of course, mirrored the decline of the movement nationally, yet it would seem that the decay was less marked in London than in many other districts with the result that the metropolis remained, as it had become in 1842, one of the principal Chartist centres in the country. This was reflected in developments such as the migration from Leeds to London of the *Northern Star* in 1844, the establishment of the Land Company in the metropolis, where the London Chartists T. M. Wheeler and Philip McGrath carried out its secretarial work, and by the fact that from 1843 onwards Londoners secured the majority of seats on the annually-elected national executive of the National Charter Association. After 1842 Chartist organization was to a large extent London-based and London officered.[13]

What, then, was the condition of London Chartism in the new year 1848, in the six or seven weeks before 'the three days of February ... without exception, the most glorious in the annals of the human race', as the *Northern Star* characterized the Paris revolution?[14] There is ample evidence that its organizational machinery was both intact and active. The Metropolitan Delegate Council met regularly, publicized itself in the *Northern Star*, and busied itself with organizing public meetings such as that held at the Royal British Institution in January when Ernest Jones, the chief speaker, made a special plea to the people of London to 'agitate and organise' as they were so 'close to the seat of power'.[15] In February, sixteen delegates formed the Council[16] with, in addition, William Tapp as their secretary. They had been chosen by NCA localities and other Chartist societies in sympathy with the NCA, which can be identified as meeting, often weekly at this time, in Marylebone, Somerstown, Shoreditch, Tower Hamlets, Bermondsey, Lambeth, Limehouse, the City and Finsbury, Camberwell, and Walworth – both especially active NCA localities – Greenwich and Woolwich. In most of these districts, too, there were branches of the Land Company also meeting regularly. All were served by a pretty regular band of visiting speakers,[17] the most prominent of whom were Philip McGrath, an East End tailor,[18] who described himself as 'a collier by trade' and a Chartist of eight years' standing,[19] Thomas Clark, Edmund Stallwood, a Hammersmith activist of nearly twenty years' standing,[20] and Ernest Jones.[21] No doubt these bodies represented the core of London Chartism, but not its totality.

There were also societies whose members while certainly favouring the Charter had other preoccupations or were out of sympathy with the National Charter Association, and hence were, in effect, on the fringes of the movement. This applied, though he would not have admitted it, to Julian Harney's special interest, the heterogeneous body of continental exiled would-be revolutionaries, the Fraternal Democrats and their cousin the Democratic Committee for the Regeneration of Poland. Both met from time to time, usually in Soho, to listen to long and impassioned speeches denouncing the evils of contemporary continental regimes and demanding the establishment of Democracy, Liberty, and a variety of new economic systems. Both of these bodies, at least, had some connection with the mainstream of the London movement, if only through the presence at their meetings of figures prominent in London Chartism, such as Philip McGrath, Thomas Clark, and Harney himself. The latter also ensured publicity in the *Northern Star*.[22] Much more remote from the main body, indeed hostile to it, yet still having a commitment to the Charter, were the followers of William Lovett at his National Hall, Hetherington and Watson of the John St. Institution; G. J. Holyoake at the Hall of Science in Finsbury and Thomas Cooper who early in 1848 was regularly but peri-patetically lecturing in London in the cause of infidelity while retaining a general sympathy for the Chartist cause.[23] Much more important than these, however, were the London Irish.

Throughout the 1830s and 1840s the strength of metropolitan radicalism was considerably affected by their attitude. Their hero for many a long year was Daniel O'Connell. When he found himself in harmony with metropolitan ultra-radicalism, those of the London Irish who were sufficiently bold to ignore priestly discouragement from joining trade societies and political organizations, became enthusiastic collaborators with London working-class leaders – as, for instance, in the Friends of Civil and Religious Liberty in 1828[24] or in the National Union of the Working Classes in 1833 in common antagonism to Grey's coercive Irish policy.[25] Frequently such collaboration was not forthcoming. O'Connell showed himself to be an enemy of trade unionism;[26] his tactics often involved co-operation with the Whigs or with middle-class parliamentary radicals, neither of whom had much appeal to metropolitan ultra-radicals. Also, when Feargus O'Connor emerged as the Chartist chieftain it became impossible to worship at his shrine and at the Liberator's, their antagonism and rivalry was total.[27] However, by the early weeks of 1848 O'Connell himself was dead, his followers, Old Ireland, were being increasingly challenged by the breakaway forces of Young Ireland organized as the Confederates, and there is clear evidence that the bulk of the politically active among the London Irish had thrown in their lot with the Confederates. The Old Irelanders led by Denis Dwaine seem to have had just one gathering, at the Bull's Head, Vere St. Lincoln's Inn Fields, whereas the Confederates had at least half a dozen clubs linked together in a Federation with Francis Looney[28] of the Thomas Davis Club most active as their leader. He was their reporter for the *Northern Star*, thus ensuring full publicity for their activites. Moreover, even before the February days in Paris the evidence points to the London Irish becoming increasingly inclined to side with the militant and radical John Mitchel against the moderate Gavan Duffy in the dissensions within the Confederation. Feargus O'Connor directly encouraged[29] this and had his reward in the close collaboration that was developing between the London Irish Confederates and the Chartists.

One should be careful, however, not to exaggerate Chartist revival. The *Northern Star*'s claim on 5 February that 'the metropolis has pre-eminently exerted itself' was only partly true. Leaving aside the Confederate Clubs, there is no evidence of more than a small increase in the number of Chartist societies – the Mason's Chartist Society of Lambeth appears to have been resuscitated,[30] and though there was much talk of the need for a Chartist Hall to serve the whole metropolis and become the home of the already projected National Convention, the cash collected for it was scarcely impressive. In the event Hetherington and Watson's John St. Hall had to be used. There are also signs that the Chartist leaders were less optimistic about progress than the *Northern Star*. At 'an important public meeting' early in February, to pay tribute to Thomas Wakley, T. S. Dunscombe and, inevitably, Feargus O'Connor, Philip McGrath hoped that the meeting 'would lead to the reorganisation of Chartism in London' and Julian Harney praised the virtues of patience and perseverance.[31] And, finally, there is little evidence that the authorities were in any way impressed by the revival of Chartism at this stage. In February they were far more concerned by the agitation against the increase in income tax which was largely inspired by middle-class radicals.[32]

The fall of Louis Philippe and the establishment of the Second Republic certainly had profound effects in the United Kingdom. The polite world, by early March, aided by extensive and highly biased press reporting became prey to a new bogy: instead of invasion, the Chartists were preparing for revolution in London. When it became known that it was intended to present the third National Petition on 10 April, that date became the expected 'February days' for Britain and great was the alarm. In contrast, Chartists and Confederates were immensely cheered by the news from Paris and sought substantially to increase their agitation.

Press reporting of events in France contributed greatly to fostering the hysteria which eventually gripped London. Most of the London dailies and even papers of moderate radical tendencies such as the widely circulated *Illustrated London News* carried more and more hostile stories about events in France following the proclamation of the Republic. The basic theme was that social chaos and, in particular the destruction of property, would be the upshot of the revolution in France. For instance, in its number for 4 March the *Illustrated London News* carried lurid engravings of villainous-looking rogues, clutching stolen wine bottles, engaged in what was captioned as 'orgies in the Palace wine cellar'.[33] Greville summed it all up on 25 March when he wrote, 'France marches on with giant strides to confusion and ruin.'[34] By an easy transition the bogy emerged. If this was happening in France, if, as was being complained by *The Times* by mid March, 'we now announce that a sovereign state is in the hands of a mob in about a dozen lines. We cannot afford more space' so numerous were the Continental revolutions,[35] then it could also happen in Britain. You had only to look about you and Chartists could be found under every bed. Hence one began to find what is familiar in such situations, the attribution to Chartists of responsibility for all troubles regardless of the facts of the case. A prime example of this, as the advanced radical *Nonconformist* pointed out, was *The Times*'s capacity for editorializing against 'the Chartist rabble' as being responsible for Trafalgar Square rioting early in March even though its reporters stated explicitly that 'no political cries were heard; and politics had nothing to do with the eruption'.[36]

Indeed, far from the Chartists having called the Trafalgar Square meeting it is perfectly plain that it was Charles Cochrane's doing and his purpose was to protest about the income tax increase. It is true that when speakers failed to materialize to address the crowd G. W. M. Reynolds, a middle-class journalist of dubious reputation, at least in some quarters,[37] who had taken no previous part in Chartist affairs, did take the opportunity to address the gathering and declare himself a new recruit to the cause. Nevertheless, the clashes that occurred between the police and the crowds in the square and surrounding streets which went on for two or three evenings quite clearly appear to have been the product of some police aggression – to which the young Matthew Arnold, who happened to get mixed up in the crowd, testified – and the activities of youths and boys for whom a fight with the police was a customary sport in early Victorian London.[38] Certainly the Trafalgar Square 'riots', the contemporaneous clashes between the police and the unemployed in Manchester,[39] or even the more serious riot in Glasgow in which several lives were lost,[40] were not the omens of approaching Chartist-inspired revolution as the London dailies suggested.

The government was certainly affected by such talk. It took precautions, though not of a drastic kind. In London the Trafalgar Square rioters were restrained from approaching Buckingham Palace by large bodies of Metropolitan Police; the Life Guards were ordered to be saddled in case of need; a nervous Chancellor of the Exchequer (Sir Charles Wood) pressed the Prime Minister to return to the capital from his holiday at St. Leonards; patrols of mounted police were instituted;

the Magistrates of Bow St., Westminster, and Marlborough St. were requested by the Home Office to 'swear in such respectable persons as present themselves as Special Constables' and to ensure that one of their number was constantly available.[41] One of the respectables who did so present himself was evidently the young Mr. Gladstone, since among the interminable obsessive listing of his reading and letter-writing in his diary one finds the laconic entry for 11 March 1848 'sworn in as special constable'.[42] Paving authorities in the West End were requested to desist for the time being from road works since 'much mischief has been caused, windows broken and the Police wounded by the ready missile which is afforded by the newly-laid broken granite used to repair the roads'.[43] And, although the Home Secretary was reported to believe that the police could cope with the Chartists,[41] nonetheless, further preparations against disorder were taken. Inquiries were made of the Electric Telegraph Company as to the cost of connecting the Home Office with the Company's Head Office in the City so that speedy intelligence would be assured.[45] And, when the Chartists announced the holding of a public meeting to celebrate the French Revolution on Kennington Common on 13 March,[46] the Police Commissioners put out a proclamation warning people against attending.[47] The meeting itself, according to press reports, was watched over by more than 2,000 police and upwards of 20,000 Specials, with the military under arms and the bridges over the Thames carefully guarded.[48] Indeed, it was almost a dress rehearsal for the much more elaborate measures taken on 10 April. The small group of mischief-makers arrested for rioting and housebreaking, following what had been an entirely decorous meeting said to have attracted an audience of 14–15,000, were energetically pursued by the Home Office who requested the Treasury Solicitor to prosecute.[49] However, in March the government was reassured by many reports from the provinces and London that, in spite of increasing Chartist activity, all was quiet and most authorities had taken the precautions advised by the Home Office. Furthermore, Lord John Russell had repaired some of the damage his financial statement had caused – by timely concession, and a highly successful parliamentary performance.[50] Also, fear that the new French Republic might embark on a highly aggressive foreign policy were considerably allayed by assurances to the contrary that were reaching the Foreign Office.[51] The only really black spot appeared to be Ireland, from whence increasingly gloomy and alarming reports of an impending rising reached the cabinet.[52] By the end of the month, it was this subject, rather than Chartist activities, that was the key topic for its consideration.[53]

However, as the days moved on towards 10 April the fear of the propertied classes continued to grow – though, be it noted, theirs was no paralysing fear: on the contrary, they demanded greater and firmer action by the government against the Chartists, offered to help it and requested arms to enable individuals and institutions to defend themselves on the coming day of revolution. For example, a Mr. J. Mason of Finsbury complained bitterly to the Home Secretary that instead of trying to disperse the March meeting at Kennington the authorities should have prevented it altogether by ordering the military to occupy the Common. He warned that, 'the lower orders are going armed with staves and stones and it rests with you to deliver London from anarchy, bloodshed and pillage'.[54] Offers of help were many and varied: the almost bankrupt Duke of Buckingham told Palmerston in mid March that:

> he wished to place himself and his Corps of Yeomanry at the disposal of Her Majesty's government for service in any part of the kingdom. The Corps, he said, consisted of 400 men of whom he would undertake to bring three hundred with two six-pounder field pieces into service.[55]

More modest offerings came from Mr. Curtis of Camberwell, who forwarded plans for a portable wrought-iron Mortar; or Commander Smith R N, who suggested that the crews of vessels in the Port of London might afford valuable assistance; or a suspicious gentleman in Temple Chambers, who reported that he had seen two howitzers passing along Bishopsgate.[56] The imagination of some of those requesting arms for the defence of public buildings certainly worked overtime on occasion. Sir Henry Ellis of the British Museum, for instance, bewailing his lack of arms for his 200 Specials, enforced his request for muskets, cutlasses, and pikes by asking the Home Office 'to remember that if it by any accident happen that the building of the Museum fell into the hands of disaffected persons it would prove to them a Fortress capable of holding Ten Thousand men'.[57]

Finally, the Duke of Wellington joined in with a weighty memorandum dated 5 April which began by saying that he had '... seen in the newspapers statements that 200,000 Chartists are to be assembled in and about London on Monday next' and that he had not heard that the government had done anything to prevent this, he felt it his duty to outline the measures that should be taken for 'the protection of the Tower, the Royal Palaces and the government of the country'. There followed a mass of detail as to where troops were to be disposed so that the Parks and Whitehall should be kept clear of 'mobs' and lines of communication be kept open between headquarters at the Horse Guards and the various barracks and temporary quarters where the troops would be stationed. Wellington, however, did not contemplate using the army as the first line of defence: 'the police should act first if there is trouble', he advised, and the troops should be available to back them up, 'but if not required it would be best not to show them'.[58] The following day the seventy-nine-year-old Duke told Russell that he had consulted Police Commissioner Rowan and could assure the Prime Minister that the Chartist procession could be stopped at whatever point was convenient to government, adding his own opinion that the further out of town the better.[59]

The weekend before the Chartist demonstration saw the hysteria reach its peak. Lord Campbell, a minister, wrote to his brother saying, 'many people believe that by Monday evening we shall be under a Provisional Government'.[60] Lord Malmesbury, a Protectionist peer of some standing, sent for his gamekeepers to come to London suitably armed and recorded in his journal on 9 April that 'the alarm was very general all over town'.[61] And in the early morning of the 10th, as Colonel Phipps, the Prince Consort's Household Comptroller, was leaving Windsor to observe events in London, he was told 'that immense bodies of people were collecting, that all the bridges were occupied by troops and guns posted and that an immediate battle was expected'.[62]

In reality, of course, the Chartists, notwithstanding some excitable rhetoric from a few delegates to their National Convention, clearly never intended, 10 April to be a day of revolution but a moral force demonstration of a kind already familiar from the experiences of 1839 and 1842. The Convention issued a statement, signed by all forty-nine delegates, that 'our procession will be an unarmed moral demonstration'[63] and on Friday afternoon, 7 April, a deputation consisting of G. W. M. Reynolds, Thomas Clark, and H. J. P. Wilkinson, on behalf of the Convention, carefully assured the Home Secretary of their peaceable intentions although insisting on their right to hold a 'Procession for the purpose of presenting the People's Petition to the House of Commons.'[64] O'Connor himself went to great lengths to impress on his followers that peace and order must be maintained.[65] It was authority, not the Chartists, that was armed to the teeth on 10 April and if any force had actually been employed it was far more likely to have emanated from an over-enthusiastic policeman, pensioner, or special constable or an hysterical member of the general public. The young Hector Berlioz's comment on witnessing the events of 10th that 'the poor Chartists knew as much about starting a riot as the Italians about writing a symphony' quite missed the point: such was certainly not their intention.[66] Nothing happened on the 10th to justify preceding hysteria, because nothing was intended. The enormous rejoicing – and self-congratulation – among the propertied classes, coupled with the belief that all was now over and that ridicule was the appropriate weapon with which to dismiss Chartism, was simply yet another sign of what *The Times*, two days afterwards, admitted was the case, 'the meteoric, unsteady condition of the public mind'.[67]

Two questions, however, remain. What precisely was the role of government and what exactly did the Chartists do on the 10th? Briefly, the government, I believe, knew better than the Press or its propertied readers what would happen but ultimately found it convenient to behave as if it shared its illusions. There was a substantial political dividend to be earned by a minority government going out and slaying a paper tiger which so many thought was real. What is the evidence to back this view? First, let us note that Lord John Russell, it is plain, was far from keen to implement the Duke of Wellington's elaborate plans for the capital's defence.[68] Contrary to Mr. Ward, I do not regard this as odd.[69] The truth was simple: Russell and Sir George Grey kept their heads – everyone agrees that this was so – for the good reason that they were amply informed about the Chartists' activities and anyone with sense could see there was nothing to fear in the way of violence and disorder, a few threatening speeches notwithstanding. Russell, however, was eventually persuaded to let the Duke have his way and post soldiers since it dawned on him that credit was to be got by appearing to be 'firm and vigorous' as all the 'be up and at 'em' brigade from the Duke downwards were demanding. It would raise British prestige abroad enormously and wipe out the impression of feebleness that the government had given earlier in the year by its mishandling of financial questions.

What is the evidence that the government was so well informed as to be confident that no serious trouble was to be expected from the Chartists? Let us remember first that at this stage there was nothing clandestine about their proceedings. Their National Convention's debates were extensively reported in the Press of all shades of opinion, and just to make sure not a word of what was said was missed government employed Mr. Gurney and his shorthand experts to take everything down for the benefit of the Police Commissioners.[70] Then, too, as far as the provinces were concerned the government had established much more careful liaison with local authorities than in earlier years of Chartist activity. For weeks before 10 April the Home Office was in frequent touch – often daily in sensitive districts – with the mayors of many towns and local military commanders, seeking information about possible disturbances of the peace and urging precautions which were generally carried out. Eventually, on 10 April, such communications would be ensured by a government takeover of the Telegraph Company for a week.[71] Until 10 April, what came back to the Home Office from the provinces goes a good way towards explaining the celebrated composure of Sir George Grey. It was a succession of 'all quiet' reports, with a few exceptions which on investigation turned out to be either chimeras in the minds of informants or disturbances unconnected with the Chartists.[72]

In short, the government had good reason to believe that no very extraordinary preparations were really required for 10 April. It was a combination of pressure from the hysterically excited and a consciousness of how this might be exploited to the government's political advantage that led to the massive overkill of 10 April. How many tens of thousands of Special Constables were enrolled will never be known – the returns that survive are too fragmentary[73] to check contemporary estimates, most of which are in the 100–250,000 range.[74] Probably such figures are exaggerated.

The returns do show, as might be anticipated, that numbers and organization among the Specials were greatest in the parishes of the West End. For instance, St. James and St. Martin-in-the-Fields had 999 and 1,500 sworn in, were described as 'efficient', and were organized into companies under their overall leaders, Earl de Grey and the Earl of Arundel and Surrey respectively. By contrast Mr. Drysdale led ninety-five in St. Pauls, Shadwell and St. John's parish, Wapping, mustered fifty-seven with no named leader.[77] Neither were judged efficient. A number of large employers, Cubitts, the builders, Barclay and Perkins, Truman and Hanbury, brewers, Vicars of Southwark, a distiller, Bacon and Hepburn, both tanners in Southwark, Maudsley, the engineer, and the railway companies, arranged to have their employees sworn *en bloc*. Whether a penalty faced an employee who refused is not known for certain but there is evidence that in some cases the purpose was, as a note attached to Maudsley's return shows, to prevent employees 'from taking the wrong side as they are on ill terms with the police'. There is also some evidence of refusal by working men to be sworn in. Mr. Bingham reported to Sir George Grey that this was the case with 'most of the workmen building the Geological Museum and Lord Ellesmere's house' and the Marquess of Salisbury was so discouraged by refusals, or by those who would only undertake to protect their master's property, that he declared that 'no reliance can be placed upon the co-operation of the Artisans who are all Unionists'.[78] Nevertheless, what struck most contemporaries was the scale and enthusiasm of the volunteering to be a Special: one of the delegates to the National Convention said that he had heard that the turners in Gosport Dock Yard were working night and day making truncheons for them.[79]

However, to the experienced military eye, the Specials were scarcely material to stand up to Chartists, especially if the latter were armed. A day after Kennington Common, Wellington was calling for them to be better organized, arranged in divisions, and so on. For the Duke it was the troops that counted. And indeed, precise details of their numbers employed in London on the 10th survive: 8,148 regulars and 1,231 Pensioners. Both Horse and Foot Guards were heavily involved, and two infantry regiments were also brought up from Dover and Chatham and six six-pounders and nine howitzers from Woolwich. They were stationed in a variety of public and private buildings ranging from the stables of great aristocratic houses, such as Berkeley and Stafford House, to prisons such as Millbank and the Bridewell in Blackfriars, with rations of salt pork, biscuits, and spirits sufficient to last for 10–15 days stored at places such as Somerset House and the Tower.[80]

The troops, as Wellington advised, stayed out of sight, as did the regular police for the most part. Altogether 4,012 of the Metropolitan force were expected to parade at 10 a.m. on the 10th. Their distribution reflected the tactics to be pursued, of which more in a moment. 1,650 of them were to be stationed at or near Westminster, Waterloo, Blackfriars, Vauxhall, and Hungerford Bridges while forty-two from the Thames Police were to man seven boats belonging to them. A thousand were to be massed close to the Houses of Parliament in Palace Yard and Great George St., while 700 occupied Trafalgar Square with eighty more constantly patrolling Whitehall.[81] Close liaison had been established between the Home Office and the Police Commissioners and the City of London authorities; their police force was expected to guard Southwark and London Bridges over which Chartist contingents from the City and East End were expected to cross *en route* for Kennington.[82]

Every public building of note – the Bank of England, the Mint, all the gaols, government offices, the British Museum, the Mansion House – was provided with armed guards, usually a motley array of Specials and Pensioners. The magistrates at all the principal courts were on continuous standby, and even the gas lights were put on half an hour earlier than usual.[83] In view of Chartist intentions and of what actually happened there was something slightly comic, to put it mildly, about the earnestness with which elderly men about town like Charles Greville went about trying to be a soldier, barricading his office with

Privy Council registers, shouldering muskets, and so forth.[84]

So what did happen on the 10th? The authorities had decided their tactics:[85] the Chartists were to be allowed to assemble on the Common, but they were to be prevented from crossing the Thames in their procession behind the two specially-constructed vans drawn by horses from O'Connor's Land Plan farm at Snigs End in Gloucestershire[86] and conveyed to London by train, in which were to be carried the huge Petition and the members of the National Convention. Instead, a small number of them were to be allowed to take the Petition by cab over Blackfriars Bridge and thence to the House of Commons. If there was any attempt to frustrate this, the authorities anticipated it might take the form of an effort to force Blackfriars Bridge: hence the greatest concentration of police and troops was stationed there. In addition every endeavour was to be made to persuade people not to join the Chartist meeting. As in March, the Police Commissioners issued a public warning against doing so.[87] This time it was supplemented by private enterprise flyposting of bills aimed at discouraging the uncommitted – one of which read as follows:

WORKING MEN
STOP AND READ

The Chartist leaders presume to assert that nothing has been done to relieve the burdens of the Working classes. Read the following and let your own good sense decide:

Is your Bread Taxed? No!
Are your Flour, Vegetables and Meat Taxed? No!
Is your Clothes Taxed? No!
Are your Coals and Wood Taxed? No!
Is your House Taxed? No!
Are your Windows Taxed? No!

Many of these were formerly Taxed but are now totally Repealed to Small-Class Houses.

   Place no reliance on these Men who would deceive you by falsehoods.

Tea, Coffee, Sugar, Beer, Soap.

These are still partially Taxed but doubtless will soon by patient endurance be repealed totally also.

   Prove that you are good and faithful subjects. Avoid attending the meeting at Kennington on Monday.

Remain Quiet! and this country must be the Manufactory of the World.

What good has revolution done for France?[89]

The Chartists had also made their preparations. Between 9 and 10 a.m. on the 10th, a fine spring morning, they gathered at a number of open spaces, Clerkenwell Green, Russell Square, Stepney Green, Finsbury Square, and so forth, and formed themselves into processions; seven or eight abreast, often with arms linked, many wearing the tall hats favoured at this time which gave the demonstration an air of dignity. Banners, cockades, tricolour caps of liberty, and even bands were in evidence.[90] The processions crossed the bridges nearest to their assembly points, converged on the Elephant and Castle and from thence proceeded to Kennington Common (which it should be noted was already surrounded by buildings on all sides). All the evidence agrees that order and good humour prevailed. The Chartists themselves had their equivalent of the Specials in the form of marshals,[91] and when one or two foolhardy spirits were found to be carrying weapons they were rapidly disarmed by the Chartists themselves.[92] The police reports consistently refer to the absence of arms or even bludgeons.[93] The National Convention itself held a brief session at the National Hall, John St., before setting off for Kennington, where Christopher Doyle, its secretary, told delegates that the Commissioners of Police had informed Mr. McGrath that, while the Petition would be allowed to be taken to the House of Commons, no procession would be allowed through the streets. Delegates reacted by agreeing that they had no option at this stage but to carry on, but they were determined at all costs to avoid a confrontation with the authorities: this would be simply to play into the government's hands, and the latter was just looking for a chance for 'a bloody slaughter'. The lengths to which O'Connor was prepared to go to avoid a collision are indicated by his advice that if, when they arrived, the Common was already occupied by the police and military, the Chartists should disperse quietly and leave him to present the Petition.[94]

In fact this was not the case. However, when the Chartists had assembled on the Common, almost at once at about 11.30 a.m., Police Commissioner Mayne and Superintendent Malalieu intervened to ask O'Connor to meet them and hear the terms on which the Petition might be presented. Mayne himself described the upshot succinctly: 'there was considerable excitement amongst the people as Mr O'Connor came to see me. It was really supposed he was taken into custody. I never saw a man more frightened than he was and he would, I am sure, have promised me anything'.[95] As it was, O'Connor accepted the terms and all went off as the authorities intended. As early as 2.00 p.m. the Queen was being informed by telegraph that the meeting at Kennington Common had dispersed quietly and by 2.30 p.m. the Lord Mayor was reporting to the Home Secretary that people were streaming back across the bridges and dispersing quietly to their homes; by 4.30 p.m. he was complaining that 'my chief embarrassment has been ... that of having too many Special Constables to control' and by 9.00 p.m. his report was 'everything is perfectly peaceful'. So much for London's day of revolution.[96]

How many were actually present on the Common will never be known for certain. The official estimates varied from Mayne's 12,000 to Malalieu's 20,000,[97] the former figure being that accepted by the Prime Minister in his report to the Queen, who with her recently-born child had been spirited away to Osborne out of harm's way.[98] The Press reached more varied conclusions: roughly speaking, the more conservative the paper the smaller the estimate and vice versa. At opposite poles were *The Standard*, 9–10,000, and the *Northern Star*, 'not less than 250,000'; *The Nonconformist* and the *Sun* plumped for 150,000 but the *Examiner*, *Morning Chronicle*, and *Illustrated London News* believed only 20–25,000 were there, and *The Times* put it at 20,000[99] but with only half that number forming the demonstration. Certainly it is not easy to believe in the higher figures since the Common was surely too small a venue to accommodate such numbers. As far as can be judged its greatest extent was 13,640 square yards and at a density of four per square yard, surely the maximum possible, the greatest possible number would have been 54,560.[100] The higher figures remain plausible only as an estimate of how many Londoners looked on or took part in the demonstration throughout its entire length as it wound through the streets.

What was the upshot? As everyone knows the Petition was received by the Commons, a Select Committee was appointed to scrutinize it which reported that instead of the boasted five million signatures, it contained only 1·9 million. Much ridicule both then and since has been directed at this revelation – not to mention the bogus signatures – but it should be noted that the reduced figure still put the 1848 petition well ahead in numbers of signatures to that of 1839 and nearly two-thirds of the way towards that of 1842, neither of which were subjected to similar scrutiny. Certainly the exposure by the Select Committee and still more the absence of revolution on the 10th sent the polite world into transports of delight. Sir Benjamin Hall's comment was representative: 'it was one of the most glorious days of English history'.[101]

Was Chartist morale shattered as a result? Opinions differ. Professor Saville has maintained that 10 April had little immediate effect on Chartist morale and that the following months saw a growth in their numbers and militancy which was ultimately curbed and defeated by 'the stability and strength of bourgeois society' which gave the government confidence to carry out a counter-revolution aided by new repressive legislation, the police, the army, an 'extraordinarily' biased judiciary, spies, and *agents provocateurs*. The upshot was the total demoralization of the Chartists, further increased by O'Connor's abdication of leadership and the vacuum at the top created by the early arrest of Ernest Jones.[102] Recently, too, Mr. Goodway has argued that the importance of 1848 in London was not the events of 10 April but, to quote his words, that 'it marked the high point of turbulence and revolutionary potential of London Chartism', which culminated in a conspiracy in the summer of 1848 aimed at overthrowing the authorities by force and seizing London. Although this was a complete failure, nevertheless, this last of a series of revolutionary attempts in London spread its tentacles more widely than ever before and gathered more support thanks, in part at least, to the close collaboration between Chartists and the London Irish of the Confederate Clubs.[103]

There is certainly more truth in these contentions than is allowed by the conventional view of 10 April as a fiasco which put paid to Chartism, although considerable qualification is needed particularly of Mr. Goodway's interpretation. All was not over for the London Chartists after their demonstration and the rejection of the Petition by the House of Commons. Indeed, the National Convention had anticipated rejection and had sketched a plan to meet the eventuality. Missionaries were to tour the country, simultaneous meetings were to be held everywhere on Good Friday, 21 April, to elect members of a new Convention to be called the National Assembly which was to meet in London on 24 April, in order to memorialize the Queen, to dismiss her present parliament and to call to her councils only persons favouring the Charter while the National Assembly remained in permanent session. A motion to this effect had been carried unanimously at the Convention's meeting on 6 April. The response among Chartists in the country as a whole to the new call was more mixed than Professor Saville appears to imply: well-attended simultaneous meetings were held in some places on Good Friday, notably in Liverpool, but in Manchester, Birmingham, and Nottingham, for instance, the response was poor. In London such meetings were duly held to choose the eight delegates allocated to it,[104] the best-attended appearing to be that held in the newly-formed Tower Hamlets NCA locality where the experiment of holding Sunday afternoon meetings on Bonners Fields – an open space to the east of Bethnal Green – had been inaugurated with such success that it was decided to make them a regular feature. It was claimed that 14–16,000 turned up and it was at a gathering at this venue on Good Friday that chose John Shaw and Alexander Sharp as its delegates, with Williams and Drake as substitutes should the delegates themselves be arrested.[105] Almost certainly, in view of the much more restricted sites at which meetings were called, delegates for the rest of London were chosen by smaller gatherings,[106] an indication that the main support for Chartism in London was by now chiefly to be found in the east central districts such as Clerkenwell and Bethnal Green. Certainly there were plenty of signs that keeping up the pressure after 10 April was a problem. At the continued sittings of the depleted National Convention, it was pointed out that it would cost about £300 a week for 100 men to sit as a National Assembly in London and the present Convention had an empty exchequer. Also to meet on 24 April, Easter Monday, was rather pointless as ministers would be out of London. A postponement until 1 May was agreed.[107]

The truth was that when the National Assembly did finally meet, the Chartists became even more divided as they gradually realized that their aristocratic rulers were armed to the teeth, not prepared to give an inch and, indeed, were planning an offensive – albeit in the first instance directed at the militant leaders of the Irish Confederates, John Mitchel, T. D. Meagher, and Smith O'Brien.[108] Some Chartists, showing all the signs of angry frustration, grew more militant making an increasing use of threatening language (threatening the use of force), collecting arms, drilling in secret, forming units of what were called National Guards, planning the reorganization of the NCA on lines that would enable it to mobilize rapidly without warning to the authorities and, inevitably, given past tradition, secretly plotting an armed rising. Others, however, drew the lesson from the 10th that wider support was necessary for success and, in particular, that co-operation with middle-class radicals such as Joseph Hume and his Little Charter Movement or Edward Miall and his Anti-State Church organization was the way to achieve this.[109] Encouragement for such a course might be found in the widespread feeling among middle-class Radicals that if they did not step up pressure for constitutional reform the aristocracy would consider its triumph complete on the 10th.[110]

Both the militant and the moderate response can be found in London in the months following the Kennington Common demonstration. The moderate response was exemplified by the separate, if parallel, activities of the veteran Chartists, Lovett and Hetherington. Hetherington, in company with Thomas Cooper, G. J. Holyoake, James Watson and W. J. Linton, J. D. Collett, and others had enthusiastically welcomed the revolution in France, sent a deputation to Paris, launched a new organization, the People's Charter Union, on 5 April, lent the John St. Hall for the National Convention, preached total passive resistance in face of government's armed might on the 10th, and for the moment at least had sunk their differences with the NCA although remaining separate from it. They had turned out with everyone else on the 10th. In the following months, however, the People's Charter Union kept itself severely aloof from the NCA, avoided all militancy, and while protesting against Whig harshness towards the physical force men, preached that the only hope of obtaining the Charter was by a union of the middle and working classes. By the end of the year Hetherington, who for so long had been an uncompromising advocate of universal suffrage, was ready to second a motion committing the People's Charter Union to supporting Hume's Little Charter of household suffrage, the ballot and triennial parliaments.[111] Lovett, by now at loggerheads with the People's Charter Union group, launched his own organization, the People's League, following what he was to regard as 'the blundering demonstration on the 10th', with the aim of uniting all radicals, middle and working class, behind a programme of the Charter, reduced government spending, and the abolition of indirect taxes in favour of progressive taxation on property. To its banner there rallied veteran Chartists such as Robert Lowery and Henry Vincent, Lovett's friend, the barrister, J. H. Parry, and radical Nonconformists such as Edward Miall.[112] But, all told, little support was gathered in London by either of these organizations: the growth of militancy was much more striking.

In London this first showed itself in a new development which soon began to reawaken the fears of respectable society: nightly gatherings in May on Clerkenwell Green, followed by processions of men marching through the streets, sometimes after nightfall, in the districts of London east of Regent Street to the boundaries of the City. In June the focus of alarm shifted to projected Chartist mass meetings in Bethnal Green and surrounding districts and sharp clashes there between Chartists and the police, the climax being the Chartist attempt to demonstrate on Bonners Fields on 12 June (Whit Monday). Indeed, the Metropolitan Police found by no means all of their problems to be over on 10 April. Colonel Rowan, the very experienced Commissioner, realized this the very next day when he analysed the situation in this way: 'the Revolution went off wonderfully yesterday – Feargus O'Connor was dreadfully frightened. It would be difficult to overestimate the good that may be anticipated by the result.' The Chartists, he went on to say, 'are now very angry and cry that nothing can be done without arms', but this he thought futile, 'as two sides can arm, they would not gain much by that'. Nevertheless, amidst his rejoicing he was constrained to observe that there was a great deal of distress and unemployment in the capital and he feared this might provide the politically active with much support. 'I wish to God,' exclaimed Rowan, 'it were possible for the Government to do something towards employing the people who are out of work.' Needless to say, he hastened to add that he was *not* thinking of National Workshops ... 'I do not mean employing them French fashion but I mean [he explained] carrying on the Public Works that have been determined on.' He concludes, significantly, '... unless something can be done in that way we shall not be tranquil'.[113]

Rowan was quite right about the lack of tranquillity and probably about its underlying cause. London does appear to have suffered exceptional distress in the early summer of 1848, or so its working folk thought. A report prepared for the Committee of Metropolitan Trades claimed that, of 200,000 skilled tradesmen in the capital, a third were out of work, another third on short time, and the rest in employment but on reduced wages.[114] Even *The Times* acknowledged that all was not well.[115]

The first evidence of disturbance, the meetings in May on Clerkenwell Green of several thousands in the evening after work, presented Rowan's police with problems. It was difficult to discover why they were being held and why they went on night after night. No prior notice of meeting was given and it was not easy to smuggle a properly accredited shorthand reporter close enough to secure accurate reports of the short, sharp speeches that were being made in the open air from the tops of vans or even lamp-posts to crowds of working men and 'very dirty and very ragged' members of 'the lower orders' hailing from insalubrious districts such as Clerkenwell, then enjoying the reputation of being the most lawless district in the capital.[116] All that could be gathered was that the purpose of such meetings was to assert the rights of Chartists and Confederates to meet freely and express their opinions and, in particular, to give encouragement to the Irish to rise against British rule and to raise such a protest as to force the government to countermand the transportation of the unjustly condemned John Mitchel.[117]

Much more alarming to the authorities was the new tactic developed on 29 May when, without warning but on a given signal, the gathering on Clerkenwell Green formed fours and marched through the narrow streets, first to Finsbury Square and then through the outskirts of the City, turning westwards along Holborn towards the West End, collecting supporters as they went along, drawing curious onlookers, and all the time shouting and singing noisily in the late evening as night fell. A few, at least, were observed carrying long pikes. One witness alleged that as many as 50–60,000 filled the streets, although a police sergeant's estimate of 15–16,000 was probably nearer the truth. The authorities were clearly taken by surprise. The Home Secretary, as soon as he got word of what was happening – at 9 p.m. – gave orders to the police to disperse the procession, ordered the park gates to be closed and the guard at Buckingham Palace to be strengthened. Sir George Grey and Lord John Russell then sat up until after midnight until they were sure that all was quiet. They were not going to be caught napping. The next day the Police Commissioners proclaimed such meetings illegal; Life Guards were posted at strategic points; Special Constables whose period of office was about to expire were resworn; magistrates were asked to stand by and an attempt to hold another meeting on Clerkenwell Green was dispersed by police action. Preparations were set on foot to arrest and convict the speakers and organizers of the meeting on 29 May, Joseph Williams, John Vernon, and John Fussell, of riot, sedition, and unlawful assembly.[118]

Nonetheless, the polite world was certainly once more thrown into a turmoil by the Clerkenwell meetings. The Prince Consort reflected this when he wrote to Stockmar on 6 May,

> ...we have Chartist riots every night ... the organization of these people is incredible. They have secret signals and correspond from town to town by carrier pigeons. In London they are from 10,000 to 20,000 strong, which is not much out of a population of two millions; but if they could, by means of their organization, throw themselves in a body upon any one point, they might be successful in a *coup de main*.[119]

There were angry demands that effective action should be taken by the government to put a stop to the Clerkenwell meetings[120] and, indeed, their measures eventually had this effect.

However, this was not the case with Chartist meetings on Bonners Fields and other venues in Bethnal Green and Hackney which in the first fortnight in June were both numerous and rowdy, involving a major clash with the police on Sunday 4 June, followed by what threatened to be a confrontation between the Chartists and the authorities on the scale of 10 April on Whit Monday, 12 June. By this time both the language and the actions of the Chartists were, or at least so it seemed to the authorities, a great deal more violent and militant than in April.[121] In June the authorities were far more concerned than they had been in April about Chartists arming themselves. There appeared to be considerable evidence that this was the case. For instance, Superintendent Johnson of N Division reported that at 5 a.m. on 4 June, acting on information from one of his constables, he had gone to Victoria Park where he saw what he took to be a rank of men at pike drill who, when he and his men charged them, ran away. At the same time Inspector Thatcher of the same Division was dispersing 300–400 assembled in a field near Grove Lane, Hackney: given the earliness of the hour and the fact that they 'sprang over hedges and disappeared' it was not unreasonable to suppose that some military-style exercise had been interrupted.[122] These events, indeed, were the prelude to what was probably the day of greatest violence in London throughout the whole year 1848.

In mid-morning on 4 June, there was a clash between 'a mob of about 300' and some Specials in Bird Cage Fields, Hackney during which an Inspector with fifty police, including mounted, intervened and while routing the crowd were pelted with stones and ginger-beer bottles.[123] Then there was a sharp struggle between the police 'and a great assemblage of persons' at Nova Scotia Gardens, Bethnal Green;[124] but the chief collision occurred after Alexander Sharpe and Ernest Jones had addressed the regular Sunday afternoon Chartist meeting on Bonners Fields which had followed an earlier Confederate gathering. The police version was that, as the meeting was breaking up, having heard highly seditious speeches from Sharpe and Jones, an attack was made upon a near-by church in which a large body of police were stationed for the preservation of order and the observation of what was maintained to be an unlawful assembly.[125] During the attack a Superintendent, it was alleged, was badly wounded by stoning, the windows of the church were smashed, and the constables menaced with dangerous weapons such as iron bars and stones. A number were severely hurt and altogether twenty-two arrests were made for assaults on the police.[126] The Chartists and a considerable number of local inhabitants, some of whom were not Chartists, saw the affair differently. They believed that the Chartist meeting had been perfectly orderly – and indeed, the evidence of the government employed shorthand reporter who was present and provided with facilities, supports this – and that afterwards the police had behaved 'in a brutal and barbarous fashion', running amok in the streets adjoining the Fields, dragging innocent folk from their houses and wielding their batons with abandon. The accusation was that they were 'dead drunk'.[127] The Chartists themselves denied that their speeches were seditious, asserted their right to meet to discuss their grievances, and maintained that all they had done was to point out the right of an Englishman to defend himself if attacked by the police.[128] The local inhabitants set up a protest memorial and formed a committee to collect evidence of police brutality and raise funds to aid the injured.[129] The Police Commissioners, however, entirely rejected all charges, arrested Sharpe and Jones, and with the aid of local clerics and magistrates launched a public subscription for the injured police. Eventually they secured the sentencing of Ernest Jones and Alexander Sharpe to two years' imprisonment each.[130]

This was not, though, sufficient to put an end to the meetings on Bonners Fields. The Chartists had decided to hold another on Whit Monday, 12 June, partly in order to demonstrate that Lord John Russell's claim in the Commons that the people did not want the Charter was utter nonsense. In the absence of Ernest Jones, visiting the north (where he was shortly to be arrested), the lead was taken by the colourful Peter M'Douall who at once wrote to the Prime Minister saying, 'you have thrown down the gauntlet: we accept the challenge' but assuring him that peaceful meetings were intended while protesting in forthright terms about 'the murderous acts of your Police'. He ended by declaring that he trusted 'that you will not force us to defend our right of public meeting and that he was perfectly satisfied that all the Chartists will assemble and disperse peacefully if unmolested'.[131]

The authorities were certainly very far from satisfied that this would be the case. The experiences of 29 May and 4 June had seriously upset them. Such disturbances, and the threat of more to follow, raised doubts about the ability of the police, the Specials, and the Pensioners to maintain order without backing from the military. Yet this was precisely what the government did not want to be committed to because since April the situation in Ireland had deteriorated to such an extent that Lord Lieutenant Clarendon was daily writing to his colleagues in London that any time now he would be facing a formidable Irish rising, which would require substantial reinforcements of the already sizeable British forces in Ireland if British rule was to be maintained.[132]

Nevertheless, dangerous as the Irish situation was believed to be, troops had to be and were found for Whit Monday and on a scale which fell little short of the preparations for 10 April. The same regiments were employed, the only major modification being that quarters had to be found for concealing them in the East rather than the West End: a railway goods yard in Spitalfields, a large barn in Victoria Park, and even the workhouse in Bethnal Green did duty. As in April the Duke of Wellington proferred advice, this time insisting that all bay-windowed houses in the Strand should be occupied by the military to prevent marksmen using them and to secure the street as a line of communication.[133] In his concern about marksmen the Duke reflected the much greater concern displayed by the authorities about how far the Chartists were supplied with arms which characterized preparations for Whit Monday, compared with those for 10 April. For instance, no pains were spared in keeping watch on Birmingham's gun trade, Inspector Field of the Metropolitan police being dispatched there for the purpose.[134] Information was obtained of sales from the capital's gunsmiths' shops[135] and obvious possible sources of weapons such as the small arms factory at Enfield and powder manufactory at Waltham Abbey were provided with guards.[136]

The most important difference, however, between the preparations for Whit Monday and 10 April, it may be suggested, was that there was genuine and not pretended alarm in the inner circles of authority about the outcome of 12 June. There is, I think, no mistaking the note of anxiety in the memorandum Police Commissioner Rowan drew up on 10 June setting out his thoughts on how he should go about preventing Chartist mass meetings in the East End. There were, he thought, two possible methods: his police could try to occupy the meeting-place before the Chartists arrived and then stop them assembling by blocking all the streets leading to it, or the chairman of the Chartist meeting, Peter M'Douall, could be told that if the Chartists persisted after public notice had been given (as it had), that the meeting was illegal and the police would be present in force to arrest the Chairman. Rowan chose the latter course as he thought it 'more calculated to confine the riot to a particular locality'. The alternative tactic, he was afraid, might lead the Chartists to switch their place of meeting, or arrange some scheme of mischief after dark, or at some place such as the British Museum where there might be some 30–40,000 on this public holiday.[137] Anxiety on the part of the police spelled the need to mobilize the troops.

In fact, on 12 June, thanks to the powerful forces of police – many armed with cutlasses – the Life Guards and other troops (including the Pensioners standing by), the timely aid of a thunderstorm and Peter M'Douall's advice to the Chartists that it was inexpedient to challenge authority to a pitched battle, the Bonners Fields meeting petered out with no more than a series of scuffles between the crowds and the police.[138] The Government's victory on 12 June effectively drove militant Chartism underground thereafter in London,[139] and the historian is confronted with as tangled a story of alleged plotting of an armed insurrection to fire and take over London as the obscurities surrounding the connection between the Newport rising in 1839 and the sporadic outbreaks of violence in the West Riding early in 1840. As was usual in such circumstances government spies provide much of the evidence on which it relied to convict those it arrested and, not surprisingly, the Chartist press denounced the spies as government-hired *agents provocateurs*. Inevitably the truth is hard to discern, and this is not the place for a detailed analysis of the available evidence.[140] Suffice it to say that by August the police believed they had sufficient evidence that would stand up in court, to carry out a series of raids on Chartist meeting-places which they claimed contained arms and were the resort of the plotting militants, who were about to launch an armed rising. Altogether dozens of arrests were made and a fair collection of miscellaneous arms would later be produced in court.[141] What is not in doubt is the severity of the punishments inflicted on those found guilty: a considerable number, though not all, of the leaders of London Chartism found themselves imprisoned or transported during the autumn of 1848.[142] For the rest of the year, apart from not very vociferous complaints about the harshness and injustice of the authorities, Chartism was as quiet as the grave.

It may well be asked, in conclusion, why the Londoners' support for moral or physical force Chartism in 1848 was so much more muted than the far more turbulent activity of the Parisians? In Paris, as Professor Amann has recently calculated, some 50–70,000 – at the most conservative estimate – and more probably upwards of 100,000 became members of over 200 popular societies in the heady days following the fall of Louis Philippe. Several hundred new periodicals and newspapers appeared in Paris between the February Revolution and the June days, and the combined press run for all Parisian newspapers rose eightfold. In short, there was a ·social revolution in which tens of thousands of people participated in public affairs who before 1848 had remained apolitical.[143] No comparable development can be discerned in London. An elaborate return survives from all the Metropolitan Police Divisions in June 1848 listing fifty-five Chartist meeting-places and organiza-tions.[144] It is reasonable to suppose that this is a fairly complete enumera-tion. Superficially this would appear to show that support for Chartism was actually greater in 1848 than in 1842, when thirty-eight was the highest figure given in Iowerth Prothero's count.[145] However, on closer inspection, one finds that seven of the fifty-five on the police list were Irish Confederate Clubs and another nine were either, strictly speaking, not Chartist bodies at all (such as the Anti-State Church Association and Walthamstow Progressives), or they were organizations which stood aloof from the main movement, such as small bodies of Peoples' Charter Unionists grouped round Thomas Cooper, Hetherington, and

W. J. Linton. Ignoring these, in terms of organized bodies of Chartists, there was little to choose between 1842 and 1848. However, the 1848 list did include a number of very tiny gatherings, such as the dozen mechanics who met at *The Star and Garter* in Kentish Town, and the twenty women who gathered under Mrs. Davey's leadership at *The Olive Branch* in St. Pancras Road. Altogether the impression is the NCA localities of 1842, often strongly based on trade society members, were altogether better supported and more active than the miscellaneous bodies of Chartists in 1848. And quite certainly, London Chartism even at its peak in 1848, seems much closer to the political lethargy which characterized Parisian working folk *before* 1848 when the supporters of Fourier, Cabet, or the Catholic Socialists probably did not number more than 10,000 in a city of a million.[146]

Why, then, was London's response in 1848 so different from that of Paris? The answer surely cannot lie in any radical difference in social and economic circumstance. Indeed, readers of the works of such writers as Louis Chevalier, Adeline Daumard, Roger Price, Peter Amann, and others analysing the malaise affecting Paris in the 1840s must often have noted the parallels with contemporary London. By the standards of the time each comprised huge agglomerations of population – London's was twice that of Paris – swollen by extensive migration from all over the country and packed into a relatively small space, with consequent acute problems of providing sufficient food, shelter, fuel, clothing, sanitation, and above all jobs, to prevent substantial numbers from dying on the streets. Both had essentially pre-industrial revolution economic structures comprising a mass of small-scale manufacturing and commercial concerns ministering to the largest market for consumption goods and services in their respective countries. Their artisans faced similar problems of overstocking of labour in the trades and undercutting by cheaper goods from developing provincial factories or from sweated labour within the capital itself, coupled with lack of recognition from above of their worth. Each contained representatives of the new style of worker in the form of the emerging railwaymen and skilled engineers. In terms of social geography each displayed sharp contrasts between a better-off and healthier West End and a poverty-stricken malodorous East End. London west of Nash's Regent Street may be compared with the I, II, III, and X *arrondisements* in Paris, while districts such as Clerkenwell or Bethnal Green might be compared with the XII or VIII *arrondisements*. Just as many a Parisian thought of himself as belonging to his *quartier* within the *arrondisement*, so did Londoners regard themselves as belonging to their parish or district – be it Marylebone, Lambeth, or

Whitechapel. In short, Mayhew's London contained the materials and conditions to generate protest and political action every bit as much as Paris.

The all-important difference lay in the behaviour of their political élites. To put it baldly and in oversimplified fashion, in Paris, the political élite, both in and out of office, in February 1848 was more divided and substantially more maladroit than was the case in Britain. So that in February instead of producing a change of ministry, a Reform Act, and some judicious change of emphasis in foreign policy which might well have perpetuated the constitutional monarchy, the French ended up by establishing a new regime with all the consequent opportunities for new participants to step on to the stage. In London, as we have seen, it is possible that if some of the more panic-stricken had been given their head, if in the provinces the summer of 1848 had reproduced the conditions of 1842, and if Young Ireland had genuinely acquired mass support, a considerably stronger reaction from the Chartists might have been forthcoming. As it was, the government, from its point of view, played its cards with skill and force; middle-class critics of aristocracy such as those supporting Edward Miall and his *Nonconformist* remained more frightened of Chartist violence than of aristocratic misgovernment, and Chartism as an organized movement, though not as an attitude of mind, was almost destroyed.

Notes

1. J. K. Laughton (ed.), *Memoirs of the life and correspondence of Henry Reeve*, i. p. 190.
2. *Parl. Debs.* 3rd ser. XCVI c. 901.
3. For the economic history see D. M. Evans, *The Commercial Crisis, 1847–8* (1848). C. N. Ward-Perkins, 'The commercial crisis of 1847', in *Oxford Economic Papers*, new series (1950) ii. 75–95; A. D. Gayer, W. W. Rostow and A. J. Schwartz, *The Growth and Fluctuation of the British Economy, 1790–1850*, i. chap. vi.
4. As Cobden observed, this was the first time such a bizarre and unfounded notion had been foisted upon and taken up seriously by the public. His attempt to ridicule the panic fell singularly flat and Greville tells us that he received 'innumerable compliments' when he wrote to *The Times* to refute Cobden (See R. Cobden, *The Three Panics*, (1862) p. 13 and G. L. Strachey and R. Fulford (eds.), *The Greville Memoirs, 1814–1860*, vi. p. 12).
5. *Northern Star* 1, 8 January 1848.
6. Hetherington, Treasurer of the LWMA, was present to assert London's priority at the stormy debate in the BPU's council when the decision was taken. He intervened to point out that their 'grand error' was in not going for universal suffrage in 1832, as he reminded them he had personally come to them and urged them to do at the time. Now they had accepted his advice, so he welcomed them as allies. (See Lovett MSS., Birmingham Reference Library vol. i. f. 153.)
7. For which see P. Hollis (ed.), *The Pauper Press* (1970) and J. H. Wiener *The War of the Unstamped* (1969).

8. There has been some controversy over the role of Place and his middle class radical friends in the drawing up of the Charter, see D. J. Rowe, 'The London Working Men's Association and the People's Charter', in *Past and Present*, 36 (1967) and I. J. Prothero's comment in 38 (1967). Suffice it to say that whether or not the Charter should be seen as having a dual origin, the LWMA's leaders soon incurred Place's sharp disapproval by the manner in which they campaigned for it.

9. For this see my 'William Lovett' in P. Hollis (ed.), *Pressure from Without* (1974), pp. 124–6.

10. The audience seems to have been 30,000 if one counts all who came and went during its five-hour duration or 15,000 if one counted the maximum present at any one time. Accounts of the meeting can be found in Lovett MSS., vol. i. ff. 242–52; R. C. Gammage, *History of the Chartist Movement, 1837–1854*, pp. 47–53; R. Lowery's autobiography in *The Weekly Record of the Temperance Movement*, 9 August 1856.

11. For this see A. R. Schoyen, *The Chartist Challenge* which, however, needs reading in conjunction with D. J. Rowe, 'Chartism and the Spitalfields Silk-weavers', in *Econ. Hist. Rev.* XX (1967).

12. According to T. S. Duncombe in his speech introducing the petition to the House of Commons; see G. M. Young and W. D. Hancock, *English Historical Documents*, XII (1) pp. 442–9.

13. For these two paragraphs see especially I. J. Prothero, 'Chartism in London' in *Past and Present*, 44 (1969) and the same author's 'London Chartism and the trades', in *Econ. Hist. Review*, XXIV (1971), pp. 202–19.

14. *Northern Star*, leader 4 March 1848.

15. *Northern Star*, 15 January 1848.

16. *Ibid.*, 4 March where they are named as signing an address to the people of Paris adopted by the NCA Executive supported by the Secretary of the Fraternal Democrats.

17. *Northern Star*, January, February.

18. He had been elected to the Metropolitan Delegate Council in 1841, had represented Tower Hamlets at the Sturge Birmingham Conference in 1842 and in 1843 had been elected a member of the NCA Executive on which he had served continuously ever since. He contested Derby at the general election in 1847 (*Reynolds Political Instructor*, 20 April 1850).

19. In evidence at the Old Bailey in the Cuffey case: T.S 11/140, file 387.

20. He had attended meetings at the Rotunda and become a class leader and committee member of the NUWC, walked in the Fast procession, formed a Lodge of Operative Gardeners in the GNCTU, had been imprisoned for his part in the unstamped press agitation, helped form the Hammersmith Working Men's Association in 1839 led that district's NCA locality in the forties and served on the NCA Executive (*Reynolds Political Instructor*, 27 April 1850).

21. See J. Saville, *Ernest Jones* (London, 1952).

22. For Harney, see A. R. Schoyen, *The Chartist Challenge* and F. G. and R. M. Black, eds. *The Harney Papers* (Amsterdam, 1969); a valuable examination of the Fraternal Democrats is H. Weisser, 'Chartist Internationalism, 1845–8', in *The Historical Journal*, XIV (1971), pp. 49–66.

23. Thomas Cooper's well-known autobiography is reticent about his activities in 1848: the police were certainly interested. HO 45/2410 Part II contains a precis of 'blasphemous lectures by one Cooper' (i.e. Thomas) by a police sergeant who reported that he lectured at 81 High St., Whitechapel.

24. For this body, progenitor of the better known Radical Reform Association in which Henry Hunt was active, see *The Morning Herald, Cobbett's Weekly Political Register* and *The Trades Free Press* for July–October 1828.

25. For this collaboration see police informer's reports in HO 64/12; *Poor Man's Guardian*; *Cosmopolite* and *The Working Man's Friend* especially for January–March 1833. Feargus O'Connor, still then a follower of O'Connell, made what was probably his first appearance before a large audience of London working men when he was main speaker at an open-air meeting of 7,000 called by the National Union of the Working Classes to protest against Whig coercion of Ireland (HO 64/13 for 120 page report of the meeting).

26. For this see F. A. D'Arcy, The artisans of Dublin and Daniel O'Connell, 1830–1847, in *Irish Historical Studies*, XVII (1970), pp. 221–43.

27. Lovett, who could stomach neither, had little or no support from the London Irish in the later 1830s.

28. He was a cabinet-maker (*Place Newspaper Collection*, set 47, vol. ii, f. 343).

29. See his letter to the Irish people in *Northern Star*, 15 January which printed the Duffy-Mitchel correspondence and attacked the *Nation* for being hostile to Chartism.

30. *Northern Star*, 29 January.

31. *Ibid.*, 5 February.

32. MEPOL 2/59: Police reports of 24–26 February on anti-Budget meetings at Islington and Marylebone. The former was chaired by David Wire, Under Sheriff of Middlesex, and speakers included Thomas Wakley MP. Police both in uniform and plain clothes were present at the latter. For reports of other meetings of this kind, see e.g. *Nonconformist*, 2 February, leader. Men active in the earlier phases of Chartism are to be found speaking, e.g. Collins, A. O'Neill, Henry Vincent etc., alongside Cobden, Sturge, Miall etc.

33. *Illustrated London News*, 4 March 1848.

34. G. L. Strachey and R. Fulford (eds.), *The Greville Memoirs, 1814–1860*, vi. 159.

35. *The Times*, 13 March 1848.

36. *The Nonconformist*, 15 March; *The Times*, 7, 8, 9 March 1848.

37. R. H. Watson, proprietor of the Patent Kamptulicon Works, Greenwich, to Grey denounced him on 10 April, as 'the most wicked and dangerous man in London... well known at the Old Bailey as a member of the Swell mob ... an avowed atheist, naturalized Frenchman ... in the pay of the *Weekly Dispatch* as writer of revolutionary articles' etc. A similar characterization came from Captain Vincent RN, a Magistrate of the Cinque Ports, who gave details of Reynolds' family background and of his 'swindles' (HO 45/2410 Part II). G. W. M. Reynolds deserves a full-length biography. For a basic outline see *D.N.B.*; for a check-list of his vast literary output see D. Kausch, G. W. M. Reynolds, a bibliography, in *The Library*, XXVIII (1973).

38. G. W. E. Russell (ed.), *Letters of Matthew Arnold*, i. 3–4, Matthew Arnold to his mother, 7 March: 'I was in the great mob in Trafalgar Square yesterday, they did not seem dangerous, and the police are always, I think, needlessly rough in manner'. Disraeli's summary was 'the cockney riots of little boys' (W. F. Moneypenny and G. E. Buckle, *The Life of Benjamin Disraeli*, iii. 95).

39. The basic sources for the Manchester disturbance are HO 45/2410 Part I (Manchester); and Part IV (Military correspondence of Lt. Gen. Sir T. Arbuthnott, C. in C. Northern and Midland Districts) and the Manchester press.

40. A. Wilson, *The Chartist Movement in Scotland* (1970), pp. 218–21 has shown that the inspiration of the Glasgow rioting was not Chartist as the London press alleged and that after it was over the Glasgow Chartists went on meeting without creating disturbances or even particularly alarming the authorities.

41. PRO 30/22/7B, Russell papers: Sir Geo. Grey-Russell 7 March (twice) 8 March C. Wood-Russell 8 March; HO 65/16: S. M. Phillips to Commissioners of Police, 7, 8 March 1848.

42. MRD Foot and H. C. G. Matthew (eds.), *The Gladstone Diaries*, iv. 17. For a list of those

sworn at Marylebone, many of them railway employees see HO 45/2410 Part II: 13 March.

43. HO 65/16: S. M. Phillips to Mr. Farrant, Vestry and Paving Clerk, St. Martins, 9 March.

44. PRO 30/22/7B, Russell papers: Earl Spencer to Duke of Bedford 6 March.

45. HO 45/2410 Part II: I. L. Ricardo-D. Le Marchant 9 March, informing government that the charge would be £1,000 p.a.

46. It would appear from Ernest Jones's remarks at the meeting that an over-enthusiastic G. W. M. Reynolds had called it without consulting the NCA Executive.

47. There is a copy in HO 45/2410 Part II.

48. *The Nonconformist*, 15 March 1848; *The Times*, 13, 14 March.

49. HO 65/16: D. Le Marchant to G. Maule, 5 April; HO 45/2410 Part II: R. Mayne to D. Le Marchant, 4 April refers to twenty-five arrests of labourers, seamen, painters etc. who were accused of being in a crowd of 400 or so who left the meeting on a prearranged signal and attacked small shopkeepers in Camberwell.

50. PRO 30/22/7B, Russell Papers: C. Greville to Duke of Bedford, 14 March 'last night was a great triumph for John and the Government ... the division was capital'. So also thought Tufnell, the chief whip, Tufnell to Russell, 15 March, *ibid*.

51. L. C. Jennings, *France and Europe in 1848*, pp. 18–20.

52. See the almost daily reports in March by Lord Lieutenant Clarendon to Grey in Clarendon papers, Letter Book II in the Bodleian.

53. As is clear from Lord John Russell's major memorandum on Ireland of 30 March, in which he required written comments from all his colleagues (PRO 30/22/7B, Russell papers).

54. HO 45/2410 Part II: J. Mason to Home Office, 11 March.

55. PRO 30/22/7B, Russell papers: Palmerston to Russell, 13 March.

56. HO 43/75: D. Le Marchant to W. I. Curtis, 7 April; HO 65/16: S. M. Phillips to Commissioners of Police, 8 April, enclosing Smith's letter; HO 45/2410 Part V (Middlesex): T. Atchison-Grey, 6 April.

57. HO 45/2410 Part V: Sir H. Ellis to S. M. Phillips 9 April; Sir Henry was issued with fifty muskets and a quantity of cutlasses.

58. WO 30/81: Wellington's memorandum, 5 April.

59. *Ibid.*, Wellington to Russell, 6 April.

60. Cited by Lady Longford, *Wellington, Pillar of State* (1972), p. 379.

61. 3rd Earl of Malmesbury, *Memoirs of an ex-Minister* (1884), p. 166.

62. Royal Archives C56/21: Colonel Phipps to Prince Albert, 10 April 5.30 p.m., describing the whole day.

63. *Northern Star*, 8 April.

64. HO 45/2410 Part V (Middlesex) for the delegates' letter to Sir G. Grey, 7 April; M. Creighton, *Memoir of Sir George Grey* (1901), p. 72 says they were received with 'cold civility' by the under-secretary.

65. D. Read and E. Glasgow, *Feargus O'Connor* (1961), pp. 131–2.

66. D. Cairns (trans. and ed.), *The Memoirs of Hector Berlioz* (1969), p. 44.

67. *The Times*, 12 April 1848.

68. John, Earl Russell, *Recollections and Suggestions*, pp. 267–8.

69. J. T. Ward, *Chartism* (1973), p. 201.

70. MEPOL 2/59 contains an example transcribed into longhand and signed by William Hunt who from previous references by Gurney was plainly one of his assistants.

71. HO 45/2410 Part II. The Company presented the government with a bill for £500 which included the cost of erecting and maintaining apparatus at a number of places not hitherto served including Harrow, Clapham, Watford, and Kingston.

74. I hope soon to complete a study of the year 1848 in Britain and Ireland which will provide the evidence for these statements on the provincial situation.

75. One *Return of Special Constables in Metropolitan Police Districts* (HO 45/2460 Part II) seems to be a fairly complete return parish by parish of the numbers sworn and their leaders up to 6 April. According to a note pencilled on it these totalled 27,774 to which there was to be added 9,113 sworn on 7–8 April with 2,037 in reserve, giving a total of just under 39,000. In addition, however, more were sworn on 9–10 April and, as a further list of their places of assembly shows, there were bodies of Specials acting independently of the Parish who were not included in the return, not to mention those who were sworn in in the City of London. There are also scattered returns from the courts where swearing was carried out, e.g. Thames Police Court, 5,636 in March and April, and Marlborough St. 4,465, but these are also incomplete.

76. Contemporary estimates include *Ann. Reg. Chronicle*, p. 52, 170,000; *The Times*, 10, 11 April, 150,000; *Nonconformist*, 12 April, 150,000; *Standard*, 10 April, 250,000; *Fraser's Magazine*, May 1848, 200,000 and *The Quarterly Review*, June 1848, 200,000.

77. It was reported that on 10 April many Specials in the Kingsland Road district (Hackney) failed to report for duty, and Mr. Young of Limehouse said 'the call is chiefly responded to by alarmists and men of Conservative politics' and 'there was an almost universal unwillingness among our shopkeeping population who are chiefly Whigs and Radicals. He went on to claim that he had converted them (HO 45/2410 Part II and Part V, Middlesex).

78. HO 45/2410 Part II: Bingham to Grey, 8 April, and Part V (Middlesex): Marquess of Salisbury to same, 8 April; Police Commissioner Rowan, commenting to the Master of the Household on 11 April on the loyalty of all classes nonetheless added 'with the exception of the lowest class' (Royal Archives C56/30). Lord John Russell told the Prince Consort 11 April that the masons were an exception to the general loyalty (Royal Archives C56/28). Claims of victimization for refusing to serve were made in letters to *Northern Star*, 22 April, by employees of Cubitts.

79. MEPOL 2/59: William Hunt's report, *op. cit.*

80. WO 30/81: Duke of Wellington's memo. of 11 April and return of military arrangements; WO 30/111: memo. on rations available and where.

81. WO 30/111: memo. on police distribution on 10 April.

82. HO 45/2410 Part V (Middlesex): Draft letter probably from Grey to Lord Mayor, 9 April; *c.f.* HO 41/26: Grey to Lord Mayor, 9 April.

83. HO 45/2410 Part II and V contain details of all these preparations as does the Press.

84. G. L. Strachey and R. Fulford (eds.), *The Greville Memoirs, 1814–1860* vi. 169.

85. The draft letter referred to in note 1 gives a clear summary of Home Office planning *c.f.* memo. in HO 41/26: ff. 83–4.

87. *Gloucester Journal*, 8, 15 April for the Snigs End contribution.

88. There is a copy in HO 45/2410 Part II.

89. HO 45/2410 Part V (Surrey): enclosed in F. T. Shee of Russell St. Bermondsey to D. Le Marchant, 9 April.

90. In addition to the press reports, typical of the police reports was 'Police Station, Stepney 9 a.m.: about 2,000 on Stepney Green forming a procession with flags and music; no appearance of arms *c.f.* reports of 3,000 at Clerkenwell and 10,000 moving off from Russell Square (HO 45/2410 Part II).

91. Cuffey described these in a report to the National Convention on 6 April (MEPOL 2/59: William Hunt's report).

92. Daniel Burn, a sofa maker, in evidence at the Old Bailey in the Cuffey case, incidentally mentioned that two armed persons on the Common were ordered into the van and made to give up their arms by the Chartist Executive. (TS 11/140 file 387: transcript of evidence for the defence in the Cuffey case).

93. E.g. Mayne told Rowan, his fellow Police Commissioner, at 12.45 on the 10 April that 'the police who have been amongst them [on the Common] state no appearance of

arms, only a few foreigners'. Another report from Bales Livery Stables at 10.45 a.m.
spoke of the procession filing on to the Common with many flags and banners but
'not the slightest appearance of arms or even bludgeons' (HO 45/2410 Part II).

94. MEPOL 2/59: 10.30 a.m., 10 April, memo. by C. Yardley, Chief Clerk of a message
from Gurney.

95. HO 45/2410 Part II:.Mayne to Rowan, 11.45 a.m. (Kennington), 10 April.

96. HO 45/2410 Part V (Middlesex): Lord Mayor Grey 10 April, 2.30 p.m., 4.30 p.m.,
4.00 p.m. Royal Archives, C56/18.

97. HO 45/2410 Part II: Mayne to Rowan, n.d or time but from internal evidence
clearly about midday on Kennington Common.

98. Russell to Queen Victoria, 2 p.m. 10 April (A. C. Benson and Viscount Esher (eds.),
Letters of Queen Victoria, ii. 168–9). Palmerston was not so sure Osborne was safe: he
anxiously inquired of Russell whether security measures had been taken, observing
'it is rather an unprotected place and the Solent sea is not impassable' (PRO
30/22/7B, Russell papers: Palmerston to Russell, 7 April).

99. *The Standard*, 10 April, evening edition; *Northern Star*, 15 April; *Nonconformist*, 12
April; *Sun*, 11 April; *Examiner*, 15 April; *Morning Chronicle*, 11 April; *Illustrated London
News*, 15 April; *The Times*, 11 April; characteristically O'Connor claimed 'rather
under than over 400,000' (*Northern Star, ibid.*).

100. *The Standard, op. cit.*, claimed that the Common only measured 2,500 square yards
and hence could only accommodate 10,000. My estimate is based on measurements
derived from *Collins Illustrated Atlas of London* (1851), reprinted by Leicester U.P.
1973 (ed., H. J. Dyos).

101. Royal Archives C56/32.

102. See e.g. his introduction to the Cass edition of R. G. Gammage, *History of the Chartist
movement* (1969), and the Merlin Press reprints of *The Red Republican*; his article,
'Chartism in the year of Revolution, 1848' in *Modern Quarterly* (1952), pp. 22–33 and his
Ernest Jones, Chartist (1952).

103. D. Goodway, *Bulletin of the Society for Labour History*, 20 (1970), pp. 14–16.

104. It was an indication of the importance of London Chartism in the total movement
that its allocation was not far short of the twelve for the whole of Lancashire, ten for
Yorkshire, thirteen for Scotland and eight for Ireland. All other places were
allocated one or two delegates. (*Northern Star*, 15 April).

105. *Northern Star*, 22 April.

106. E.g. Westminster and Marylebone chose Vernon and Child at a gathering in
Portland Place near Regent's Park, watched over by the whole of S Division of the
police, and the S. London Chartists assembled at Bricklayers Arms to choose T. M.
Wheeler and Bassett. Both were much smaller venues than Bonners Fields.

107. *Northern Star*, 22 April.

108. The major evidence, in Chartist eyes, of the government's counter-offensive was, of
course, the Gagging act, i.e. the Crown and Government Security Act which made
'open and advised speaking' of treasonable matters, that is 'compassing, imagining
and levying war against the Sovereign', felonious with a penalty of transportation
for life or not less than seven years. Although government and parliamentary
discussion centred on its usefulness for dealing with the militants in Ireland, the Act
applied to the whole UK and both Radicals and Chartists believed it endangered
freedom of speech for those advocating a radical overhaul of the political system.

109. Before 10 April, many prominent Chartist speakers in London had denounced the
middle class in unmeasured terms; e.g. Harney declared 'the history of the last
sixteen years proclaims ... the iniquitous and monstrous ingratitude of the middle
class. United with the middle class? Unite rather with wolves.' Kydd, denounced
the new aristocracy of manufacturers as 'more to be feared than the old feudal
barons' and Ernest Jones asked 'who built the bastilles, who pulled wages down;

who propounded the hellish doctrine of competition, who opposed the Ten Hours Bill; who passed Co-ercion? ... who but the middle class'. (*Northern Star*, 5, 12 February).

110. For example, see leaders in *Nonconformist*, 12 April.

111. The history of the People's Charter Union can be traced in *The Reasoner*; W. J. Linton, *Prose and Verse*, vii; G. J. Holyoake, *Bygones worth remembering; Holyoake diaries* at the Bishopsgate Institution; *The Spirit of the Age*; F. B. Smith, *Radical artisan*; *The Life of Thomas Cooper by himself*.

112. For the People's League the chief sources are W. Lovett, *Life and Struggles*, pp. 335–49; and *The Nonconformist*, 1848 *passim*.

113. Rowan to General Bowles, Master of the Household, 11 April (Royal Archives C56/30).

114. *Northern Star*, 29 January, claimed that 'the destitute, houseless, fireless, foodless and hopeless, in London alone, are computed at near fifty thousand'. For the report, *ibid*.

115. *The Times*, for instance, in a leader of 27 April, observed that there were 'some millions who possess neither property nor comfortable nor regular employments sufficient for a decent existence ... These men as a body will be revolutionists in one form or another. The special constables have routed O'Connor ... but they have not vanquished hunger ... The time has come for the state to be more emphatic about its duty to give the destitute either relief or employment.' In fact *The Times* remedy was state-guided emigration.

116. E.g. Hepworth Dixon, *The London Prisons* (1850), pp. 224–5 'we take it for granted that Clerkenwell is known to every breakfast table in the kingdom ... It is low London of low London ... more murders and attempts at murder take place in Clerkenwell than in any other part of the kingdom.'

117. For the Clerkenwell Green meetings see especially M E P O L 2/59: Information given on oath by Horace Hardy, Sgt. 15G, on 6 June; Royal Archives C56/84, 86: Russell to Queen, 1 June, and Grey to Queen, 4 June, explaining the difficulty of securing prosecutions for seditious speaking.

118. The chief sources for the events of 29–30 May are Queen *v*. Fussell and Queen *v*. Williams and Vernon in J. E. P. Wallis (edited', *State Trials*, new series, VI. 723–74, 775–82; HO 45/2410 Part II: 29/30 May, *ibid*. Part V; for reswearing of Specials; M E P O L 2/59. Notice issued by Rowan and Mayne declaring Clerkenwell meetings illegal; Royal Archives C56/79 and 82: Russell to Queen, 30 May, Grey to Queen, 31 May.

119. K. Jagow (ed.), *Letters of the Prince Consort* (1938), Prince Consort to Stockmar 6 May, p. 141. It may be noted that by incorrectly attributing this letter to *before* 10 April, C. Woodham Smith in her *Queen Victoria*, i. 287 fails to bring out the revival of alarm in polite circles in May.

120. The Queen expressed her feelings by inquiring of the Prime Minister 'Does not Lord John think some of the speeches outrageously violent and seditious?' (Royal Archives C8/17: Queen Victoria to Russell, 31 May).

121. L. Strachey and R. Fulford (edited), *The Greville Memoirs*, VI. pp. 73–6.

122. HO 45/2410 Part II: J. Johnston, N Division report, 4 June.

123. HO 45/2410 Part II: Johnston's second report, 2 p.m., 4 June.

124. *Ibid*., Report from H Division, 4 June.

125. *Ibid*., R. Mayne to Grey, 10.15 a.m., Sunday; see Attorney General's speech in Queen *v*. Ernest Jones in J. E. P. Wallis (edited), *State Trials*, new series, VI. 784–830.

126. *Ibid*., Return of persons taken into custody ... 4 June and G. Maule to A. Waddington, 23 June. After a three-day trial at the Old Bailey, seventeen were sentenced to upwards of two years' hard labour.

127. *Ibid*., e.g. William Higgins to Grey, 5, 10 June, who declared 'he was no Chartist'. Evidence of James White in Queen *v*. Ernest Jones, *op. cit*.

128. Speech of Serjeant Wilkins and the defendants in Queen v. Ernest Jones, *op. cit.*
129. HO 45/2410 Part II: Memorial signed by 265 inhabitants; placard 5 June; Arthur Nelson to Home Office, Gloucester Coffee House, Church St. Shoreditch, 8 June.
130. *Ibid.*, memo. 12 July and enclosed printed bill.
131. HO 45/2410 Part II: P. M. M'Douall and McCrae to Lord John Russell, 6 June. On 8 June they informed Grey that a public meeting would be held on Whit Monday on Bonners Fields, assuring him that it would be peaceable and orderly.
132. Clarendon papers, Letter Book ii, *passim.*
133. WO 30/81: Wellington memo., 9 June and note on military arrangements for 12 June; PRO 30/22/C Russell papers: Grey to Russell, 11 June, detailing preparations.
134. MEPOL 2/59: Inspector Field's reports, June to August.
135. HO 45/2410 Part II: Return of number of fire arms sent from Birmingham . . . in June and sales of arms in London in the last six months. This last showed:

London, Last six months	Guns	Pistols	Swords	Other weapons
To gents, respectable Tradesmen, Gamekeepers	378	467	71	0
To Mechanics, Labourers who are believed and others known to be Chartists	122	162	22	18

136. *Ibid.*, Ordnance to Home Office, 8 June.
137. MEPOL 2/59: memo. by Rowan, 10 June.
138. Grey to Queen Victoria, 7 p.m. 12 June (Royal Archives C56/97) for official description and satisfaction at the outcome. See reports in *Nonconformist*, 14 June; *Illustrated London News*, 17 June; *The Greville Memoirs*, vi. 77; *The Times*, 13 June; *Northern Star*, 17 June.
139. According to police informants a committee of twenty-four delegates (probably the Metropolitan Delegate Council) with M'Douall in the chair, met at the Albion in Bethnal Green Road in the early evening of 12 June and decided to abandon all outdoor meetings. Chartists and Confederates were to meet in their localities every evening and to arm themselves so that within the next ten days 'the Government could be taken by surprise at midnight'. A committee consisting of four of the delegates – Henslow, Pitt, Honeyfold, and Percy – three members of the NCA Executive, two Confederates, and two trade union members was to form a secret body in permanent session to co-ordinate preparations and 'appoint the day and the hour when the final struggle is to take place'. Special messengers were to be used to communicate with the various localities (HO 45/2410 Part II: T. R. Reading to Mayne, 12 June (7.30 p.m.), and George Davis's report at Greenwich Police Station, 12 June, to Malalieu).
140. Briefly, the authorities, on the evidence of their spies, particularly George Davis and Thomas Powell, principal witness for the Crown in the subsequent trials, maintained that plotting an armed rising against the government went on intermittently from 12 June until 16 August when the signal for an attempt was about to be given. (HO 45/2410 Part II: reports of George Davis, 14 June (two reports), 14, 15 August and reports of F Division 13, 17 June; Queen v. Dowling and Queen v. Cuffey and others in J. E. P. Wallis (edited), *State Trials* (new series) VII, 382–466, 468–82.)
141. E.g. The Orange Tree, Orange St., Red Lion Square, the meeting place of the Metropolitan Delegate Council, was raided and 11 arrests made. One of these Joseph Ritchie, a bricklayer was a delegate. The police alleged they found 117 ball

cartridges and all the apparatus for bullet-making at his lodgings in Drury Lane. (HO 45/2410 Part II: Report of F Division, 16 August.)

142. E.g. William Cuffey, who was sixty, a West Indian and a tailor, was sentenced to twenty-one years' transportation; Alexander Sharpe and Joseph Williams, who both received two-year prison sentences, did not survive the experience of Westminster Bridewell. The severity of the silent and solitary system carried on there is well described by another Chartist prisoner, W. J. Vernon in *Reynolds Political Instructor*, 9, 16 March 1850.

143. P. H. Amann, *Revolution and Mass Democracy: the Paris Club Movement in 1848*, (Princeton, 1975), pp. 33–5, 47–8.

144. MEPOL 2/59: Returns from the Metropolitan Police Divisions of where meetings are held, 21–22 June 1848.

145. I. Prothero, 'Chartism in London', in *Past and Present*, 44 (1969), p. 101.

146. P. H. Amann, *op. cit.*, pp. 28–30.

Bibliographical Note

The essential point of departure for the history of London in this period are the two volumes of The History of London, G. Rudé, *Hanoverian London, 1714–1808* (London, 1971) and F. Sheppard, *London 1808–1870: The Infernal Wen* (London, 1971). R. R. Sharpe, *London and the Kingdom* (London, 1895), vol. iii provides a valuable chronology of City politics with extracts from the sources. Also important for City politics are A. B. Beaven, *The Aldermen of the City of London*, 2 vols. (London, 1913) and *Addresses, Remonstrances, and Petitions to the Throne* (London, 1865). For eighteenth-century politics, see L. S. Sutherland, 'The City of London in Eighteenth-Century Politics', in *Essays presented to Sir Lewis Namier* (ed. R. Pares and A. J. P. Taylor, London, 1956) and G. Rudé, *Wilkes and Liberty* (Oxford, 1962). G. Rudé, *Paris and London in the Eighteenth Century* (London, 1969) examines aspects of popular movements and contains valuable comparative material.

For political movements in London during this period see J. H. Plumb, *Sir Robert Walpole*, 2 vols. (London, 1956, 1961); I. R. Christie, *Wilkes, Wyvill and Reform* (London, 1962); G. S. Veitch, *The Genesis of Parliamentary Reform* (London, 1913); S. Maccoby, *English Radicalism 1786–1832* and *English Radicalism 1832–52* (London, 1955 and 1935). See also D. J. Rowe (ed.), *London Radicalism, 1830–43* (London, 1970); E. P. Thompson, *The Making of the English Working Class* (2nd edn., London, 1968); and G. A. Williams, *Artisans and Sans-Culotte* (London, 1968). On the London Corresponding Society see also H. Collins, 'The London Corresponding Society', in *Democracy and the Labour Movement* (ed. J. Saville, London, 1954).

For Westminster Radicalism see J. M. Main, 'Radical Westminster, 1807–1820', *Historical Studies: Australia and New Zealand* 12 (1966). Information on trade union organizations and their development can be found in H. Pelling, *A History of British Trade Unionism* (London, 1963); S. and B. Webb, *The History of Trade Unionism* (London, 1920); and J. L. and B. Hammond, *The Skilled Worker* (London, 1919).

The economic development of London is examined in Sheppard and Rudé, but also useful are J. E. Martin, *Greater London: An Industrial Geography* (London, 1966) and J. Pudney, *London's Docks* (London, 1975). Social developments are examined in M. Dorothy George, *London Life in the Eighteenth Century* (London, 1925); J. J. Tobias, *Crime and Industrial Society in the Nineteenth Century* (London, 1963); and L. Radzinowitz, *A History of English Criminal Law* (London, 1956). For the later nineteenth century see E. P. Thompson and E. Yeo, *The Unknown Mayhew* (London, 1971) and G. Stedman Jones, *Outcast London* (Oxford, 1971). See also R. Glass (ed.), *London, Aspects of Change* (London, 1964) and H. J. Dyos and M. Wolff (eds.), *The Victorian City: Images and Realities* (London, 1973).

For urban development see K. Grytzell, *Population Changes in London, 1801–1901* (Lund, Sweden, 1969) and J. Shepherd, J. Westaway, and T. Lee, *A Social Atlas of London* (Oxford, 1974).

SHEFFIELD CITY
POLYTECHNIC LIBRARY
PSALTER LANE
SHEFFIELD S11 8UZ